P9-BIB-583

THE
AVALANCHE
BOOK

THE AVALANCHE BOOK

Betsy Armstrong

Knox Williams

Book and Cover Design
by Bob Schram
Cover Photo by
Richard L. Armstrong

Library of Congress Cataloging-in-Publication Data

Armstrong, Betsy R.
The Avalanche Book

Bibliography: p.
Includes index.
1. Avalanches — North America. I. Williams, Knox.
II. Armstrong, Richard L. (Richard Ley),
III. Title.
QC929.A8A69 1986 363.3'49 86-7560
ISBN 1-55591-001-7

FULCRUM, INC.
GOLDEN, COLORADO

TABLE OF CONTENTS

San Juan Mountains, southwestern Colorado (Steven J. Meyers photo)

PREFACE

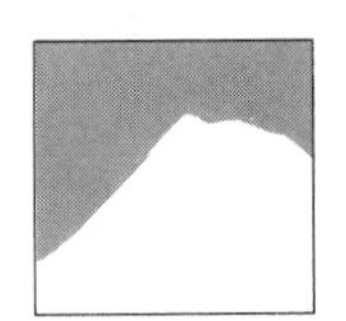

AS NATURAL HAZARDS GO, THE DE-structive effects of snow avalanches do not match up to the consequences of hurricanes, floods and tornadoes. However, avalanches are of deadly importance for those whose activities regularly bring them in contact with snow-covered mountain terrain. Avalanches not only generate a fear among those who must constantly confront them, but these same people often find avalanches truly fascinating, as well as a scientific challenge. The intrigue comes not only from the awesome beauty displayed by a fast-moving powder avalanche, but also from the fact that scientific theory has yet to explain all of the mysteries of the snow avalanche.

The community of avalanche professionals is a small one, yet a sizeable body of literature has been written on the subject. We have read a good portion of these works — most of them scientific papers on snow metamorphism, stress in an inclined snowpack, fracture mechanics, fluid flow, and related subjects from meteorology and geology. We've contributed to this library by writing our share of papers. Yet there are few good non-technical books in English on snow avalanches.

A writer's problem does not change.... It is always how to write truly and, having found what is true, to project it in such a way that it becomes a part of the experience of the person who reads it.
ERNEST HEMINGWAY

The 1961 *ABC of Avalanche Safety*, by Ed LaChapelle (rewritten and republished in 1985) was the first contemporary pocket guide to the field. In 1966 Colin Fraser wrote *The Avalanche Enigma* (later revised as *Avalanches and Snow Safety*), an excellent account of avalanche history and research in the Alps. In 1968 Monty Atwater penned *The Avalanche Hunters*, which told the story of his pioneering years as the first snow ranger in the United States. In 1967 Dale Gallagher wrote *The Snowy*

Torrents, a documenting of avalanche accidents in the United States and the safety lessons to be learned from these incidents, which was followed in 1975 by the second volume written by Knox Wiliams, and followed again in 1984 by *The Snowy Torrents, Volume III* by Williams and Betsy Armstrong. In 1961 the U.S. Forest Service published the first *Avalanche Handbook,* an authoritative guide to all aspects of the avalanche problem, followed in 1976 by Ron Perla and Pete Martinelli's revised version. In 1983 Tony Daffern authored *Avalanche Safety for Skiers and Climbers*, a handbook of avalanche information with a slant toward the Canadian experience. The Alaska Department of Natural Resources published *Snow Sense*, written by Jill Fredston and Doug Fesler, in 1984. Beyond these, all other written works are strictly technical papers or books designed to further the state of the art among snow scientists and practiitioners. Even Hollywood has tried its hand at avalanche fiction in the movies, with spectacular but unconvincing results.

Through our careers, we've long been active in presenting evening talks and field seminars on avalanche safety. In conversations with hundreds of people at these gatherings, one question has been repeatedly asked: Is there a good book on avalanches that I can understand and enjoy?

Robert Baron and Hunter Holloway of Fulcrum Inc., too, felt this subject deserved to be written about in a fashion that would entertain and teach at the same time. While on a backpacking trip in the summer of 1984 in the Yellowstone National Park and during an all-day rain storm which kept them tent-bound, they had plenty of time to gaze at the steep slopes surrounding their campsite and consider the consequences: what if this were winter and the falling rain was instead heavy snow. They later approached us with their ideas, and we jumped at the chance .

The Avalanche Book is a non-technical description of snow avalanche science, protection, survival, and lore, written for anyone having a general interest in the subject. Topics include the basic what's, why's, and where's: what properties of snow contribute to avalanche formation, what triggers an avalanche, why are avalanches deadly and destructive, and where and when do avalanches occur. We also talk about practical solutions to avalanche problems: ways to minimize avalanche risk, safe travel tips, survival methods, rescue, control efforts, legal considerations, and current research. Actual avalanche incidents — mainly from the United States but drawn from around the world — are used as examples throughout the text to illustrate the dangerous and fickle nature of snow avalanches.

Many people have contributed to this book, offering support, knowledge, patience and timely opinions. First, to Bob Baron and Hunter Holloway for believing in us when sometimes we didn't; to Richard Armstrong for his chapter three, his editing, his translating and his graceful tolerance during this entire project; to Ed LaChapelle for reviewing several chapters and for being our glacier and avalanche guru; to Walter Good of the Swiss Federal Institute for Snow and Avalanches, for providing us with old Swiss avalanche stories; to Jim Kennedy of Ketchum, Idaho, for reviewing chapter eight; to those who contributed their photographs; and finally, to Suzie and Johanna — thank you.

K. W. and B. A. 1986

Large slab avalanche in motion at Loveland Pass, Colorado. The truck escaped without damage (U.S. Forest Service photo)

1 WHY TELL OF AVALANCHES

CATASTROPHE IN CALIFORNIA

AT 3:45 P.M. ON MARCH 31, 1982, the snow broke loose on the slopes above the California ski resort of Alpine Meadows. A crack 10 feet deep and 3,000 feet wide split open, and a massive avalanche began its death-dealing descent toward the buildings below. The people working inside and a few walking through the parking lot could not know of their imminent peril, for a raging blizzard trimmed visibility to just a few yards. Seconds later the falling wall of snow had grown to 30 feet high and had accelerated to 80 miles per hour. It smashed into the base area, crushed ski lifts, buildings, and people, then fell silent as the air-borne dust cloud slowly settled to earth. In about 10 seconds — certainly no more than 15 — a mountainside of snow weighing more than 65,000 tons had rushed about a third of a mile downslope, demolished a chairlift and a steel girder building, damaged another building, caused property damage of $2 million, and killed seven people. It was the worst ski-area disaster in United States history, and the headlines that blared across the nation's newspapers and airwaves shocked the American public into realizing that avalanches are not confined to Europe's Alps but also lurk in our backyard.

"Begin at the beginning," the King said gravely, "and go on till you come to the end; then stop."
LEWIS CARROLL

What is this thing we call "avalanche"? The word is enough to strike a cold fear in the hearts of mountain people, for they know the fate that awaits the unwry. Avalanches have been falling in the mountains of the world as long as snow has blanketed those mountains. No doubt avalanches claimed their first victims when prehistoric man ventured out of tropical climates and set foot in a hostile environment of snow-covered mountains. Avalanches have been the scourge of mountain dwellers and travelers

1.1 Total destruction of a building at Alpine Meadows, California, on March 31, 1982 (Dick Penniman photo)

throughout recorded history. For centuries avalanches threatened only those who lived and worked in the domain of the aptly named white death. But with the coming of the 20th century, there also came a new breed of avalanche victim — the tourist. These days an avalanche victim is much more likely to be a skier, climber, snowmobiler, or a person in pursuit of some other form of winter recreation. Consider the following scenario of a hypothetical, modern avalanche accident.

WHAT THE SKI TOURERS FOUND

It is a Saturday afternoon in midwinter, one of those days it's great to be outdoors. The air is crisp; the sun, warm. A light breeze sends small, puffy clouds drifting silently overhead, their shadows rolling across vast fields of sparkling fresh snow that fell yesterday and the day before. Three ski tourers are breaking trail in one foot of new snow. They are young, athletic, and in good shape. Already this day they have skied about five miles, some of it through woods on a gently climbing trail packed by other skiers, some breaking trail on moderately steep traverses, and some on exhilarating downhill runs making sweeping telemark turns through knee-deep powder and occasionally taking soft spills. There is even the infrequent but inevitable face-forward head plant, but always the skier rises laughing, shakes the snow from inside his parka and goggles, and pushes off kneel into the next turn. All their runs have been on slopes of 25 to 30 degrees, enough steepness to attain good momentum but with enough new snow to provide braking for balance and control.

Now, though, they are traversing toward a farther and steeper slope of untracked snow. On an even farther slope, they spy a fracture line, a scraped surface, and a mound of rough snow at the bottom — a fresh avalanche. They remark that it would have been fun to have seen it run. Suddenly a booming sound erupts from the snow beneath their skis. Simultaneously the snow all around them collapses about an inch, and cracks shoot in all directions for 10 to 20 feet. The skiers, startled, freeze in their tracks, their hearts racing and a chill running down their spines. No one says a word, but their expressions convey their unasked question: What was that? After several seconds of silence, one man offers his opinion: "Maybe we should turn back." But a short discussion shows he is outvoted, and not wanting to be a party pooper, he begins moving forward with his friends. They reach the top of the slope without further incident.

All agree that maybe it would be safer if they ski one at a time. The first skier carves his first turn along the near edge of the slope, a descent line that offers the gentlest pitch on the slope but which is still steeper than anything they have skied so far. He skis well and makes about 10 smooth turns before stopping along the edge of the slope. He shouts encouragement to his friends, and the second skier zips up his parka then glides on a shallow traverse toward the center of the slope. It is steeper here, and the snow a little deeper. He links two pretty turns before losing his balance on the third and falling with a thud in the soft snow. At once a spiderweb of cracks shoots silently across the snow, and 50 feet above the fallen skier, a fracture two feet deep and 100 feet wide yawns open. The shout of "Avalanche!" does the fallen victim no good, for he is helpless lying on his side in the middle of the slope. The avalanche quickly gains a churning momentum and engulfs its victim, the whole time emitting a surprisingly soft whooshing sound. The two survivors strain to glimpse their companion but manage to see only the briefest flash of a red parka in a tumbling river of white.

Inside the maelstrom, the victim quickly gains speed, starting out in a head-first, slide but is abruptly flipped over onto his back. His head pops free to the surface, and he gulps a breath of air but mostly gets a mouthful of air-borne snow. The snow rips off one ski pole. With his arms now free, he flails at the snow and manages to turn his body slightly, but a terrible pressure and pain is building in his left leg as the attached ski is gripped firmly in the dense snow flowing at the bottom of the avalanche. He is being dragged under when suddenly his ski is ripped off, and once more his head pops free of the snow. The sensation of speed is terrifying. With one ski attached, the victim can barely control his rolling and tumbling, and his fear of smashing into an unseen rock or tree is very real. A moment later, he feels the snow around him begin to slow down rapidly, with a simultaneous sensation of its becoming very heavy. With one final effort, he thrusts upward with his arms and bursts through to the surface, just as the avalanche crunches to a stop and seals its victim from the chest down in a vise-like grip. He is one of the lucky ones, for this avalanche returned its victim alive.

The incident we've just described was not real; instead it was a composite of facts and details taken from many real accidents occurring in recent winters, all combined to create a typical modern avalanche accident. The victim in this incident was a survivor. He survived a terror-filled ride lasting 10 seconds on which he traveled some 200 yards at speeds up to 50 miles per hour. How typical is this incident? Typical enough to enable us to predict that in the next 10 years about 100 skiers per year will be caught in a similar avalanche in similar circumstances and that about 10 of these skiers will die per year.

This is a scary statistic, for here is an act of nature that has killing power in a sport that is so much fun. But it is not only the sporting public that are prey for avalanches. Although avalanches take their greatest toll among winter sports enthusiasts, they also claim lives among those at home and at work in the mountains. As you will learn later in Chapter 6 which deals with avalanche accidents, most encounters are avoidable and, therefore, not truly accidental. It makes good sense then to learn something about this thing we call "avalanche!"

DEFINING OUR TERMS

An avalanche is a mass of snow — sometimes containing ice, water, soil, rock, and trees — which slides down a mountainside. The word is directly derived from the old French *avalanste*, which was in turn derived from *avaler*, meaning to let down, lower, or go downstream. Earlier Latin derivatives are *labi*, meaning to slip or glide down, and *labina*, meaning a slippery place. The Latin derivatives easily give rise to the German word for avalanche which is *lawine*, especially when one considers that the letters b, u, v, and w were frequently interchangeable in Germanic languages. Our main topic in this book is the snow avalanche, which of course means an avalanche composed mostly or entirely of snow. There are other types of avalanches, however. There are rock avalanches, which can bring down millions of tons of granite or other mountain-forming materials, which change the landscape forever, and which you can read about in geology texts. There are soil avalanches, and there are mud avalanches (commonly called mudslides), which are caused when water-saturated soils break loose and ooze down a mountainside. There are also ice avalanches, which always contain some snow but are primarily made up of glacier ice. In this book we will talk some about ice avalanches, for they are indeed a product of snowfall, but one in which the snowfall has occurred over years or even centuries causing the snow to become glacier ice. Mainly we will concern ourselves with the science, the beauty, and the danger of avalanches that build up and release in the seasonal snow cover. By seasonal snow cover, we mean the snowpack that accumulates and melts away in one winter's season.

You will find as you read that we use several synonymous words in referring to avalanches. Sometimes we substitute the word snowslide for avalanche; the two mean precisely the same and are used interchangeably. We're even partial to using slide as a contraction of snowslide; again, no difference is implied. However, one word does imply a difference: when we speak of a sluff (a common, phonetic spelling of slough), we mean an avalanche that is quite small and most often harmless — not always harmless, though, as we shall see in the coming chapters.

Avalanches come in different forms, types, and sizes. These will be explained in detail in Chapter 3. For now, though, let's begin our journey through the world of avalanches by looking at where they occur, why they are worth studying and writing about, and why they are so fascinating.

WHERE AND HOW MANY

The mountains of the world make up about 20 percent of the continental land mass. Those mountain ranges that are situated in cold enough latitudes or that reach high enough elevations to favor an enduring, deep mantle of winter snow are the habitat of avalanches. In the simplest terms, an avalanche requires only two ingredients: a snow cover and something for it to slide down. Nature has been generous in providing both. The mountains, with their lofty peaks reaching up and catching the winds, have the ability to create their own weather. This means snow, and lots of it. The great mountain ranges wring out the moisture of passing storms, frozen moisture which falls as snow and covers the rugged peaks in a blanket of white. With the snow comes the wind, which howls over the peaks and funnels through the passes, scouring the snow from its resting places and driving it in swirling clouds to new resting places which become ever-deepening drifts on steep slopes. With every passing hour, the drifts grow layer by layer into straining snow pillows, until that critical moment when one more snowflake is one too many. Cracks explode across the slope, the snow breaks its tenuous hold against gravity, and the avalanche begins its churning rush toward the valley floor — and heaven help the poor tourist or mountain dweller in its path below.

So it is that mountains provide the real estate on which snow and wind — the architects of avalanche — design their creations. Not surprisingly, the world's largest mountains produce the largest avalanches. The Himalayas of Asia, with numerous peaks above 20,000 feet, spawn awesome avalanches. Many of these are ice avalanches which shear loose from the snouts of glaciers adorning these magnificent peaks. Many more are avalanches of snow falling from massive snowfields. Certainly tens of thousands of avalanches — and conceivably hundreds of thousands — fall annually in these high, stark landscapes. Most fall unobserved. The world hears of avalanche events in these parts mostly when mountaineering expeditions take on the big ones — Everest, K2 (Godwin-Austen), Makalu, Dhaulagiri, and Annapurna, to name a few. High altitude sickness, frostbite, falls, and avalanches take a horrible toll upon this hardy breed of men and women who are driven to conquer the highest summits. In *The American Alpine Journal,* 1981, David McClung presents data on avalanche deaths in the Himalayas. From 1895 to 1979, 198 mountaineers and porters had died by avalanche, making this the greatest killer of members of expeditions to the world's highest mountains. Everest leads the list with 34 killed, followed by Nanga Parbat (20), Dhaulagiri (17), Manaslu (17), and Annapurna (12).

No part of the world, though, has seen a longer and harder struggle against avalanches than the Alps of Austria, France, Italy, and Switzerland. The first historical record of avalanche encounters may have been in the third century B.C. when the Carthaginian general Hannibal led his army on an epic crossing of the Alps during the Second Punic War. There have since been some 22 centuries of battle between man and avalanche as the people of the Alps have fought to prosper while living in the shadow of mountains. Nowhere is this history better chronicled than in Colin Fraser's excellent work, *Avalanches and Snow Safety.*

With the coming of the tourist, avalanches have found a

whole new breed of victim, thus ensuring ample statistics in the future. Data taken from Fraser's book indicate that some 17,500 avalanches fall annually in the Swiss Alps alone. This is a statistic which we view as a conservative estimate, for surely many thousands of avalanches go undetected in remote, unpopulated areas or during storms. Nonetheless, it provides a good basis for estimating the number of avalanches falling in the Alps altogether. That estimate would be at least 100,000. To a lesser (and unknown) extent, avalanches fall in the other great mountain range of Europe, the Caucasus of southern Russia. The Scandinavian countries, too, must deal with avalanches, especially in the mountains and glacier-carved fjords of Norway. Scotland and Iceland have been the sites of occasional avalanche encounters.

Still other mountainous countries of the world face avalanche hazards. Japan, with a maritime climate which brings heavy snowfalls to its plentiful mountains, must cope with a significant problem, especially on the main island of Honshu, where heavy snowfalls, and large populations often combine to produce destructive avalanches. New Zealand is the Southern Hemisphere counterpart of Japan: it lies at similar latitudes, has a similar land mass, and has impressive mountain terrain and snowfall. The avalanche hazard is considerably less than that faced by Japan, however, mainly because of a much smaller population, which translates into fewer avalanche encounters. Still, the mountains of the South Islands of New Zealand — the Southern Alps — produce avalanche hazards in the ski fields and national parks which require watching. To an even lesser extent, the mountains of southeast Australia create avalanche hazards for its winter tourists. Another home of world-class avalanches is the Andes of South America. From the high ranges and volcanos of Columbia and Ecuador to the Patagonian icefields of southern Chile, the high cordillera (many peaks above 15,000 ft.) rise abruptly from the Pacific Ocean, trapping heavy snowfalls and generating avalanches on a vast scale.

Our main purpose in this book, though, is to focus on avalanches in North America, and especially in the United States. North America is home to one of the greatest mountain systems on earth, the North American Cordillera, which stretches for 5,000 miles from Panama to Alaska. This is an extension of the South American Cordillera — the Andes. Combined, the two create a mountain chain some 10,000 miles long. In North America, the cordillera is composed of the Coast Range, the Sierra

Nevada, the Cascades, and the Rocky Mountains, itself a mountain chain that extends more than 3,000 miles from central New Mexico to northwest Alaska. Within these major ranges lie smaller, individual ranges, each extending ten to hundreds of miles in length and each possessing its own climate, personality, and beauty. Throughout our book, we will refer often to individual ranges, each time giving new facts as needed to tell our story. For now let's name some of the better known mountain ranges of America and look at the characteristics that shape their personalities.

THE MOUNTAINS OF AMERICA AND THEIR AVALANCHES

The west coast of North America from Baja to Alaska is protected by an irregular chain of mountains known as the Coast Ranges. In southern California, many peaks top 7,000 feet, with San Gorgonio Mountain the highest at 11,500 feet. The high peaks carry a wintertime snow cover and are home to several ski and winter sports areas. Significant avalanching comes only sporadically, when massive, cold, Pacific storms bring heavy snowfalls or when spring thaws turn the snow to slush. Mount Baldy, situated some 50 air miles east of Los Angeles, is a popular resort with clearly defined avalanche areas. The tourists that flock there have frequently ignored the signs warning "Avalanche Danger." These signs are often carted away as souvenirs or even used on the site as toboggans! Regardless of whether it's ignorance or a cavalier attitude toward the danger, it's not nice to fool with Mother Nature. Inevitably, accidents have occurred.

On April 4, 1965, at least seven recreationists found themselves caught up in a wet snowslide that had pulled loose from the rocks at the top of the slope. The scene was chaos after the slide stopped, as at least 100 spectators who had witnessed the avalanche milled around the debris, some helping to pull out victims buried to the waist or neck. Soon everyone was accounted for except a teenage boy. An organized rescue team located him three feet deep some three and a half hours later. Miraculously, he was alive, conscious, and suffering only from shock and exposure.

Not so lucky was David Merrill, a nine-year-old Cub Scout on an outing with his troop on January 20, 1977. At 4:08 p.m. a wet avalanche released on the same slope as the 1965 incident. Seven people, including four Cub Scouts, were swept downhill. All were recovered quickly except Merrill, who was totally buried. A probe team located the boy 30 minutes later under three feet of dense, wet snow, but rescue came too late: the boy had suffocated. Both these accidents happened when the snowpack was thawing, and typify the avalanche danger of the coastal mountains of southern California.

The Sierra Nevada is the major mountain range of California, stretching 400 miles from Tehachapi Pass on the south to Lassen Peak on the north. Most peaks rise to about 9,000 feet in the northern range and 12,000 to 13,000 feet in the central and southern range. In fact, more than 500 peaks rise above 12,000 feet, with 14,495-foot Mount Whitney rising above all. These mountains are capable of wringing out enormous amounts of rain and snow from Pacific storms — five to 10 feet of snowfall in just a few days. These are the times, generally four or five each winter, when avalanche hazards reach an extreme state. Destructive avalanches such as the one that devastated Alpine Meadows Ski Area in 1982 are the unwelcome harvest of too much snow in too few days in the Sierra.

The Cascade Range starts at Lassen Peak in northern California and stretches for 700 miles across Oregon and Washington into southern British Columbia. Most peaks in this range top out at 6,000 to 10,000 feet, but studded throughout its length are the magnificent volcanos of the Pacific Northwest — Lassen, Shasta, Hood, Adams, Rainier, Glacier, and Baker. Frequently only these volcanic peaks rise above the clouds, all lesser peaks being enshrouded in thick mists that roll in from the Pacific. Lying among the lesser peaks now is Mount St. Helens. Once a

1.2 Mount St. Helens, Washington, where an avalanche killed five climbers in 1975. The arrow shows the position of the camp (Roland Emetaz photo)

proud, symmetrical cone of a mountain rising to 9,677 feet — some considered it the most beautiful of all the volcanos — it literally blew its top in a catastrophic eruption on May 18, 1980. The upper 1,270 feet of the mountain was blown away, thus destroying the site of one of the worst mountaineering avalanche tragedies in the United States.

It was on April 26, 1975, that a party of 29 climbers, 17 of them members of a mountaineering class taught at the University of Puget Sound in Tacoma, set up camp on the Forsyth Glacier on the north slope of Mount St. Helens. Skies were partly cloudy and fair, but winds gusting to 60 miles per hour drove swirling snow plumes across the face of the mountain. The next day, weather permitting, the party would attempt a summit ascent. At 8:26 p.m., when most of the group had retired to their tents or snow caves, a particularly large and growing snow cloud moved down the slope toward the camp. It quickly became clear to the few climbers who saw the cloud that it was not being driven by the wind. Then they heard the rumble. A cry of "Avalanche!" preceded the leading edge of snow by seconds. Tents were instantly flattened or ripped from their anchors and tumbled downhill. It was over in 15 seconds, but what had been an organized camp dug into contours of the glacier was now a rubble-strewn mess with tents swept as far as 200 yards away. The survivors surveyed a shocking scene: most of the tents were gone, with only small blotches of color showing in the fading light. Rescue began immediately as survivors threw themselves into a heroic effort of probing and digging, lasting through the night. At least 18 people had been completely buried, most inside their tents. Within hours, all but two had been found. Of these, three did not respond to resuscitation efforts and did not survive. The bodies of the remaining two victims were recovered three days later. In all, five men and women, aged 18 to 30 years, died in the avalanche, an avalanche that can never kill again, for its steep lair was wiped from the face of the earth in the violent eruption five years later.

Most of the volcanos of the Cascades have, at one time or another, brought down avalanches fatal to climbers. It is Mount Rainier, Washington, though, at 14,410 feet, that has registered the greatest toll of climbers lost to avalanche. To achieve its hostile, glaciated summit is a challenge that has drawn climbers from far and wide. Some highly skilled, some not so skilled, many have perished in the attempt. On March 9, 1969, John Aigars, a

1.3 Mt. Rainier, Washington (National Park Service photo)

31-year-old ski mountaineer traveling alone, triggered an avalanche in a treacherous area known as Panorama Point. He was buried and killed. On November 18, 1974, two climbers were picking their way down Success Cleaver in white-out conditions when David Taylor, 27, in the lead, kicked off a shallow slide that instantly swept him out of view of his companion, over a cliff, and onto the Success Glacier, 100 feet below. His body was never found. On December 31, 1977, 17-year-old Mike McNerthney was caught in a slide while descending the Panorama Point slope. He died in the same spot as Aigars had eight years before. Five months later on May 31, 1978, 24-year-old Todd Davis died in an avalanche in a steep couloir known as the Fuhrer's Finger on the south side of the mountain.

On March 4, 1979, famous mountaineer Willi Unsoeld, 52, and Janie Diepenbrock, 21, one of 28 students being led by Unsoeld, died in an avalanche on a chute above the Cowlitz Glacier bearing the grim name of Cadaver Gap. Ironically, this was to have been Unsoeld's last climb of Rainier, for severe arthritis had kept him in constant pain for several years. Unsoeld took a calculated risk in descending Cadaver Gap. Two days of storm had worsened the avalanche conditions since their ascent, but Unsoeld had a group of students who had been battered by snow and wind, were tired, and in some cases were becoming hypothermic and perhaps on the verge of frostbite. The safe haven of Camp Muir was not far away if they could successfully negotiate Cadaver Gap. With no good alternatives, Unsoeld led the first rope team and stepped into a death trap.

The worst accident in the history of mountaineering on Rainier (and in the United States), however, came on June 21, 1981, in the form of a death-dealing ice avalanche. A party of 22 climbers were resting below a steep ice wall of the Ingraham Glacier, when in a moment of extraordinary bad timing, a huge chunk of ice broke off the glacier. Eleven climbers were caught in the open with no place to run: they died a horrible death beneath the crushing, grinding blocks of blue ice.

We don't want to leave the impression that only the volcanic peaks of the Cascades are the haunts of avalanches. In severe winters, some of the heaviest snows on earth fall over these rugged mountains, and there is no shortage of avalanche paths. In fact, the worst avalanche disaster in United States history occurred at the abandoned townsite of Wellington, Washington, in 1910. In Chapter 2, you can read details of this avalanche, which in seconds snuffed out the lives of 96 men, women, and children.

Rising west of the Cascades and west of the city of Seattle and Puget Sound are the Olympic Mountains, a dramatic upheaval of the Coast Range. With water on three sides, the range dominates the Olympic Peninsula. The high point, Mount Olympus, rises nearly 8,000 feet above the nearby ocean. Impenetrable rain forests and jagged ridges of rock and ice make this one of the most difficult mountain areas to travel. Heavy snows assure plenty of avalanches, but human encounters have been few. No fatal avalanches have been recorded in the Olympics this century.

The western Canadian provinces of Alberta, British Columbia, and the Yukon Territory are stitched north to south by those two great barriers, the Coast Mountains and the Rocky Mountains. The Coast Mountains, with abundant snows and a long winter season are known for their glaciers and ice fields. The highest peaks lie at the northern end of the range in the St. Elias Mountains. Here, Mount Logan at 19,850 feet and Mount St. Elias at 18,008 feet look down upon the massive Malaspina Glacier, itself larger than the state of Rhode Island. The high point in the Canadian Rockies is 12,972-foot Mount Robson. Though not as high as the Rockies of the United States, these are magnificent with sheer, axehead-shaped peaks rising above the plains of Alberta. These Rockies are made up of several ranges whose names have been popularized by the rapid growth of helicopter skiing in recent years: the Bugaboos, Cariboos, Monashees, Purcells, and Selkirks. In the Yukon, the Selwyn and Mackenzie Mountains become the northern extension of the Canadian Rockies.

Certainly the mountains of Alaska, seen by so few and visited by fewer still, are among the most awesome of the continent. The Coast Range rises out of the Pacific and looms over Juneau, the state's capital, in the southeast panhandle. The residents of Juneau live literally in the shadow of mountains, and no city in the United States has as severe an avalanche potential (see Chapter 8). Though Juneau has so far been spared from avalanche disaster (except for a snow and rock slide in 1936 that killed 14), it seems only a matter of time until conditions become ripe for the avalanche that could claim dozens of lives.

North along the coast, beyond the St. Elias Mountains and the Malaspina Glacier, lie the Chugach, Kenai, and Wrangell Mountains. It is the Chugach, though, where many avalanches have killed. The Chugach are Alaska's most accessible mountains, closing in on Anchorage, the largest city, and on Valdez, the terminus of the Alaska oil pipeline on Prince William Sound. Chugach State Park provides not only a great playground for the restless of Anchorage but also a great opportunity for avalanche encounters. Climbers, ski tourers, and hunters have been dying by avalanche at the rate of one a year for 15 years in the Chugach, making this one of the highest-risk avalanche areas in the United States. Most of the accidents have been like the one in 1971 that killed two climbers on the Eklutna Glacier; the church outing in 1973 on Flattop Mountain in which one died; the bear hunter in 1975 who died along the Twenty-Mile River when he became the prey of the avalanche; or the four ski tourers who died in one avalanche near Turnagain Pass in 1978. Some of the incidents, though, have been a bit more bizarre. On April 14, 1973, a large avalanche fell 3,000 feet into the Passage Canal on Prince William Sound, creating a 15-foot tidal wave which rolled one and a half miles across the canal and struck a barge moored at Whittier. The wave lifted the barge violently and broke the three-inch-thick steel mooring lines. Four smaller boats were sunk. A more freakish accident occurred in Valdez on February 6, 1977, when a slab of snow broke loose from the domed roof of a giant oil storage tank, falling on and killing a 40-year-old workman below.

Alyeska Ski Area lies in the Chugach Mountains. Tucked in the shadow of 4,000-foot peaks, it is an area with formidable avalanche problems requiring constant attention and control. Despite several close calls, there has never been an avalanche death at the area. Chair lifts have not been so fortunate; there have been two instances of major damage by avalanches. The first was a particularly fascinating avalanche event. Late on the afternoon of April 12, 1969, after the lifts had closed, an artillery control team trained their gun on the steep slopes rising above the ski runs. One shot released a massive slide that roared down onto the trails, threw an enormous cloud of powder snow into the air, then seemingly came to a stop. In fact it had not come to a stop but instead had plowed into the wet snow at lower elevation, gouged out a thick layer of this snow, and set it into motion as an ultra-slow-moving wet avalanche that was oozing toward the base facilities. Startled employees and guests looked up to see a wall of snow 25 feet high and crunching along at the pace of a brisk walk come out of the mouth of a canyon and take dead aim on the lower lift terminal, several buildings, and the parking lot. Hastily, one man drove a snowcat out of the path of the avalanche, others warned people to abandon the buildings in the way, and others headed to the parking lot to drive away parked cars. The avalanche hit the lift, crushed the operator's building, and slowly twisted and bent the steel towers of the lift. The avalanche then threatened the ticket office. The snow mass crept to the edge of the building, pressed against walls and windows, and stopped without breaking a single pane of glass.

The Alaska Range cuts across south-central Alaska north and west of Anchorage in an arc 600 miles long. This range separates the south-central portion of the state from the great plateau of the interior. It also is home to North America's highest peak, 20,320-foot Mount McKinley. (Recently the proper name of this mountain has reverted to its original name — Denali, the Indian word for "great one.") Looming next to Denali is a second giant, 17,400-foot Mount Foraker. Avalanches falling from these peaks have taken a heavy toll on mountaineers — especially Japanese — trying to conquer the summits. Recent incidents include three Japanese climbers killed in 1976, two more in 1978, and one more in 1979. American climbers have been involved in numerous avalanches on these peaks, frequently suffering injury but so far no deaths.

Alaska claims two more great mountain ranges, both so remote that avalanche encounters have been few. The Aleutian Range begins on the mainland and stretches in a broad arc some 1,500 miles into the stormy North Pacific. These relatively low volcanic peaks form the backbone of the Alaska Peninsula and the Aleutian Islands. The other range is the vast, aloof Brooks

Range, planet Earth's farthest north mountains. Lying entirely north of the Arctic Circle, the Brooks Range encompasses some 150,000 square miles, portions of which likely remain unexplored.

From the northernmost reaches of the Rockies, let's head south 3,000 miles to New Mexico and check out the Rockies in a region more familiar to us all. The Southern Rocky Mountains extend from central New Mexico to southern Wyoming. The principal ranges in this region are the Sangre de Cristos of New Mexico and Colorado, the San Juans of southwest Colorado, the Elk, West Elk, and Sawatch Ranges of central Colorado, the Front, Gore, and Park Ranges of northern Colorado, and the Medicine Bow and Laramie Ranges in Wyoming. This system of ranges is the highest in America. Some 1,200 peaks top 10,000 feet in elevation, and 53 exceed 14,000 feet, with Mt. Elbert at 14,433 feet the highest of all. Indeed there may be no mountain barrier so formidable as the Sawatch Range with its immense lineup of "fourteeners": Massive, Elbert, La Plata, Huron, Oxford, Belford, Missouri, Harvard, Columbia, Yale, Princeton, Antero, Tabeguache, and Shavano. It is terrain like this which helps make Colorado the highest state, having an average elevation of 6,800 feet.

The Central Rockies are composed of the Wasatch and Uinta Ranges of northern Utah and the Bighorns, Wind Rivers, and Tetons of western Wyoming. To many no mountains have such stunning beauty as do the Tetons, which rise abruptly from the meadows of Jackson Hole in cathedral-like spires reaching to 13,766 feet. The Uintas are unique in the "lower forty-eight" in that they are the only range having an east-west orientation.

The Northern Rockies, though not as lofty as the Rockies to the south, offer dramatic scenery in an undulating series of north-south oriented ranges and valleys. Extending across central and northern Idaho and western Montana, this system is composed of the Clearwater and Salmon River Mountains, the Sawtooth and Lost River Ranges, and the Bitterroot, Madison, and Absaroka Ranges. Glacier National Park, on the United States-Canadian border boasts some of the most spectacular scenery in all the Rocky Mountains, offering its own special collage of sheer granite peaks, glaciers, lakes, and valleys. Indeed, these mountains with their rows of ledges, striations, and facets take on the appearance (at least to snow eaters who have looked at thousands of ice grains under a microscope) of enormous cup crystals. (We'll tell you all about cup crystals in Chapter 3.)

Collectively, the Rockies are a mid-continent mountain system dividing the Great Plains on the east from the Great Basin and Columbia Plateau on the west. The Continental Divide, running its full length, separates the Atlantic and Pacific Ocean watersheds. Situated far from oceanic storm and moisture sources, the Rockies generally have less abundant and drier snowfalls than the mountains nearer the Pacific. This leads to a preponderance of dry-snow avalanches, as we shall see in more detail as our story unfolds.

The final — actually first, given their great age — major mountain range of America is, of course, the Appalachian Mountains. Stretching more than 1,000 miles from northern Georgia to northern Maine, the Appalachians never achieve great heights, especially when compared to their much younger cousins out West. From central New York to Virginia, elevations range from 2,000 to 4,000 feet in the Catskills, Poconos, Shenandoahs, and Alleghenies. The Great Smoky Mountains of Tennessee and North Carolina, however, rise with regularity above 6,000 feet. The beauty of these parts of the Appalachians is one of craggy mountains, densely mixed deciduous and coniferous forests, cascading rivers, dark hollows, and misty vistas. It is not avalanche country, despite a sometimes severe and snowy winter climate.

Avalanche country in the Appalachians comes farther north in the White Mountains of New Hampshire. Here, in the Presidential Range, are a cluster of peaks rising above 5,300 feet, and above timberline — Adams, Clay, Jefferson, Madison, Monroe. Topping out at 6,288 feet, Mount Washington stands well above the rest and is notorious for having one of the harshest climates on earth. Indeed, on April 12, 1934, the weather station at the summit was blasted by a wind gust of 231 miles per hour, the highest wind speed ever recorded at the earth's surface.

The rocky slopes of Mount Washington are snow-covered and wind-swept much of the year and have thus been the sites of several serious avalanche encounters. On February 18, 1956, a party of five climbers triggered a slide while descending Tuckerman Ravine. One died. On April 4, 1964, two climbers died when an avalanche swept them down and buried them in Huntington Ravine. Much more recently, on January 25, 1982, two related incidents took the life of one man and caused crippling injuries to two others. On the 22nd, Hugh Herr, 17, and Jeffrey

Batzer, 20, set out for a weekend of ice climbing. Caught in a typical Mount Washington blizzard with the temperature hovering near five below zero and winds howling to 73 miles per hour, they became disoriented, headed down the wrong ridge, and ended up floundering through waist-deep snow for hours in a vain search for shelter. Not able to travel, they bivouacked in the snow for three days, suffering the ravages of cold, eventually being unable to put back on frozen boots, knowing their frostbite was at a life-threatening stage, and losing strength and hope.

A rescue was in fact underway, but it led to tragedy for one of the searchers. Albert Dow, 28, and Mike Hartrick, 30, were traversing a steep wooded slope on Lion Head near Tuckerman Ravine when they released an avalanche that carried them through the trees. Battered, bruised, and partly buried, Hartrick survived. Dow did not; other rescuers summoned to the site pulled his lifeless body from the snow one and one half hours later. The following day, January 26, searchers found Herr and Batzer. The two young men would survive their ordeal but would pay a terrible price: both lost both legs to frostbite.

Mount Washington is not alone in the Appalachians in bringing down avalanches on unwary climbers. Mount Katahdin, Maine, got into the act on February 8, 1984. Until this date there had never been a fatal avalanche recorded on Maine's highest peak. Five climbers triggered a slide near the rock buttress called First Cathedral; all five were swept downhill and buried. Three of them survived shallow burials, but the other two, Ken Levanway and Steve Hilt, had died of suffocation by the time they were dug from beneath the hard-packed snow.

Thus ends our introductory tour of the mountains of the world, and especially those of America. As we continue, we'll bring you back to selected portions of these mountains to learn more of their personalities, weather, and avalanche histories.

THE AVALANCHE PROBLEM IN PERSPECTIVE

Since the early 1970s, a group of avalanche scientists with U.S. Forest Service Mountain Snow and Avalanche Research Project (located in Fort Collins, Colorado, until the project's demise in 1985) gathered data on from 60 to 70 mountain sites scattered throughout the western states, including Alaska. The purpose was to gain a national perspective on the avalanche problem. The data sites were comprised of ski areas, highway passes, national parks, state parks, touring centers, heli-ski operations, mining operations, and various backcountry venues.

The Westwide Network, as the data sites were collectively called, reported roughly 9,000 avalanches a year. To answer the more difficult question — how many avalanches actually fall in the United States — let's do a little guesswork. We know that at even the manned Westwide Network sites, not all avalanches observed get recorded. Second, we can be certain that during major storms lasting several days, some avalanches break loose and slide downhill only to be totally obscured by falling and drifting snow by the time the observer gets out a day or two later. Third and most significant, there are vast wilderness areas in which thousands of avalanches fall without being observed. Indeed, we remember one episode in 1973 following a major avalanche cycle in Colorado. Our observers had reported several hundred avalanches during a five-day storm period. On the first clear day after the storm, we hitched a ride on the Forest Service twin-engine airplane and went looking for avalanches. Our flight over the Elk and West Elk Mountains around Aspen and Crested Butte and over the San Juan Mountains around Ouray, Silverton, Telluride, and Durango was stunning: literally thousands of avalanches had rained down in these remote ranges. Almost every major slope showed signs of fracture lines and piles of debris. The point is this: for every avalanche written down and reported by an observer, at least ten had actually run.

If we apply this rough ratio of ten to one to the national statistic of 9,000 avalanches recorded, we get an estimate of 90,000 that actually fall. Since we're dealing in crude "guesstimates" only, we're perfectly justified in rounding this number off and saying that the number of avalanches falling annually in the United States is on the order of 100,000.

We can similarly arrive at a world figure for the number of avalanches falling. Earlier in this chapter we suggested that 100,000 avalanches annually was a reasonable number for the great mountain ranges of the Alps, Himalayas, and Andes. When we total these various estimates, and make allowances for other parts of the world — Canada, Scandinavia, Russia, Japan, New Zealand, for example — it's easy to argue that the number of avalanches falling annually worldwide is on the order of one million.

Getting back to the United States statistics, about 100 avalanches a year (roughly one percent of the 9,000 reported) cause serious problems — injury, death, and destruction of property. Based on the incidents that are reported, about 140 people a year are caught in avalanches (that is, they are bodily involved in the moving snow or its effects), 60 to 70 are partly or wholly buried, 12 sustain injury, and 17 are killed. Average annual property damage is approximately $400,000.

We can borrow a statistic used by the National Weather Service that sets the economic value of a human life at $620,000. (Presumably, this figure is based on a productive wage earner averaging $20,000 for 31 years.) This would mean an economic loss to our society of about $10.5 million caused annually by avalanche deaths.

How does an annual fatality rate of 17 compare with other avalanche-prone countries? Precise statistics are hard to come by; nonetheless, Austria and Switzerland each report 35 to 40 persons killed by avalanches per year; France, 31; Italy, 20 to 30; Germany, about 10; and Norway, 10 to 15. Japan averages about 30 persons killed a year, while Canada averages seven. It's not surprising that the European countries lead the list, for there the hazard is not only to recreational tourists but also to villages sitting beneath avalanche paths. The United States, being a younger country with a lower population density, has not yet been pushed to this higher plateau of disaster potential.

GOING TO EXTREMES: HOW BIG OR SMALL, HOW FAST OR SLOW?

Avalanches, like people, come in all shapes and sizes. There are thin ones that come down in a sliver; there are broad ones that bring down a whole mountainside. There are shallow ones that peel off a top layer of snow just an inch or so thick; there are deep ones that rip out an entire winter's snow cover to the ground. There are short ones that slump just a few feet; there are long ones that fall a mile or more. And there are slow ones that crawl at two miles an hour, and the ultra-speed demons that hurtle at 200 miles an hour.

A very small avalanche is called a sluff. Sluffs are mostly harmless, and are common mountain sights. After a fresh snow, small, shallow trickles of dry snow that have sifted five, 10, or 50 feet down steep banks are routine features of the snowscape. On sunny spring days, wet sluffs and snowrollers etching trails down virgin slopes are inevitable. An example of an extremely small slide that could have easily been harmful, but in this case was not, ran on January 13, 1980. Debby Browne, age 30, was ski touring on Cameron Pass, Colorado, with her husband and two friends when the unexpected occurred. The group had toured to treeline without incident. Browne began her descent ahead of the others and stopped on the side of a shallow but steep gully, waiting for the others to catch up. A booming sound like thunder, but coming from the snow, startled the group. A second later Browne felt the snow give way underneath her, and in the next second the snow pushed her forward and toppled her over. The avalanche ran no more than 10 feet but still buried Browne face beneath one and one half feet of snow; only the tip of one ski pole remained on the surface. Her husband skied to the spot and began scooping away the snow. In two minutes he had cleared the snow from Browne, who was frightened but unharmed. Later, the skiers mentioned that they had known the avalanche danger was high and that avalanche warnings were in effect, and had been on the lookout for large avalanche paths, but did not think of the short gully wall as a danger spot.

Not so fortunate was 35-year-old Robert Wells when he was caught in a small slide. On March 17, 1984, Wells and Greg Meyer headed off on the popular Commando Run leading from the summit of Vail Pass, Colorado, toward the top of Vail ski area. About six miles into the tour, Wells and Meyer, tiring, altered their route and headed on a downhill timber-bash toward Interstate 70, planning to hitch a ride back to the summit of the pass. Their route along Timber Creek brought them to one last short, but steep, pitch within 50 feet of the highway. Wells cut across the top of the slope, and then disappeared from Meyer's view, when a small avalanche knocked him down and carried him to the creek bottom — and under the highway bridge. He had fallen only 40 feet in elevation, yet was buried three feet deep in heavy, damp snow. Seventy minutes later, Meyer and a trucker who had stopped on the highway recovered Wells' body, but it was too late. Here was an avalanche that broke one and one half feet deep, snared its victim, and carried him on a very short tumble ending in a creek bed — where it was easy to get buried without a trace. This was the perfect spot for a small slide to turn killer. Creek banks provide the ideal environment for small avalanches.

The avalanches at the other end of the spectrum — the big ones — frequently are not killers. This is because they almost always release by natural causes, that is, from their own weight. (Artificial or outside triggers, such as a skier, are much more effective in releasing small to medium avalanches in shallower snowpacks.) A typical large avalanche in North America might set 300,000 cubic yards of snow in motion. Picture a mountainside of snow having a depth of 10 feet and an area of 20 football fields; next, picture this amount of snow breaking loose and falling 4,000 feet in elevation (the equivalent of a slope distance of one and one half to two miles). Now that's a big avalanche.

Two avalanches of this size fell near the remote community of Gothic, Colorado, during a storm in March 1978. The first broke loose in a snow layer (or slab) only three feet deep, but this layer was 3,000 feet wide and 1,000 feet long. The second avalanche was three to six feet deep and 10,000 feet — roughly two miles — wide. Both fell about 2,500 feet in elevation. Neither caused damage, but wouldn't that have been an awesome spectacle to watch?

A slope near Portage, Alaska, about 50 miles east of Anchorage, has been especially active the last few years in producing stupendous avalanches. It is named the Williwaw avalanche, because it repeatedly ravages the Williwaw campground. In January 1980 this avalanche hit the campground at the base of the mountain and then ran three-quarters of a mile across the Portage Valley, destroying thousands of trees along the way. A similar release in February 1983 again clobbered the campground and piled snow 20 feet deep in the valley over an area the size of 20 football fields. In both cases the powder cloud filled the valley and rolled through the air a mile beyond the mass of avalanche debris. After the second avalanche had run, a team of avalanche practitioners flew by helicopter to the top of the avalanche to study and measure the fracture face. This required serious mountaineering skills, for they had to rappel from the top of the fracture down to the bed surface of the avalanche, and jumar (using ascenders) back up. The fracture depth ranged from 24 to 36 feet and was 1,300 feet long. It was certainly a spooky — and possibly dangerous — position to be in, tucked under the shadow of a monstrous overhanging wall of snow. This is the deepest fracture of snow know to us.

Large avalanches become killers when they overrun people, cars, and houses far below the release point. One example of a killer highway slide is the East Riverside avalanche on Red Mountain Pass, four miles south of Ouray, Colorado. The East Riverside frequently produces large avalanches that bring enormous amounts of snow crashing down onto the highway at speeds of 100 miles an hour. Four times this avalanche has killed. In February 1908, Elias Fritz was killed here when he and two companions were struck by a slide while shoveling a path through the debris of an earlier slide. On March 3, 1963, the Reverend Marvin Hudson and his two daughters, Amelia,

17, and Pauline, 12, died when an avalanche swept the three and their car, which had been stuck in snow, off the highway and into the Uncompaghre River gorge. Eighty-eight days later the last body was recovered. The third incident occurred on March 2, 1970, when an avalanche swept away Robert Miller, age 36 and father of seven, who was driving a bulldozer to clear snow from a previous avalanche. The fourth incident, occurring on February 10, 1978, was a replay of the second. Terry Kishbaugh, 28, was operating heavy equipment clearing debris from one avalanche, when a second large one swept him into the canyon. His body was recovered three months later.

One more example of a giant avalanche turned killer is the one that hit the small community of Twin Lakes, Colorado, in 1962. In the pre-dawn hours of January 21, a slab 10 feet deep and hundreds of feet wide broke loose and fell 2,800 feet in elevation down Perry Mountain. The avalanche was so large and moving so fast that, near the bottom, it jumped a 100-foot-high natural diversion dam that had always stopped or deflected avalanches in the past. The slide then mowed down a stand of 70-year-old aspen trees before crashing into the houses nestled against the woods. Seven homes and a house trailer were obliterated, with parts of houses carried 500 feet from their foundations. Nine residents were buried by the avalanche; seven died.

The largest avalanches known to have fallen in North America have done so in the Wrangell and St. Elias Mountains of Alaska and Canada. One especially large avalanche fell down the slopes of Mount Sanford on April 12, 1981. This one contained an estimated one million cubic yards of ice and snow, fell almost 10,000 feet in elevation, and traveled almost eight miles before coming to a stop. The avalanche threw up a powder cloud many thousands of feet high that was visible for more than 100 miles. Indeed witnesses from afar telephoned various authorities to report that Mount Sanford, a volcanic peak, was erupting. A helicopter flight the next day told the story. An enormous block of ice had fallen from the summit ice cap thousands of feet down a sheer cliff and exploded on impact with the glacier below, causing an avalanche of snow. The avalanche then rumbled eight miles down the glacier, in the process going up and over a 3,000-foot mountain in the way!

An average avalanche of snow (using approximate figures) is two to three feet deep at the fracture line, 100 to 200 feet wide, and will fall 300 to 500 feet in elevation. The speed of an avalanche of this size is roughly 40 to 60 miles an hour, if the snow is dry. If the snow is wet, either from heavy rain or from thaw, the speed will be less, probably in the range of 20 to 40 miles an hour. We have already seen, earlier in this chapter, the ultimate in slow-moving avalanches: a wet avalanche in Alaska, in which the speed was only three or four miles an hour, or around five feet a second — pretty much the pace of a brisk walk. This type of slide would love to come to a stop, but addiional snow keeps piling on at the top end, and like a train, a push at the back forces the front to chug along.

Larger avalanches attain higher speeds. A dry-snow avalanche of, say, four feet deep and 500 feet wide, falling 1,500 feet in elevation could easily attain a speed of 70 to 80 miles per hour. A very large slide that broke eight to 10 feet deep, 700 to 800 feet wide, and fell 3,000 feet could reach speeds of 90 to 120 miles per hour. In all cases, wet-snow avalanches would move at lesser speeds, seldom if ever going more than 60 miles per hour. The fastest avalanche speeds measured have been in the range of 230 miles per hour. These measurements have been made by Japanese scientists, and we are not certain what the conditions were that caused these avalanches to move so fast. We do know that the avalanches fell down a confined gully that was exceptionally steep — perhaps 60 to 70 degrees. Certainly no avalanche having this extraordinary speed has been measured in the United States. But, of course, avalanches don't have to possess far-out measurements to be impressive: the everyday variety are impressive enough.

July 1888 photo of a hand-dug tunnel through avalanche debris deposited by the East Riverside Avalanche in Colorado (San Juan County, Colorado, Historical Society)

2 HISTORY AND AVALANCHES

THERE WAS A TIME WHEN THE mountains of the world were uninhabited and devoid of human beings during the long winter months. Avalanches would roar down the steep slopes, ripping out trees and generally rearranging the landscape — but hazard, the threat to people and their property, did not exist. That, however, changed dramatically once settlers began to move into the higher elevations. For as long as humans have populated mountainous terrain, avalanches have threatened, often fulfilling their threat with death and devastation.

Why did groups of people voluntarily subject themselves to the unforgiving environment of long, snowbound winters marked by freezing temperatures, harsh winds, and the constant threat of avalanches? The settlers needed to find a place where they could escape the population pressures of the lower lands and where they could make a living. Hundreds of years ago those livelihoods centered around agriculture. As time went on, mountain livelihoods came not so much from the soil as from the rock, with mining writing the history of many high, rugged regions in North America. More recently, it is those "farming" the white gold — the ski industry — who keep numerous mountain areas alive with people.

Human history becomes more and more a race between education and catastrophe.
H. G. WELLS

The upsurge of winter recreation in recent decades has brought not only alpine and nordic skiers, snowmobilers and winter climbers to the mountains, but has also increased traffic on avalanche-prone roads, increased building and development in often hazardous terrain, and contributed in general to land-use pressures. The increasing numbers of people, vehicles, and property in the way of avalanches keeps danger on a continuously rising scale.

Let's first look at the earliest reported interactions between humans and avalanches, as we work our way through mountain history up to the present.

AVALANCHE HAZARD IN EUROPE

As noted earlier, we are indebted to author Colin Fraser for tracking down some of the earliest references to European avalanche accidents, including those details on Hannibal's Alpine crossing in 218 B.C. He found in Polybius' and Livy's accounts of the crossing descriptions of the snow conditions Hannibal observed — fresh snow on a crust of old snow — one sure sign of an avalanche waiting to happen, as we shall soon see. His troops were harassed and attacked by local tribesmen in their travels to the summit of the pass, which could account for some losses — but certainly not for these staggering numbers: 18,000 (out of 38,000) soldiers, 2,000 horses, and several elephants. Fraser also refers to the poet Silius Italicus's (A.D. 25-101) epic poem *Punici*, which offers another telling detail: "Detached snow drags the men into the abyss and snow falling rapidly from the high summits engulfs the living squadrons."

In 1939, Professor Paul Niggli, of the Swiss Federal Institute of Technology, wrote the introduction to a collection of pioneering research papers into snow and avalanches which was translated into English and called *Snow and Its Metamorphism.* His excerpt from Strabo's *Geographica IV 6, 6* from the year A.D. 16, is probably one of the oldest descriptions of avalanches in the Alpine region:

> *It is difficult to protect oneself against ice sheets sliding down from above which are capable of hurling entire caravans into the gaping abysses. Many such sheets lie one on top of another because one snow layer after the other turns to ice and the sheets on the surface disengage themselves from the ones below before they are melted entirely by the sun.*

Fraser found descriptions of avalanche accidents in monastic records dating from the 12th century. During this period in Europe, religious pilgrims traveled to and from Rome over mountain passes in the Alps, occasionally during winter. After a difficult December crossing of the Great St. Bernard Pass in Switzerland in 1128, Rudolf, the Abbot of St. Trond, near Liège, and his party reached the village of Saint Rhemy, having pushed through large drifts of snow enroute. While there he observed:

The small village was overcrowded by the throng of pilgrims. From the lofty and rugged heights above it fell often huge masses of snow, carrying away everything they encountered, so that when some parties of guests had found their places, and others were still waiting near the houses, these masses swept the latter away and suffocated some whilst crippling others of those in the buildings. In such a continual state of death we spent several days in the village.

The early avalanche victims were travelers and soldiers. But in time, a new group found themselves as potential targets. The earliest inhabitants of the Alpine regions of Europe settled in the lowlands, where the climate was milder than in the precipitous higher elevations, and where natural resources such as fertile land and forests were abundant. But later waves of migration found the fertile lowlands already heavily populated, and were forced to settle in the mountain valleys. Once there, they faced a hostile environment, including long snowy winters, short growing seasons, and another danger — the snow avalanche. By the Middle Ages, the mountain valleys were widely inhabited and the written history of avalanche disaster, sketchy prior to this time, begins to expand in detail and frequency.

An early chronicler of Swiss avalanche history was Flury Sprecher von Bernegg, a knight and also the local scribe in Davos, who was responsible for recording all kinds of unusual events occurring in the Davos environs. His first entry was from 1440 and described an avalanche which destroyed 4 buildings and killed 11 people. Four people were buried for 24 hours but were rescued alive. This chronicle of avalanche history of the Davos area (*Lawinenchronik der Landschaft Davos*), was continued by Sprecher's son, and by many others through the centuries. From an entry in 1606 comes this loose translation of the old Swiss German:

On January 16, 1602 there was an accident of extraordinary importance. It was Saturday night at 12 o'clock when a hideously gruesome avalanche smashed into the town of Davos, with such force that the mountain sides and valley floors seemed to shake. Uninhibited by wood or stone, the avalanche took out whole forests of larch and pine. It had snowed for three weeks and the snow was 12 shoes deep. [one "shoe" is the equivalent of 12 inches (one foot)] The rescuers were summoned by the ringing of church bells. The rescue effort continued for three days and three nights and an unbelievable amount of snow was excavated. Thirteen people were found dead under the snow; seven in one house, four in a church. A 14 year old girl was found alive after being buried in the snow for 36 hours.

In many cases, the villagers made the avalanche problem worse. Before settlement, dense forests covered many of the steep slopes above the valleys. The forests inhibited large avalanches, since catastrophic avalanches do not originate in a heavy forest, and avalanches traveling into such a forest will often slow as the snow encounters the trees. This tends to diminish the speed of the snow and break up the avalanche. However, villagers often cut down the forests for building and heating purposes. In many areas the trees never grew back, leaving the slopes bare and smooth — a perfect track for the run of a snow avalanche. A prime example of deforestation is in the valley of Ursental in central Switzerland. Above the town of Andermatt (Figure 2.1), there remains just a wedge of trees, while the remainder of the steep slope is bare. Up valley, near the Furka Pass, is the town of Hospental, which also maintains it's own protective wedge of trees. As the story is told, the inhabitants of the valley systematically cut down the forests that covered the steep slopes on both sides. Almost too late they realized their mistake: they saw that on the bare, treeless slopes, huge avalanches began descending to the valley floor, making travel between towns extremely dangerous. All tree-cutting stopped and the wedges of trees above the towns were preserved. Reforestation, the systematic planting of trees, continues today in the Ursental, to thicken the wedges that are periodically thinned by avalanches. Modern avalanche defense structures are also used, and we will discuss these in detail in Chapter 7.

Another related anecdote from Switzerland comes from the book *Balancing on An Alp*, by anthropologist R. M. Netting. He studied the village of Torbel, in the Valais Canton of southern Switzerland. This canton has been inhabited since the ninth century. Netting observed that while clearing of the forests must have occurred during the early settlement of the area, many of the slopes remained forested. "Conservation and judicious use of the forest were impressive achievements of the Torbel polity, especially since the trees also served to anchor mountainside soil, protect the watershed, and reduce avalanche danger."

Not just in the European Alps were avalanches making life difficult for the local populations. Perhaps the longest historical record of avalanche events and accidents belongs to the island

2.1 The Swiss village of Andermatt and the wedge of trees which protects it from avalanches. Note the structures in the upper part of the wedge; these are to inhibit snow from avalanching and are described in Chapter 7.

country of Iceland. Iceland has suffered more fatalities from snow avalanches than from any other single type of natural hazard in its more than 1100-year history. Much of Iceland's history is preserved in annals that date back to the 13th century. Helgi Björnsson, researcher with the Icelandic Meteorological Office, has described Iceland's avalanche history, from the annals and from other more recent sources such as newspapers and diaries. The earliest reference to avalanche deaths is from the year 1118, when five people were killed. Since then avalanches have claimed about 600 lives.

Iceland's near neighbor, Norway, also has a long history of destruction and catastrophe caused by the snow avalanche. Avalanches are most common in the western and northern parts of Norway, where steep-sided slopes end in narrow fjords and valleys, and snowfall is abundant. Two of the worst years in Norway's history were 1679 and 1755: records show that in 1679 avalanches killed between 400 and 500 people, and in 1755, about 200. Statistics compiled by G. Ramsli in Norway show between 1,600 and 1,700 avalanche fatalities, from 1836 to the present. In addition to the hundreds of fatalities, countless others have been injured, cattle have been killed, houses and other structures damaged or destroyed, forests and farm lands damaged, and travel by trail, road and railroad halted.

In many alpine villages, houses were squeezed together in safe havens between avalanche paths. All too often, the capricious nature of the beast defied the efforts of the villagers and avalanches swept away houses that had been standing for hundreds of years. Two examples from Switzerland describe this best. Colin Fraser mentions the 1459 avalanche near Disentis that totally destroyed the Church of Saint Placidus which had been standing for 655 years! The second example comes from John Friedl, an anthropologist who studied Kippel, one of four villages in the narrow, avalanche-battered Lotschental Valley. The oldest house, built in 1404, was destroyed by an avalanche in 1951, after standing for 547 years.

From the 1706 book *Description of the Natural History of Switzerland*, written by Johann Jacob Scheuchzer, come tragic stories from Switzerland's history. For example:

On January 25, 1689, a snow-break occurred near Saas in Brettigaü, in the Calmüren mountains . . . with fearful violence it carried part of the forest down with it, continued its course down the central mountain with much wood and rocks, passed through the community of Raschnal, and crossed the Lanquart River. It destroyed nine houses and many stables, killing twenty people.

Many people of the communities of Küblis, Conters, and Saas responded to the tolling of the church bells and brought relief to the sufferers. But in the same afternoon, another avalanche came down . . . it destroyed all dwellings and stables along the Sagen Brook, a total of 157. Fifty-seven bodies were found, and many people were injured.

In 1936, in a classic text entitled *Mountain Geography*, Professor Roderick Peattie recounts several avalanche catastrophies from Switzerland. On January 16 and 17 of 1594, avalanches in Bendretto tore down a church, a rectory, and several houses and barns. In 1634 the priest's house was destroyed and the priest buried. In 1695 the village was again besieged by avalanches from all sides of the valley, with the church and several houses and barns destroyed. The snow in the village measured more than ten feet deep. In the high valley of St. Antonien in the Grisons in southeast Switzerland, from 1608 to 1876, avalanches destroyed 38 houses, 200 barns, four sawmills, 43 people, and 130 head of cattle. In 1689 an avalanche wiped out the village of Saas, killing all the inhabitants. In 1719 an avalanche in the Valais district wiped out an entire town, killing 60 persons.

One final story comes from the village of Obergestelen. On February 20, 1720, an avalanche leaped over a forest situated between the slope and the village and destroyed a third of the village, killing 84 of its 200 inhabitants and 600 head of cattle. The avalanche snow blocked the Rhone River, which quickly melted through the snow and then flooded a portion of the settlement. What was left of the town was ruined by fire. "The indomitable villagers rebuilt their town, only to have it subsequently destroyed by an avalanche from the other side of the valley."

Although it sounds unlikely, the British Isles can also be mentioned in this history of avalanche accidents. R. G. Ward, professor of geography at the University of London and a keen observer of snow and avalanches, found the first recorded avalanche accident in Scotland. This took place on New Year's Day of 1800. A party of five gamehunters were inside a shooting lodge in the Gaick hills just south of the Cairngorm Mountains when an avalanche totally destroyed the building. Another incident from Scotland's history is not so well documented. It seems that "a giant snowball" fell alongside a poor man's cottage. He and his family were in luck. Uninjured, they opened the snowball and found inside "three brace of ptarmigan, six hares, four brace of grouse, a blackcock, a pheasant, three geese, and two fat stags."

The 19th century provides a continuation of Europe's devastating avalanche history, and records became more detailed. In Iceland, as population increased, people began moving into previously unoccupied areas. Before this time, Iceland's population was mostly rural. But after 1880 people settled along the deep and narrow fjords on the Icelandic coasts, establishing villages where fishing was the main livelihood. Settlers in many of the villagers soon learned that they were living in the paths of deadly avalanches which periodically swept down the towering peaks above and into the fjords. Stories come from both Iceland and Norway of fishermen in their boats who were killed by avalanches. The avalanche would race down the slope and, moving at top speed, fly across the fjord, capsizing the unwary fishermen in their boats. One of the worst avalanches in Iceland's history was on February 18, 1885, when the village of Seydisfjordur on the east coast was struck: 24 people were killed that day. Another disaster struck Hnifsdalur in the northwest peninsula of Iceland on February 18, 1910, when avalanches killed 20 people.

AVALANCHE HAZARD IN NORTH AMERICA

While avalanches were dictating the routines of many alpine villagers in Europe and Scandinavia, they were an unknown quantity in North America. For hundreds of years, native Indians inhabited the western mountains in summer, escaping the scorching temperatures of the plains and enjoying the cool climate and ample game and fish of the higher elevations. When the aspen began turning golden as winter approached, the mountains became empty of people again. Only the trees and bushes, and perhaps occasional unsuspecting coyotes and elk, suffered the wrath of the fast-moving avalanches.

The quietude and serenity of the mountains in winter was broken finally and forever with the discovery of gold. From the mid-19th century on, mining camps began popping up everywhere: California, Colorado, Washington, Utah, Montana, Nevada. The gold rush literally changed the faces of many mountain areas. No longer pristine, slopes and valleys became laced with trails, wagon roads, and then railroads and even aerial tramways. Streams of people followed the early prospectors, from mining engineers to entrepreneurs to shop keepers, packers and haulers, printers, priests, and prostitutes, to name a few. Coming from the eastern half of the country and western Europe, thousands came to make their fortune, or to capitalize on those who did.

Avalanches were but one of the perils these mountain settlers faced, but they took a distinctive toll. Hundreds have died in avalanches in the United States — close to 500 fatalities in Colorado alone — and hundreds more in Canada. Avalanche history in this country is just over a century old but it is packed with devastating property damage and loss of human life.

Newspaper accounts and diaries, some dating back to the 1870s, preserve the dramatic record. Although comprehensive record-keeping did not began until the 1950s, enough information remains to piece together the history of tragedy and destruction — and to witness the spirit to survive and overcome.

"Snowslides creep silently at first down the mighty slopes and suddenly, with an awful roar, overwhelm the unsuspecting victim." This is the awesome horror of the snow avalanche, as described by Reverend J. J. Gibbons in 1898. A constant traveler in Colorado's San Juan Mountains during all seasons, attending his parishioners in the busy mountain towns, he observed: "The farmer watches the winter's storm with joy, while the miner, fearing the snowslide and the precipice, dreads its approach."

Dr. Ron Perla, now a research scientist with the Canadian government, was a Forest Service snow ranger and researcher at the Alta (Utah) Avalanche Study Center in the1960s. Having spent many hours reading old newspapers, he provided us with the following details of Alta's avalanche history. First a description of an early disaster from the Salt Lake *Daily Tribune*, of December 26, 1872: a telegraph message from Alta, a mining town located at the head of narrow Little Cottonwood Canyon:

8:30 p.m. . . . Number killed not ascertained, seven sleighs found, four more missing. Three teamsters got out alive. Eight teamsters and some passengers reported lost. Occurred one mile below. Storm unabated." "Dec. 30, 1872 . . . 200 men probing with 12 foot rods of iron, one sleigh carried across canyon and 200 feet up mountain.

During the next winter, 1873-74, an avalanche swept through Alta, destroying about half the town and killing 60 people. The final indignity came in the form of fire, which swept through what was left of the town, decimating it. Again, on March 7, 1884, avalanches killed at least 12 people in Alta, and on February 13, 1885, the town was almost completely destroyed when an avalanche claimed 16 more lives.

From Anthony Bowman's unpublished master's thesis on the history of Little Cottonwood Canyon (from Utah State University) comes the estimate that about 225 to 250 people were killed in avalanches between 1865 and 1915 in Little Cottonwood Canyon.

Climatic studies of the western United States by Professors Roger Barry of the University of Colorado and Ray Bradley of

2.2 The three levels of the Virginius Mine, in the 1890s. The 1883 avalanche damaged the boarding house at the upper level (Library, Colorado Historical Society photo)

the University of Massachusetts revealed that cooler than normal temperatures accompanied greater than average precipitation during the years from 1850 to the 1890s. (The Norwegian and Icelandic records also note these years as being heavy snow winters.) The winter of 1883-84 was particularly vicious. The Denver *Republican* reported (as reprinted in the Animas Forks *Pioneer* of March 29, 1884) that close to 100 were killed by avalanches in Colorado, including 20 in the San Juan Mountains alone. One of the doomed sites was the Virginius Mine, perched on a steep, barren mountainside at 12,000 feet elevation, high above the southwestern Colorado town of Ouray (Figures 2.2 and 2.3). In December of 1883 snow fell continuously for three days and nights. Late in the storm an avalanche crashed into the boarding house, "carrying death and destruction in the mighty embrace," in the words of the local newspaper, the *Solid Muldoon* (December 28, 1883). Four men were killed, and it took rescuers 24 hours to find the last two survivors.

The following day, a party of 32 men from the nearby mines traveled to the Virginius to bring to town the bodies of the men killed. Pulling the "sled hearses," they approached Cumberland Basin, below the Virginius Mine. This was the most dangerous part of the route and with every step the men glanced toward the steep snow slopes above and around them. Suddenly someone cried, "Look out. . . it's coming" just as a huge avalanche, nearly a quarter mile in width, overwhelmed the group. The *Solid Muldoon* reported: "For a few minutes after the slide the snow presented a smooth unbroken surface, and it seemed that those who had risked their lives to give the bodies of their comrades burial had found a common grave with them. But Death had been satisfied for the present." Before long there was movement and noise in the quiet, charged air as every man, one by one, slowly pushed himself up and out of the snow. All of them survived. Most likely, the avalanche snow spread out in a thin cover so no one was buried deeply. The bodies of the Virginius miners were temporarily abandoned, to be recovered a few weeks later when snow conditions stabilized (Figure 2.4).

The *Pioneer* reported 75 avalanches down between the towns of Animas Forks and Eureka (both north of Silverton) with one slide running to within 150 feet of the newspaper office in Animas Forks. Burdened by printing the multitude of accident reports, the *Pioneer* on March 15 summed up the winter this way: "Since the last storm, a reign of terror has spread over all this part of the country, such as was never known before." "Silverton Closed to the World" headlined the Silverton *Standard* on January 27, 1906, announcing the beginning of the winter that would be the most destructive to life and property in that Colorado area's history. Silverton was and is the county seat of San Juan County, nestled in the heart of the San Juans. The town is completely surrounded by 12,000 to 13,000 foot peaks, and in the early mining days was accessible only by narrow-gauge railroad. "The snow fell fiercely and continuously for three days,

2.3 The Virginius Mine in the 1890s, located at 12,000 feet elevation in Colorado's San Juan Mountains (Denver Public Library, Western History Department photo)

2.4 Rescue party bringing down the bodies of the men killed in the Virginius Mine avalanche and buried again by the avalanche in Cumberland Basin (Library, Colorado State Historical Society photo)

then a howling gale eddied it into tremendous drifts that paralyzed traffic." In early January, five miners died in one avalanche while numerous other avalanches destroyed thousands of dollars' worth of property, wiping out aerial tramway towers, blacksmith shops, boarding houses, and one entire mill which was "crushed to the floor by an immense snowslide."

Cleanup and rebuilding proceeded into February and early March. Warm dry weather prevailed, which lulled the local inhabitants into thinking that winter was behind them. But March 11 heralded another storm, with blizzard conditions continuing for almost a week; winter had dealt one more devastating blow, and it gave the population a St. Patrick's Day they would long remember. When it was over, the Silverton *Standard* headlines (March 24, 1906) proclaimed: "Desolation and Death. The 17th of March a Date Long to be Remembered in This District — Storm Reaches Its Climax St. Patrick's Night and Almost a Score of Lives Lost." The tally at storm's end was 22 different locations damaged or destroyed . . . tramway towers, cabins, compressors, mine portals, miscellaneous mining buildings, powder-cache buildings, boarding houses, and an entire mill totally destroyed. But worst of all: the deadly avalanches had killed18 men.

One of the demolished boarding houses was empty. Had the avalanche struck one hour earlier, 70 miners would have been eating dinner in the dining room. Luckily, they had all returned to work in the mine portal. In the Sunlight Mine bunkhouse, the three occupants were asleep when the avalanche hit. Joe Walker had joined the other two a few hours earlier, moving in from a nearby mine, thinking the Sunlight was a safer place to be. The force of the avalanche pushed Walker out of bed and to his death. The other two were more fortunate: one was tossed out of bed unharmed, the second "'was lifted and carried along . . . with about the same sensation as reposing in a sleeping car. He was gently deposited 150 feet distant from the building, still safe and unharmed, in bed. Such are the freaks of a Rocky Mountain snowslide."

The worst disaster of all took place at the Shenandoah Mine, near Silverton, in a windswept basin high above treeline. Twenty-one occupants were eating dinner in the Spotted Pup boarding house when the avalanche struck. Only nine survived. One of them remembered that the avalanche "struck the front of the house first and I think I flopped about a dozen somersaults. It lifted the bunkhouse up, smashed it into kindling wood and we were all thrown out into the slide at one time." Only two men ended up on top of the snow and they searched all night, digging out six live men. The last survivor was found the next morning. He had been carried over a 30-foot cliff and, badly bruised and dazed, had wandered around in the snow all night.

Avalanches were also causing havoc in adjacent Ouray County just north of Silverton. Tom Walsh's famous Camp Bird Mine had a history of avalanche damage since its beginnings in 1896. However, all the previous avalanches had damaged only the mine's upper workings, located in Imogene Basin, several thousand vertical feet and a few miles south of the mill and offices. But in March of 1906, the U.S. slide, unleashing from U.S. Mountain, tore into the mill and continued 300 feet further, smashing into the boarding house. Seven men sat in the reading room of the boarding house when the avalanche came through. Four were buried, one under six feet of snow; although all were injured, they survived to tell the tale. The survivors and the other miners in the building quickly ran to the mill, but found very little left. Only the engine room was left standing. Three men had been in the mill when the avalanche struck, and more than 50 men began the search.

After nearly two hours of work in a blinding snowstorm, Frank Strickland was found, alive with a heavy timber across his head and with another across his feet, binding him so tightly he could not move. He was also buried by nearly eight feet of snow. Soon after Will Crecy was found beneath a mass of wreckage of the mill.

This report from the Ouray *Herald* noted that the third victim was not found until the next day; apparently he had been killed instantly. The final blow to the mighty Camp Bird came two days later: "Fire last Monday night destroyed what the snow-slide of Saturday night failed to do in the destruction of the Camp Bird mill . . . The remaining 20 stamps were totally ruined and all the woodwork of the mill was reduced to ashes."

2.5 Another rescue party; this group went to the aid of the victims of the Shenandoah Mine avalanche (March 17, 1906) near Silverton, Colorado (James Bell photo)

The mature coniferous forest that was destroyed by the 1906 avalanche slowly grew back. The mill and aerial tramway, which were also destroyed, were rebuilt, and the area was quiet for almost 70 years. But the sleeping giant on U.S. Mountain struck again in January 1974, when another large avalanche swept into the Camp Bird valley. This time the slide again harvested trees on the slope above the mill but the only destruction was a water flume. The avalanche stopped just three feet short of the mill!

Gold fever was also spreading in Alaska — and there too avalanches were taking their toll. Doug Fesler, avalanche specialist with Alaska State Parks and another chronicler of avalanche history, describes one disastrous time in Alaska's history. In 1898 thousands of outsiders came north to the gold fields of the Klondike, seeking "the yellow metal that white men die for." During the month of April alone, 72 gold seekers died in avalanches, while another 49 were buried or caught. Thirteen mules and 10 dogs were killed; another 12 mules, one dog, and one ox survived; and tons of equipment and supplies were lost.

The most disastrous avalanche in United States history occurred in 1910 near the town of Wellington in Washington. Dale Gallagher details this accident in *The Snowy Torrents*, a compilation of avalanche accidents in the United States from 1910 through 1966. (Two subsequent editions bring detailed descriptions of avalanche accidents up to 1980.) The Great Northern Railroad train was traveling on its route from Spokane to Seattle, through the Cascade Mountains. A heavy winter storm brought avalanches across the tracks, causing two trains — one with five passenger cars, the second a mail train — to stop in the town of Leavenworth. Workmen cleared the tracks and the trains resumed travel, but only for a short distance; gale-force winds forced the train to stop again. Winds and snowfall closed the Cascade Tunnel a few miles from Leavenworth and also disrupted electrical service in the tunnel.

It wasn't until evening of the next day — Thursday, February 24 — that the trains passed through, proceeding past the little town of Wellington, about a quarter mile from the tunnel. Railroad officials directed the trains along two parallel sidings just beyond the town, where all progress stopped. The snow had now drifted so deep that only the tops of the telegraph poles could be seen. The main railroad line was again closed. Late Thursday night, a small avalanche crossed the track where the trains had been parked hours before, sweeping away the cook shack and killing the two men inside. The 55 passengers had eaten all three meals at the shack that day. From Friday through Tuesday the trains sat stationary on the siding. The storm continued unabated. The trains were blocked in both directions. The crews worked without rest with rotary snowplows, clearing and reclearing the tracks of avalanche snow as new slides came down, undoing hours of work. Equipment failures and unhappy passengers only made the situation worse.

Passengers trudged through the deep snow to the hotel in Wellington for meals and to send telegrams. Some of the passengers wondered why the train couldn't be moved back into the tunnel to be protected from avalanches, but the conductor assured them that it was in the safest place already. On Saturday a group of passengers met with the railroad superintendent, again urging that the train be moved into the tunnel or at least closer to it. The superintendent denied the request on the grounds that the tunnel would be wet and cold, with poor ventilation for the train's coal smoke. He mentioned that the passengers would be unable to walk to the hotel because the tunnel had water running along the track. By Sunday, several days of inactivity was taking its toll and chaos was gradually taking over, as the storm increased in intensity. Several passengers decided to hike to the little railroad town of Scenic, eight and a half miles west. Railroad workers followed, irate that their demands for higher wages were refused. A railroad crew walked into Wellington from the east to report that their equipment was stranded between two avalanches on the track.

One observant passenger noticed that the mountainside above the train looked very different from when they had first arrived. Then, he could clearly see the stumps and snags of trees; now the slopes above the tracks were an "immense quilt of pure white snow." The same passenger, returning to the train, noticed "part of a hill simply fold up and start sliding with a roar." This was an ominous sign. On Sunday night, snow turned into sleet. By Monday, the trains had been stationary for five days. Everyone was "a bundle of nerves" as the sleet ended and a warm moist wind took over. By this time, some of the snow drifts were 20 feet in depth.

At 0120 hours, on Tuesday, 1 March, the white death made its call. The avalanche that many had feared swept everything in its path 150 feet down into the Tye River Canyon. Buried under the snow lay two trains, three steam locomotives, four electric locomotives, a rotary snowplow, several boxcars, an engine shed, a water tower, and telegraph poles and wires!

Rescuers looked desperately for survivors and sadly dug out bodies from their snowy vault. The town of Wellington was spared the ravages of the avalanche, and its inhabitants joined in the search, looking for the remains of the train. They found only one end of a coach, a portion of a rotary plow, and the roof of a shack; everything else was "buried in a white grave." Eleven hours after the accident, when rescuers had almost given up on finding any more survivors, they heard a faint sound. "Digging down they found a large tree trunk, and under it was a woman, just barely alive. This was the last of the survivors." The final death toll was 96, with 22 survivors, a record which still stands in the United States for avalanche tragedy.

TRANSITION: FROM MINERS AND FARMERS, TO SOLDIERS AND SKIERS

Meanwhile, in Europe, avalanches were on the attack against a new breed of mountain people. For hundreds of years, avalanche victims had been inhabitants of the steep-walled mountain valleys. Most Europeans had hurried as quickly as possible through the mountains, fearing the perils not just of avalanches but of dragons who infested the mountains; some looked like serpents with the heads of cats, others had bat wings and long hairy tails. Mountain travelers were terrified of these dragons, and also of the witches and souls of lost people who also were thought to reside on the mountain summits. But in 1741, for the first time, the mountains were invaded for pleasure rather than expediency when groups of adventurous Englishmen went to Chamonix in the French Alps to climb Montenvert, a 5,866-foot peak. This was just the first chapter of what has become the continuing saga of year-round climbing, which has played a noticeable part in raising the statistics related to avalanche hazard — and to other hazards as well.

Occasionally soldiers too found themselves in the clutches of avalanches. From Johann Scheuchzer's 1706 *Description of the Natural History of Switzerland* come the following accounts. In 1478 the subjects of Mäyland, which borders on the Lifine valley, chopped wood in the forest belonging to Lifine. This created such a stir that the people of Urj immediately declared war on the dowager princess of Mäyland, exhorting all members of the Federation to join them in their march across the mountains. "No sooner had the 1000 men from Zurich, who wanted to be in the vanguard, crossed the St. Gotthard, together with the warriors from Urnen, than 60 of their soldiers were suddenly caught in an avalanche and were crushed miserably."

In 1499, Emperor Maximilianus ordered 2,000 soldiers to invade the Engadein Valley. As the army was crossing a high mountain pass, an avalanche engulfed more than 400 soldiers. "The panic created by this occurrence soon changed to laughter, however, when the men buried under the snow emerged from it one by one as if they rose from the grave, and although many of them were injured, none were lost." In the following year, a large number of Swiss soldiers recruited by the Bailiff of Dijon were crossing the St. Gotthard Pass when they were caught in a huge avalanche which killed about a hundred of them.

The troops mentioned above were all hurrying through the mountains, to do battle elsewhere. But during World War I, soldiers were doing battle in the mountains, and avalanches were used as a weapon of destruction. It was the Austrians vs. the Italians in the Tyrol Mountains. No one knows how many lives were lost in the avalanche warfare, but estimates are in the thousands. Colin Fraser gives a range of a conservative 40,000 to as high as 80,000. He quotes a famous skiing pioneer and avalanche expert who trained the Austrian Alpine troops: "The mountains in winter were more dangerous than the Italians."

In 1943, Frank Harper, an American, wrote a handbook for ski and mountain troops called *Military Ski Manual*. In it he described the practice of "loosening snow-avalanches from their hollows and hurling them down upon the enemy . . . Patrols worked their way up the steepest mountain-walls and started the avalanches by throwing a rock, or sometimes by a well-aimed shot from a Howitzer that could be fired from a distant position."

A soldier familiar with "avalanche warfare" described the procedure to Harper:

> *Nothing simpler. Paul and I had gone up; we waited seven hours for the Alpini [the Italian mountain troops]. We had laid the rope around the snow-crest; each of us held a rope-end in his fist. When the enemy came, there was nothing left to do but saw the rope into the crest; we waited until the column was below us. There was nothing but smoking snow to be seen, and nothing but a terrible thundering to be heard. We followed the avalanche, on trouser-seats and boot-soles, and rescued seventy-five men from the snow.*

Even today in the mountains of Afganistan, guerrilla soldiers are using avalanches as weapons, purposely triggering them on Soviet soldiers in this ongoing conflict.

Aside from temporary breaks in this historical record for warfare, the transition of avalanche victims, from residents and workers to recreationists, was continuing in North America as well as in Europe. Although mining in the western United States continued to be profitable and successful until about the 1920s, it then began a long downhill course, with mines in many mountain areas closing or operating only sporadically. As mines closed, miners, their families and all the assorted populace that followed them slowly drifted out of the mountains, seeking more lucrative prospects. Fewer and fewer people were traveling the mountain trails and roads in winter. Many railroads shut down operations, and the road beds were eventually torn up. The remaining population concentrated themselves in the few mountain towns which continued to hold on through the ups and downs of occasional brief mining booms and the more frequent busts and quiet times. In the United States during the period after World War I to about World War II, avalanche incidents occurred infrequently but continuously, bringing occasional damage along the few roads and railroads still in use and sporadic destruction to the few remaining mines.

During this transition period in American avalanche history, an interesting change was taking place. While populations in threatened locations remained stable, or decreased, a different breed of adventurer began invading the mountains. Earlier, people who lived and traveled in the mountains did so due to economic necessity — but this new group came for fun! Sports-oriented people had began to experience the thrill of skiing.

Occasionally, adventurous people had taken up skiing in North America, especially in the mining communities in the latter part of the 19th century. Many of the miners were Scandinavian and had brought their skiing skills with them. They fashioned skis, generally seven or more feet in length, out of any available hardwood, and used one long pole to control their speed. Turning was not a prerequisite for skiing. The preferred technique was: point the skis downhill and go, pushing the pole into the snow only when excessive speed became terrifying. The skis used in Alta, Utah, in the early 1880s were described as "Norwegian snow-shoes — skees — 14 feet long and six inches wide."

Miners in the San Juan Mountains of Colorado soon learned to copy the skiing skills of their Scandinavian co-workers after noting how quickly the Scandinavians were able to travel in deep snow. After working several days in the high-country mines, the miners would spend hours trudging down the trails through the snow for a few days of rest and relaxation in town. Once there, they found their Scandinavian co-workers warm and settled in the saloons, having arrived long before on their skis. Mail carriers also found skis useful as a method of winter transportation. In the 1870s mailmen often used skis to deliver mail to the young town of Alta. Mailmen in the San Juans occasionally skied over the high mountain passes when the snow was too deep for horses.

After a few years, men, women and children were all trying out the new sport, and races became part of the winter's recreation. Scandinavian miner Alberta Kaugen reigned as "schuss king" after a race in 1884 on the slopes above Alta. In December of 1880, three Norwegian miners working near Silverton, Colorado, challenged anyone in the United States to a race "according to the Norwegian snow shoe rules." The invasion of the high mountain slopes for recreation was just beginning.

Avalanches were still killing and injuring miners in their rugged habitats — but a different type of avalanche accident was beginning to make the news. Once sports lovers strapped on their skis with strong leather bindings and took to the slopes, the consequences were inevitable.

In February 1905, the Silverton *Standard* reported possibly the first fatal avalanche accident to recreational skiers in the United States. Two miners at the Irene Mine near Silverton were trying out their new "snow-shoes" while a third watched from the mine cabin. The Irene was located near timberline, in the trees but adjacent to a steep, open bowl, where the two fledgling skiers were trying to stay upright. Suddenly an avalanche released above them, carrying them down the slope and burying them both. The avalanche also demolished the cabin, burying the observer, but he was able to extricate himself, and hurry down to find his two companions. Although they were buried only 30 feet downslope from where they had been skiing when the avalanche struck, both were dead.

Another skier, Jacob Stroebel, was killed in an avalanche in January 1911, while skiing down Minnie Gulch near Silverton. He was buried 18 inches deep, with his skis securely on. The first avalanche fatality of the winter of 1913-14 was Henry Castle, who was caught near the Buffalo Boy Mine near Silverton in December. He and his partner were on "Norwegian skis" when an avalanche buried him. His partner escaped unharmed.

These sporadic skiing accidents were only the tip of the iceberg. The turning point — which brought first hundreds, then thousands of adventurers into the snow-covered mountains — was the development of alpine skiing. In the 1930s, many of the mining camps were almost deserted and avalanches fell unnoticed. In Alta, Utah, George Watson, a miner and mining promoter, was the town's only resident. One long snowy winter, he occupied his time by reading magazines and learning that skiing was becoming a popular sport both in the U.S. and in Europe. He elected himself "mayor" and took upon himself the task of developing the area as a ski resort. In 1936 the first two chairlifts in North America were erected at Sun Valley, Idaho, signaling the beginning of skiing as both a popular sport and a growing industry. Mayor Watson in Alta was busily consolidating surface rights and soliciting donations from the many mining companies, to begin developing Alta for skiing. In 1938 the Alta Winter Sports Association, with Mayor Watson as one of the prime motivators, constructed Utah's first ski lift — an abandoned, aerial mining tramway that was converted into a single chair lift. Skiers no longer had to spend hours and wear themselves out climbing up a slope, only to ski back down in just a few minutes. Now for just 25 cents per trip, or an all-day for $1.50, they could ride up the slope on the Collins chair lift in just six minutes.

Once again, hordes of people flocked to the mountains in winter — this time for "white gold" — the thrill of skiing. And once again, the "white death" began stalking its victims. On February 7, 1937, in Colorado's Front Range mountains, the Berthoud Pass ski course reported its first avalanche victims: two Denver men whose bodies were not recovered until spring.

Alta Ski Area suffered its first avalanche fatality in 1941, in an area called "the Snakepit," dangerous then and now. On April 1, 1949, an avalanche caught and buried four men at the Loveland Basin ski area in Colorado, killing 17-year-old Sidney Prather. Alpine skiers at the developing ski areas were joining the ranks of avalanche victims.

Highway workers and travelers, too, fell victim to the avalanche. The Georgetown *Courier,* in March 1944, reported the story of Adam Frazer and Robert Etzler, Colorado highway department workers. They were clearing the highway of avalanche snow which was blocking traffic on Loveland Pass. Both agreed that Etzler would plow over the top of the pass while Frazer continued the original job. When Erzler was out of sight, another avalanche came down in the same place as the first, sweeping Frazer and his bulldozer down the mountainside. A rescue crew worked for two hours, digging through snow and ice, before they found Frazer's body crushed by the avalanche. In February 1945, Harold B. Willis, a salesman for the Meadow Gold Creamery Company of Denver, "was swept to his death . . . by a snowslide that carried his automobile from the highway down a steep embankment near the foot of Berthoud Pass."

From the 1940s right through to the present, the trend toward more recreation-related avalanche accidents becomes increasingly obvious. Although avalanches continued to interrupt transportation systems, destroy mine facilities, and occasionally bury and kill miners and motorists, the odds have been shifting more and more to the downhill skier, the cross-country skier, the ski-mountaineer, and the snowmobiler. As skiers become more proficient in their sport and more begin to leave the ski area boundaries to seek the thrills of wilderness skiing, avalanches will continue to claim their victims. New innovations in skiing — such as helicopters and snowcats — which take people deep into the mountains for undisturbed powder — and more sophisticated equipment are bringing increasing numbers of people into unprotected and potentially dangerous areas. And avalanches continue to prey upon even the most careful and experienced skiers.

As for the state of avalanche hazard today, those most endangered are those choosing to either live or vacation, or both, in the mountain environment in winter. Beginning in this century, dramatic changes have taken place in the social and economic lives of mountain dwellers: the tourist has come to the mountains . . . to play and to develop the land, often with little knowledge of the inherent hazards of this environment.

2.6 An 1890s congenial meeting at Mt. Sneffles, Colorado. These men are sporting their skis and snowshoes as they pass around the bottles (Library Colorado State Historical Society photo)

A slab avalanche at the moment of fracture (R. Ludwig photo)

3 Properties of Snow

Richard L. Armstrong

Physical Properties

How the snow cover develops and changes

When most people think of a snow cover, they think of just that, a blanket which covers the ground: a thick and homogeneous layer whose primary characteristics are that it is cold and white. In reality, snow is one of the most complex materials found in nature, and it is highly variable, going through significant changes even before it has accumulated as a continuous cover on the landscape. When we look closely and observe the changes that take place within a layer of snow on the ground over time, it might first appear that there is no logical explanation for the changes and that some sort of random system prevails. But just as is the case with atmospheric phenomena, those weather conditions which may appear to be chaotic are actually an orderly physical system where all changes take place according to physical laws. This chapter is concerned with a basic understanding of how and why changes take place in snow layers over time, and specifically, how these changes affect avalanche conditions.

We will trace the changes that take place from the time the snow crystal forms in the atmosphere and falls to the ground to that point in time when it melts and leaves the surface of the local landscape as melt water. The variable nature of snow begins with the initial crystals and with the familiar saying "no two snow crystals are alike." Some of the earliest studies of snow, Bentley's photographic classic from 1931 and Nakaya's study in 1954, focused on the variety of new snow types and although some classification systems have hundreds of types, one of

Interesting if true, and interesting anyway.
Mark Twain

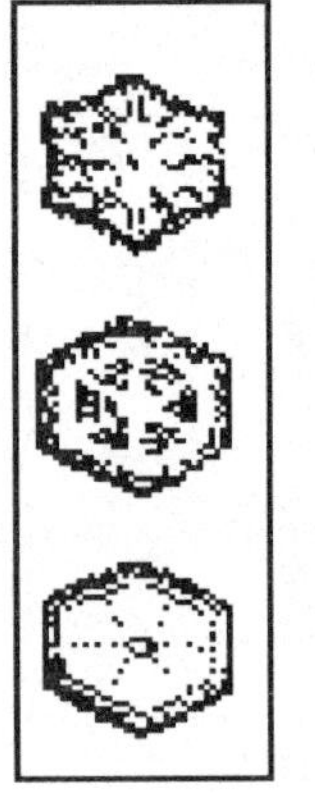

Plates *Stellar Crystals*

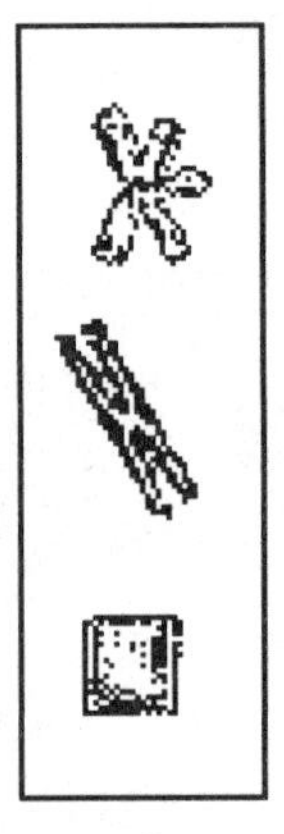

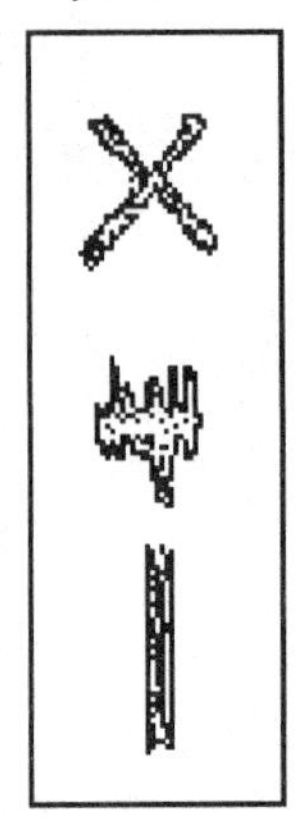

Columns *Needles*

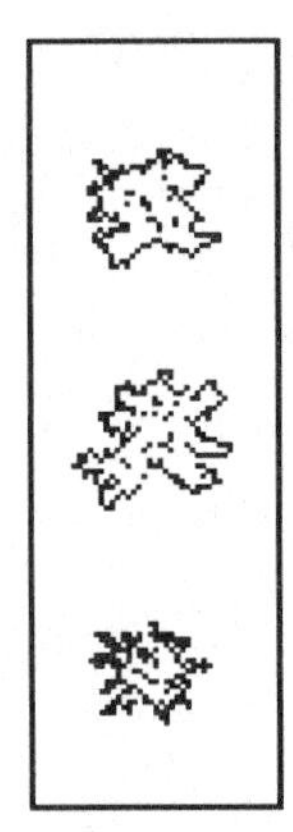

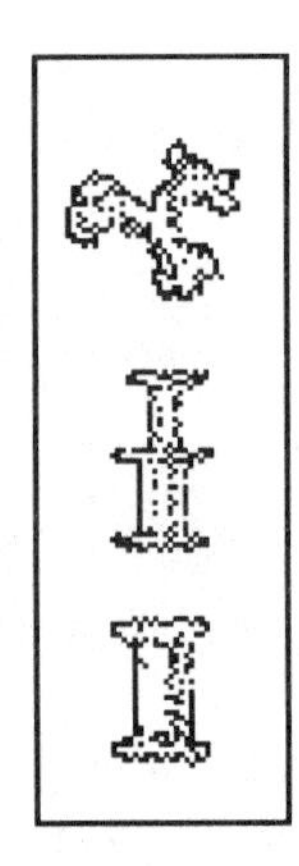

Spatial dendrities *Capped columns*

more straightforward and simple systems is shown in Figure 3.1. Bentley's work provides a vast collection of snow crystal photographs; Nakaya's is more scientific — he not only provides excellent photographs of snow crystals but he also describes the atmospheric conditions which control their formation.

In nature the snow cover is variable on both the broad geographic scale (the type of snow found in Antarctica is quite different from snow found in the Cascade Mountains of North America) and on the microscale (where snow conditions may vary greatly from one side of a rock or tree to the other). Of course, all snow crystals are made of the same substance, the water molecule, but local environmental conditions control the type and character of snow that will be found at a given location. At a single location the snow cover varies from top to bottom, resulting in a complex layered structure.

When we investigate snow cover stratigraphy by digging a snow pit and observing an exposed vertical face, some variations are obvious even to the naked eye, while others can be detected by brushing the pit wall to expose the layers of varying hardness. The individual layers may be quite thick or very thin. In general, the thicker layers represent consistent conditions during one storm, when the new snow crystals were the same type, wind speed and direction varied only a little, and temperature and precipitation were fairly constant. Thinner layers, perhaps only millimeters in thickness, often reflect conditions between storms, such as the formation during fair weather of a melt-freeze crust, a period of strong winds creating a wind crust, or the occurrence of surface hoar, the wintertime equivalent of dew. These delicate feather-shaped crystals deposited from the moist atmosphere onto the cold snow surface overnight offer a beautiful glistening sight as they reflect the sun of the following day (Figure 3.2). However, they are very fragile or low in strength, and once buried by subsequent snowfalls, may be a major contributor to avalanche formation.

One property of snow which anyone can easily observe is its strength or hardness, something which we intuitively know has great importance in terms of avalanche formation. Snow can vary from being light and fluffy — easy to shovel or sweep, and especially delightful to ski through — to being heavy and dense — impossible to penetrate with a shovel and hard enough to make it very difficult for a skier to carve a turn even with sharp metal edges. It is just one substance, the water molecule, which is responsible for this wide range of conditions, for it is the water molecule which makes up the ice skeleton whose empty spaces are filled with air — in other words, a snow layer. What is actually changing to produce this wide range of conditions? In the broadest sense, it is the density or the mass per unit volume. In the case of snow, how much of the volume is made up of ice crystals and how much is made up of air determines the density. The denser the snow layer, the harder and stronger it becomes, as long as it is not melting. What are the conditions which cause the snow to densify, and what controls how fast this process will proceed?

If we were to measure the density of the new snow as it fell we would observe a wide range of values. This difference is the result of just how closely the new snow crystals pack together, and this is controlled by the shape of the crystal. There are a variety of shapes of the initial crystals, as we saw in Figure 3.1, and some are able to pack more closely together than others. For example, needles will pack more closely than stellars and as a consequence may possess a density which is three to four times that of the stellars.

The effect of wind can alter the shape of the new snow crystals to a large extent, breaking them into much smaller pieces, which pack very closely together to form wind slabs, which in turn, may possess a density five to ten times that of new stellars falling in the absence of wind. Because these processes occur at different times and locations at the surface of the snow cover, and are later buried by subsequent snow falls, a varied and inhomogeneous layered structure results. Therefore, what may seem to the casual observer to be minor variations in atmospheric conditions can have a very significant influence on the properties of the snow.

After the snow has been deposited on the ground, what controls how and at what rate it densifies or settles? If we measure the density over a period of time we will always find that it increases — the snow layer settles vertically or shrinks in thickness. Because an increase in density equals an increase in strength, the rate at which this change occurs is important with respect to avalanche potential. First, the snow can settle simply because of its own weight. It is highly compressible because it is mostly composed of empty air space within the ice skeleton made up of snow crystals. In fact, in a typical layer of new snow, 85 to 95 percent of the material is the empty space within the ice

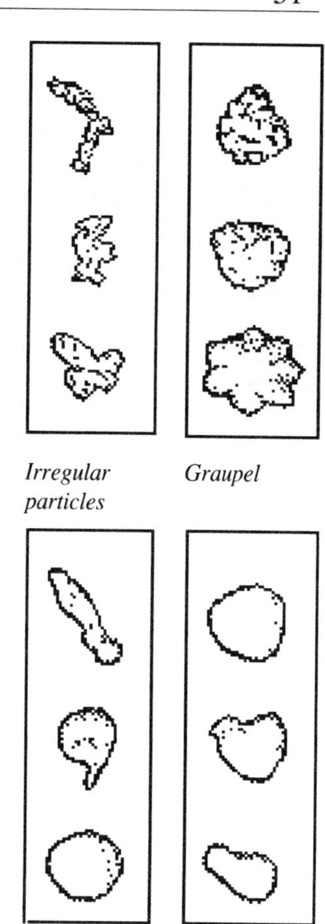

3.1 International classification system for solid precipitation. (International Association for Scientific Hydrology)

3.2 Surface hoar crystal, ten times actual size, left (R. Armstrong photo). A newly deposited layer of surface hoar, right (K. Williams photo)

skeleton. The ice crystals are able to move and slide past each other, the force of gravity causes them to move slowly downward, and the layer shrinks. The heavier the weight of snow above, and the warmer the temperature, the faster this settlement proceeds.

At the same time, the complex, intricate shapes which characterized the new snow crystals begin to change. They become more simple, or rounded in shape, and thus an additional means for closer packing results. The intricate crystals change because they posses a shape which is naturally unstable. This is because new snow crystals have a very large surface area-to-volume ratio — simply another way of saying that their shape is complex — and are composed of a crystalline solid close to its melting point. In this way snow crystals are rather unique compared to most materials found in nature. The surface energy physics involved dictates this to be an unstable condition and the initial shapes change; the warmer the temperatures, the faster the change. Under very cold conditions, one might be able to recognize the original shapes of the snow crystals after they have been in the snow cover for several days or even a week or two; but as temperatures warm and approach the melting point, such shapes would disappear within a few hours to perhaps a day. These changes in the shape or texture of the snow crystals are examples of initial metamorphism. This term, metamorphism, is borrowed from geology and has the same meaning as it does in that field: changes which take place due to the effects of temperature and pressure. As the crystal shapes simplify, they can pack more closely together and further settlement is enhanced (Figure 3.3).

The changes we have just described generally occur within the time frame of hours to a few days. What happens to the structure of the snow cover over a period of weeks to months involves

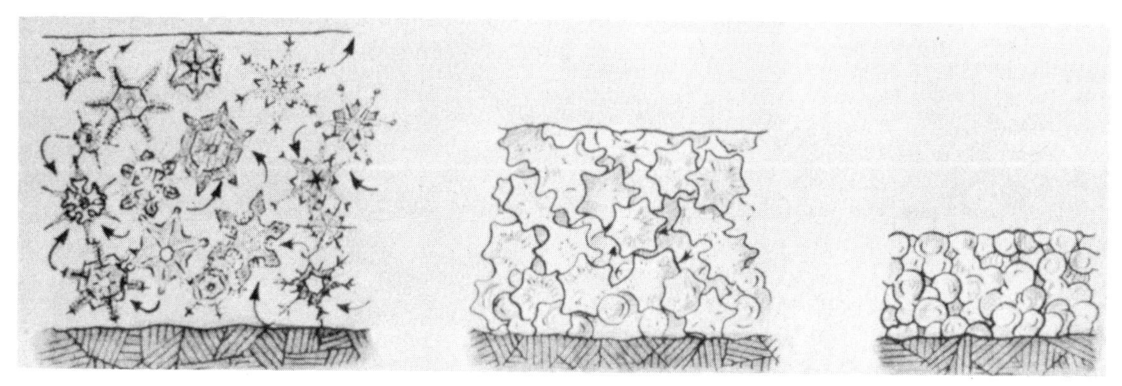

3.3 *As the crystal shapes become more rounded, they can pack more closely together and the layer settles or* ***shrinks*** *in thickness.*

other processes. Settlement, which may have been rapid at first, will continue but at a much slower rate. At this stage other factors will start to exert the dominant influence on metamorphism. These conditions include temperature — not just the average temperature of the layer itself, but the difference in temperature measured upward or downward in the snow layer. This difference is called the *temperature gradient* (TG).

Averaged over the period of a day snow temperatures generally are coldest near the snow surface and warmest near the ground at the base of the snow cover. Thus we have a temperature gradient across a layer of snow sandwiched between the cold winter air and the relatively warm ground (Figure 3.4). At this point we need to remember that we are dealing not just with

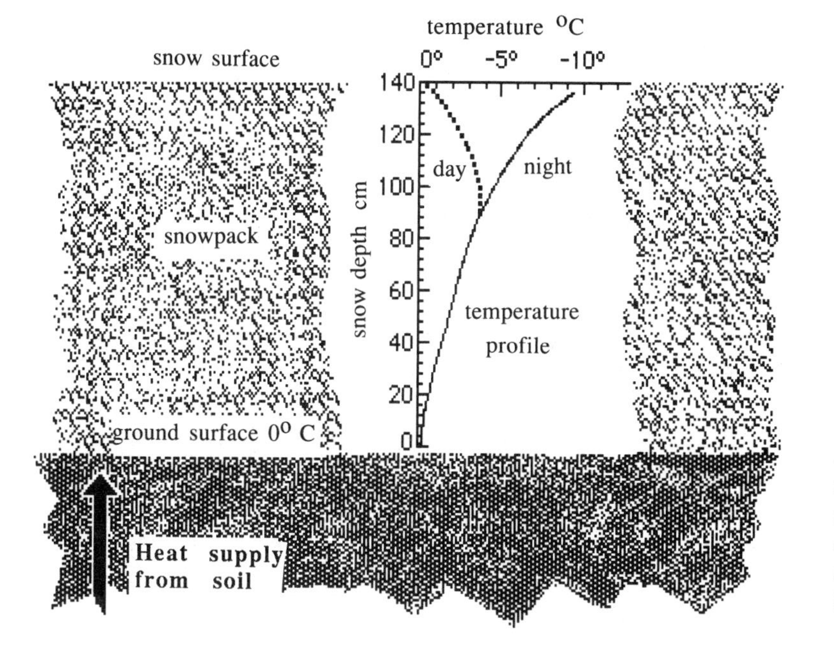

3.4 *When an insulating layer of snow separates the warm ground from the cold air, a temperature gradient develops across the snow layer.*

3.5 In the presence of a strong temperature gradient, the shape of the snow crystals is completely changed. The crystals are cohesionless, or loosely bonded to one another and the layer is very weak.

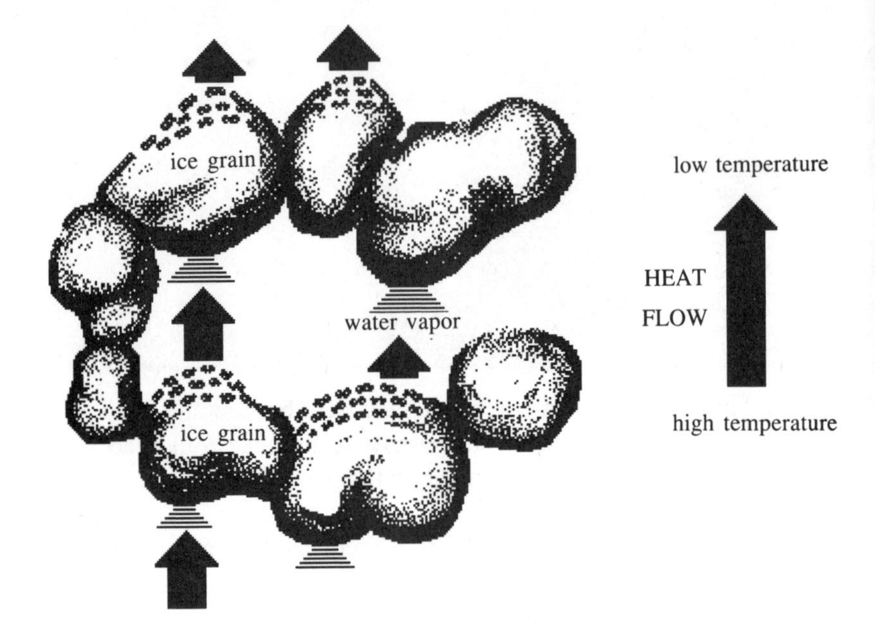

snow crystals but also with a material that is primarily composed of air. Thus the temperature gradient is across large void spaces filled with air as well as across the ice. Within the ice skeleton, snow layer next to the ground, the temperature within the air spaces is warmer than the snow layer just above it, which is just slightly closer to the much colder air at the snow surface. In general, this pattern continues as you move upward through the snow cover — warmer near the ground and steadily colder as you approach the surface.

It is a basic principle of our environment that warmer air contains more water vapor than colder air, no matter whether it is the air within a room in a house, the air outside the house, or the air within the snow cover. Water vapor exerts a pressure: the greater the amount of water vapor, the greater the pressure. Therefore, a pressure gradient, as well as a temperature gradient, exists through the snow cover. If a pressure difference exists, there will be a natural tendency to equalize the difference (just as adjacent high and low pressure centers in the atmosphere produce the movement of air masses from one place to another) so the pressure difference within the snow causes vapor to move upward through the snow layers. The air within the layers of the snow cover is saturated with water vapor, which means that the relative humidity is 100 percent. However, when it moves upward to a colder layer, the amount of water vapor that can be supported in the air space diminishes. The result is that some of the vapor must change its state from vapor to solid, and be deposited on the surrounding ice grains.

While this process may be a bit difficult to imagine, we experience a similar process inside our homes during winter. When the warm moist air in a heated room comes in contact with a cold windowpane the water vapor in the air, which we cannot see, is cooled to its ice point, and some of the vapor changes state, going directly from vapor to solid, and is deposited as frost on the window. This same process is occurring within the snow cover, as vapor moves upward from warmer to colder layers where fewer numbers of water molecules can exist as vapor.

Figure 3.5 shows what is happening during this temperature-gradient process in terms of the changing texture of the snow layer. Water molecules sublimate (similar to evaporation, but in this case the change is directly from solid to gas, without passing through the liquid stage) from the upper surfaces of a grain, and the resulting vapor moves upward along the temperature (and vapor) gradient, and is deposited as a solid ice molecule on the under side of the colder grain above. If this process continues long enough — and it will as long as a strong temperature gradient exists — all of the grains in this snow layer will go from solid to vapor and back to solid again; that is, they will totally recrystallize. The new crystals are completely different in texture from their initial form. They become large, coarse grains with facets and sharp angles and they may eventually evolve into a hollow cup form. Examples of these crystals are shown in Figures 3.6 through 3.8. Well developed examples are commonly known as *depth hoar*.

Depth hoar is of particular importance to avalanche formation because of its very low strength. This is because there is little or no cohesion or bonding at the grain contacts. The depth hoar or TG snow layers could be compared to dry sand. Each grain may possess significant strength but as a layer it is very weak due to the lack of "connections" between the individual grains. This is why depth hoar is commonly called sugarsnow.

Depth hoar usually develops whenever the temperature gradient is equal to or greater than about 10 degrees centigrade per meter (Figure 3.4). In the cold, shallow snow covers of a continental climate, such as that of the Rocky Mountains, a gradient of this magnitude is common within the first snow layers of the season. Therefore, a layer of depth hoar is frequently found at the

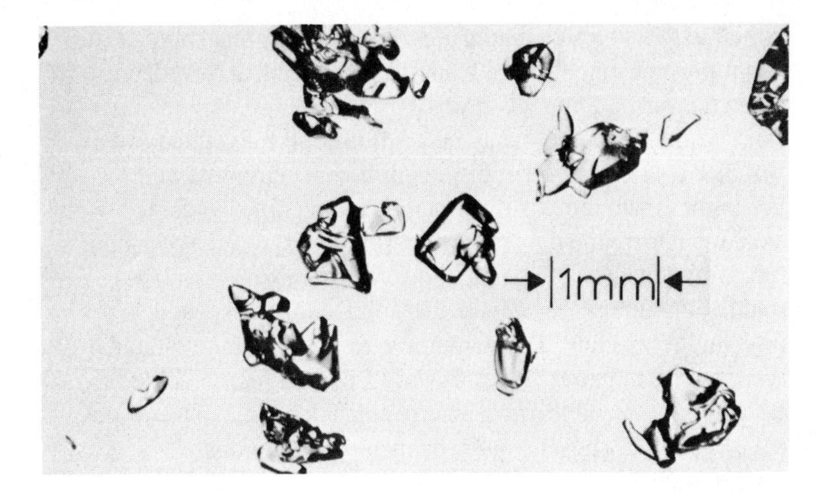

3.6 Beginning temperature gradient process; facets and angles are visible (R. Armstrong photo)

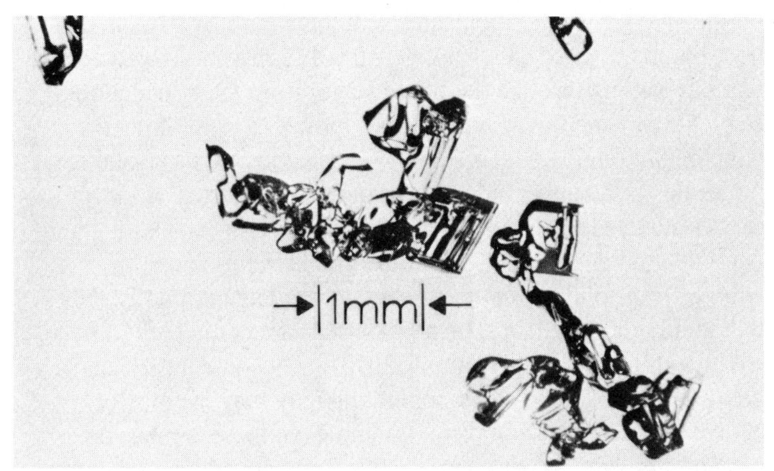

3.7 As the temperature gradient process continues, the crystals grow in size and stepped features are visible (R. Armstrong photo)

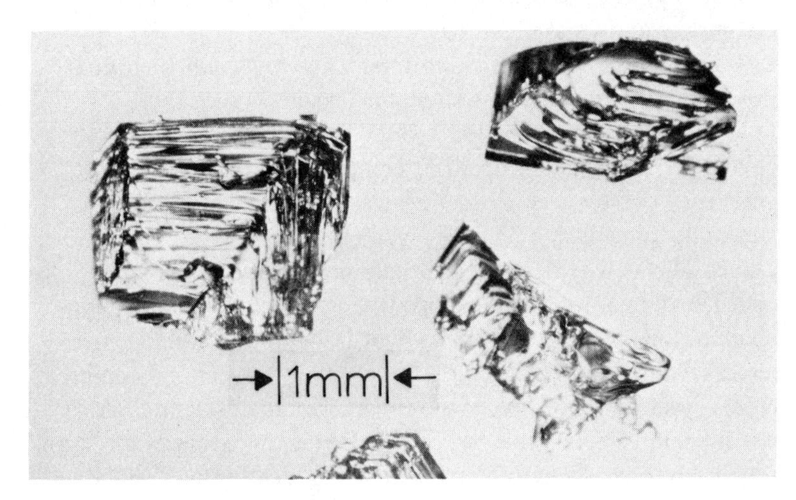

3.8 Advanced temperature gradient crystals attain a hollow cup-shaped form (R. Armstrong photo)

bottom of the snow cover and the resulting low strength becomes a significant factor for future avalanches.

In the absence of a strong temperature gradient, a totally different type of snow texture develops. When the gradient is less than about 10 degrees centigrade per meter, there is still a vapor pressure difference and still a movement of vapor upward through the snow layers but at a much slower rate. As a result the water vapor which is now deposited on the colder grains tends to cover the total grain in a more homogeneous manner, rather than showing the preferential deposition that was characteristic of the depth hoar. This process produces a grain that has a smooth surface and is more rounded or oblong in shape. Over time, more vapor is deposited at the grain contacts (concavities) than over the remaining surface of the grain (convexity). As a result, connecting bonds form at the grain contacts and this snow layer gains strength over time (Figure 3.9). This bond growth, called sintering, results in a cohesive texture which is in complete contrast to the cohesionless texture of depth hoar. This type of grain has been referred to by various specific terms over the years (*destructive metamorphism, equi-temperature metamorphism,* and *equilibrium metamorphism*), but it can generally be described as fine-grained or well-sintered (bonded) snow. An example of these rounded and interconnected grains is shown in Figure 3.10.

The preceding paragraphs describe the "big picture" in terms of what happens to snow layers after they have been buried by subsequent snowfalls. If the layer is subfreezing — that is if no melt is taking place — one of the two processes described above is proceeding, or perhaps a transition exists between the two. This basic distinction is truly one of the most fundamental discoveries that has been made regarding how snow changes with time. Within the total snow cover, either of these processes may be taking place simultaneously, but only one can take place within a given layer at a given moment in time. It is interesting that both processes take place faster the warmer the snow temperature. Because water vapor is involved in both of these changes — and the warmer the temperature the greater the amount of water vapor available — the process will occur faster as temperatures approach the melting point. It is the temperature gradient or temperature difference across the layer which determines whether the process will involve the growth of the weak depth hoar crystals or the development of a stronger snow layer with a sintered, interconnected texture.

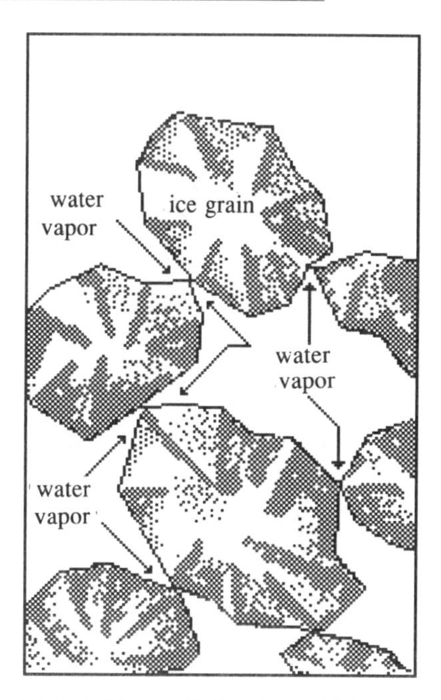

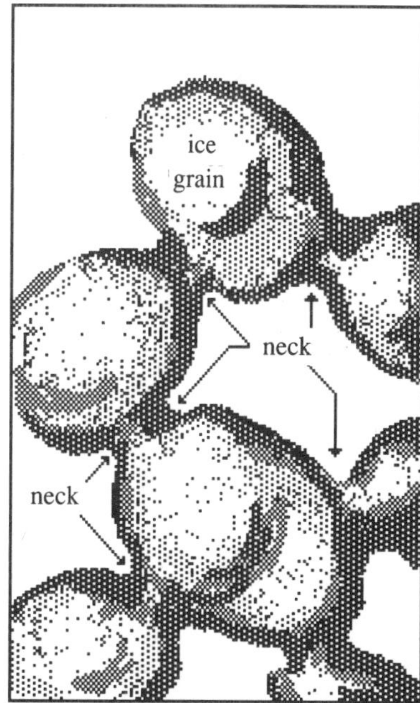

3.9 Equi-temperature grain growth. In the presence of weak temperature gradients, bonds grow at the grain contacts.

3.10 Bonded or sintered grains resulting from equi-temperature metamorphism (S. Colbeck photo)

Figure 3.11 provides a general example of how, as the snow cover gets deeper over the winter, the temperature gradient across the snow diminishes. In order to keep the example simple, let's say that the air temperature is kept constant at minus 10 degrees centigrade (in fact, this is not far from reality, for during mid-winter, mean monthly air temperatures do not vary little while snow depth varies considerably). The example in Figure 3.11 represents conditions during early- to mid-winter, perhaps late October through January. The initial layer of new snow, 50 centimeters in depth, experiences a very strong temperature gradient of 20 degrees per meter and eventually becomes well-developed depth hoar. The second layer develops in the presence of a weaker gradient — about 10 degrees per meter — and consequently reaches only the beginning stage of TG metamorphism. By the time the third layer accumulates, the gradient has dropped well below the critical value of 10 degrees per meter and this layer develops into a sintered, fine-grained, cohesive layer which densifies and strengthens much more than the layers below. Note that while the air temperature remains unchanged in this example, the snow cover increases in thickness, causing the average temperature gradient to decrease.

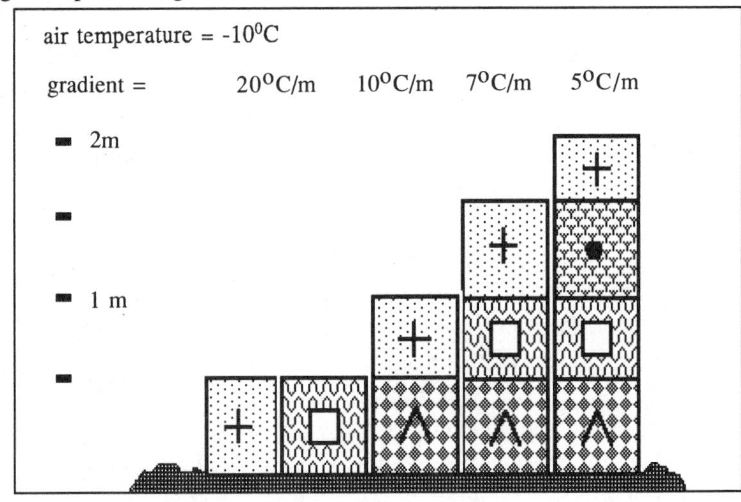

3.11 As the snow cover becomes deeper over the winter, the average temperature gradient diminishes and the opportunity for TG metamorphism decreases.

Now that we are getting closer to the actual process of avalanche formation, we should point out that there are two basic types of avalanche release. First, there is the point or loose snow avalanche (Figure 3.12). The loose snow avalanche involves cohesionless snow and initiates at a point, spreading out laterally as it moves down the slope, forming a characteristic inverted V-shape. A single grain, or a clump of grains, slips out of place and dislodges those below it on the slope and they in turn dislodge others. The avalanche continues as long as the snow is cohesionless and the slope is steep enough. This type of avalanche usually involves only small amounts of near-surface snow. In contrast, the second type of avalanche is called a slab avalanche and requires a cohesive snow layer which is poorly anchored to the snow below due to the presence of a weak layer below. In the case of the slab avalanche, the cohesive blanket of snow breaks away simultaneously over a broad area (Figure 3.13). A slab release can involve a range of snow thicknesses, from just the near-surface layers to an event which includes the entire snow cover down to the ground. Therefore, in contrast to the loose snow avalanche, the slab avalanche has the potential to involve very large amounts of snow. (Chapter 5 opens with an excellent example of a large slab avalanche.)

3.12 Loose snow or point avalanche.

In order to understand the conditions in the snow cover which contribute to slab avalanche formation, it is essential to re-emphasize that the snow cover develops layer by layer. We noted previously how this layered structure could develop by metamorphic processes, but there are numerous other ways in which distinct layers develop, most of which will have some influence on avalanche formation. The reason that the layered structure is of such prime importance is that it is directly tied to the two ingredients essential to the formation of slab avalanches: the cohesive layer of snow and the weak layer beneath. Both of these ingredients are required; just one will not suffice. If the snow cover is homogeneous from the ground to the snow surface, there is no danger of slab avalanches, regardless of the snow type. If the entire snow layer is sintered, dense and strong, stability is very high. Even if the entire snow cover is comprised of a very weak layer of depth hoar, there still is no hazard from slab avalanches because the cohesionless character of the depth hoar does not allow the propagation of the cracks necessary for slab avalanches to form. However, the combination of a basal layer of depth hoar with a cohesive layer above does provide exactly the ingredients

3.13 Slab avalanche.

3.14 Snow layer combinations which often contribute to avalanche formation.

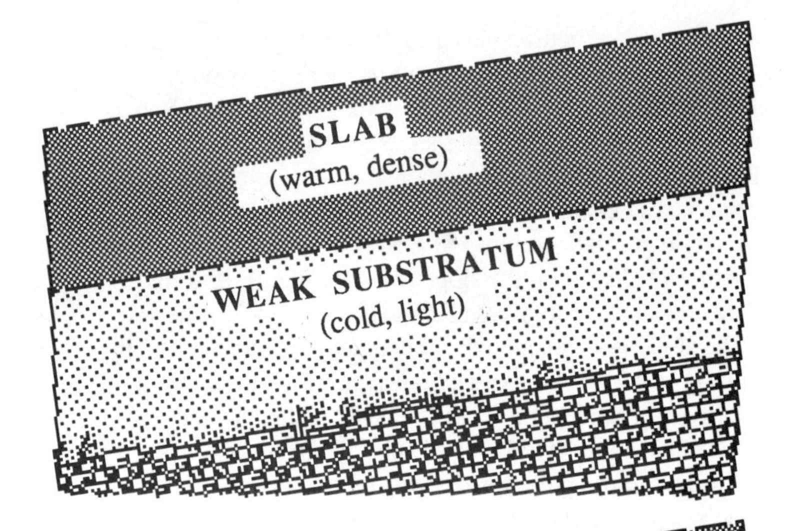

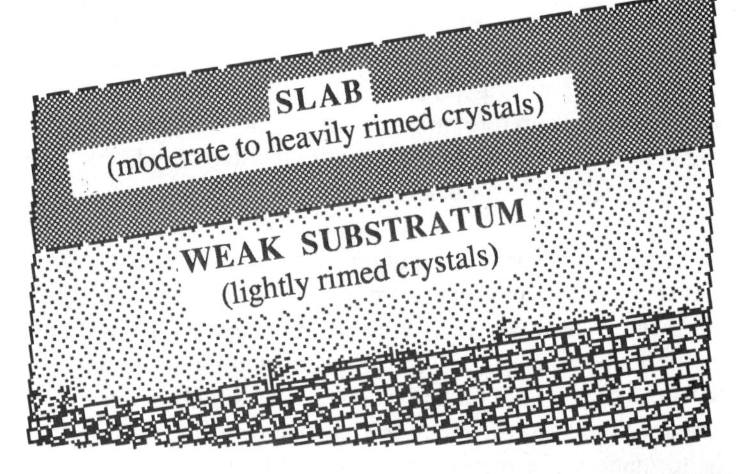

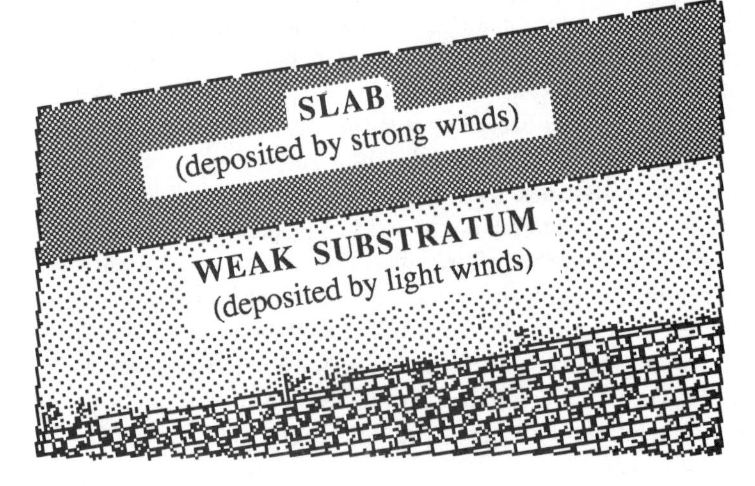

for slab avalanche danger. In order to successfully evaluate the slab avalanche potential, we need information about the entire snow pack, not just the surface. A hard wind slab at the surface will seem strong and thus safe to the uninitiated, but when it rests on a weaker layer, which may be well below the surface, it may fail under the weight of a skier and release as a slab avalanche.

What are some of the typical snow structure combinations which contribute to slab formation? Thick layers of weak snow often result from the development of depth hoar early in the season, as described above. The typical combination of climatic factors which produce these layers are: early winter snowfalls followed by several weeks of clear, cold weather. Even at the higher elevations in the mountains, the snow cover on the slopes with a southerly aspect may melt off during this period of fair weather. However, in early to mid fall — October and early November — the sun angle is low enough so that steep slopes with a northerly aspect will receive little or no direct heating from the sun. The snow remains on the ground, but as we have seen, not without changing. The snow on the north-facing slopes experiences the optimal conditions for depth hoar formation: a thin, low-density snow cover (maximum opportunity for vapor flow) is sandwiched between the warm ground, still retaining much of its summer heat, and the cold air above. This snow layer recrystallizes over a period of weeks and when the first large storm of winter comes in November, for example, cohesive layers of wind-deposited snow accumulates on a very weak base, setting the scene for a widespread avalanche cycle. Figures 3.14 describes other combinations which result in brittle or cohesive layers of snow developing above a weak layer.

MECHANICAL PROPERTIES

How Snow Deforms on a Slope

In the previous section we focused on the structural makeup of the snow cover, or its physical properties. Almost all of these properties we can easily see or measure. For example we "feel" the difference between low density soft new snow layers and a hard, cohesive wind slab as we travel over the snows whether, it be on skis, snowshoes, or snowmobile. We can identify various crystal types and we have the means to measure temperature or density. When we dig a snow pit, we get a wealth of information regarding these physical properties, layer by layer, throughout the thickness of the snow cover. What we learn about all of these physical properties contributes a great deal to our ability to evaluate the avalanche hazard potential. However, even a detailed knowledge of these properties does not provide all the information we need. The current mechanical state of the snow cover must also be taken into consideration. Unfortunately, for the average person, these properties are virtually impossible to measure. As we learn more about avalanche hazard evaluation, we will see that nature does provide us with some direct evidence of the mechanical state of the snow cover. This information is presented in Chapters 4 and 5.

The purpose of the following section is to present a conceptual overview of the role of mechanical deformation within the snow cover just prior to its failure and the start of a slab avalanche. We noted earlier in this chapter that the snow cover has a tendency to settle simply from its own weight. When this occurs on level ground, the settlement is perpendicular to the ground and the snow layer densifies and gains in strength. The situation is not so simple when the snow is resting on a slope. In this case the force of gravity is divided into two components, one tending to cause the snow layer to shrink in thickness as in the level ground example, and a new component, acting parallel to the slope, which tends to pull the snow down the slope. This type of downslope movement within the snow cover is occurring at all times, even on gentle slopes. The speed of movement is slow, generally on the order of only a few millimeters per day up to perhaps millimeters per hour within new snow on steep slopes. However, the evidence of these forces is often clearly visible in the bending of trees and damage to structures built on snow-covered slopes. Although the movement is slow when deep snow pushes against a rigid structure the forces are significant and even large buildings can be pushed off of their foundations.

We cannot describe how snow deforms in terms of a single material because it tends to respond in a highly variable fashion. Consequently, snow is generally described as being a visco-elastic material. This means that there are times when it deforms as if it were a liquid (viscous), while at other times it responds more like a solid (elastic). A viscous deformation implies a continuous and irreversible flow, as when a jar of warm honey is knocked over on a table and the honey flows slowly across the surface. In terms of snow, this type of slow deformation is not difficult to imagine after even a brief introduction to its properties. In contrast, an elatic deformation implies that once the force

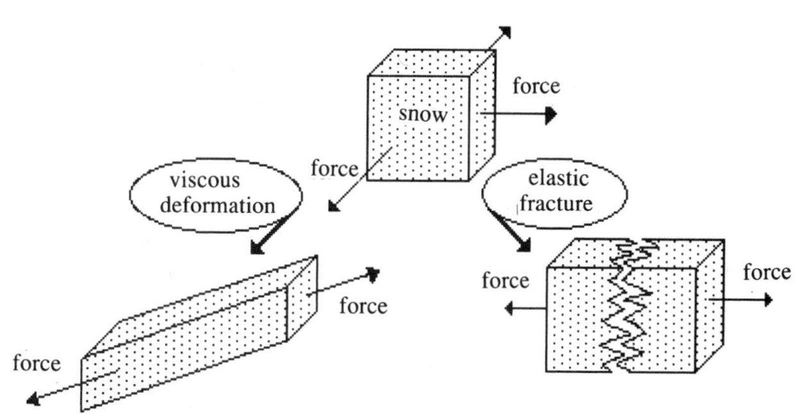

3.15 Depending on prevailing conditions, snow may deform and stretch in a viscous or flowing manner (left arrow) or it may respond more like a solid and fracture (right arrow).

ties. In contrast, an elastic deformation implies that once the force causing the deformation is removed, some small part of the initial deformation will be recovered. Everyday examples of this are common and often involve total rebound — as when a rubber band is stretched and released — or when one billiard ball strikes another and rebounds. The elasticity of snow is not so obvious, primarily because the amount of rebound is very small compared to more familiar materials.

In terms of avalanche formation, it is important to understand when snow will act primarily as an elastic material and when it will respond more like a viscous substance. These conditions are shown in Figure 3.15. From laboratory experiments it has been clearly determined that the conditions of warm temperatures and the slow application of force favor viscous deformation. In nature, we see examples of this, as snow slowly deforms and bends over the edge of a roof or sags slowly from a branch of a tree. In this case the snow deforms but does not crack or break. In contrast, when temperatures are very cold or when the force is applied rapidly, snow tends to react like an elastic material. Although we would not expect it to happen in the previous example of the billiard ball, we know that if enough force is applied to an elastic material, it will fracture. When this happens we think of the substance as being brittle, and it is the release of the stored elastic energy which causes the brittle fractures to move through the material. In the case of snow cover on a steep slope, the forces may increase, in the form of accumulating snow or the weight of a skier, until the snow fails. At that point, the stored elastic energy is released and is then available to drive the brittle fractures over great distances through the snow slab. When we look for elastic deformation in the snow cover, it is the slab avalanche

3.16 The consistant 90 degree angle between crown face and bed surface of the avalanche shows that slab avalanches result from an elastic fracture (K. Williams photo)

itself which provides the best example. While we cannot actually see the elastic deformation, the evidence of the resultant brittle failure is clearly present in the form of the sharp, linear fracture line and crown face of the slab release (Figure 3.16). The crown face is perpendicular to the bed surface in virtually all examples of the slab avalanche, evidence that the snow has failed in a brittle manner.

Therefore, if we are to begin to understand the slab avalanche condition or the stability of the snow cover, we must "view" it in terms of its mechanical state. It is now necessary to go beyond examples drawn from a generalized snow cover; we must try to imagine what is happening in the actual starting zone of an avalanche just prior to a slab release. We know that the snow is always deforming downslope, but throughout most of the winter the strength of the snow is sufficient to prevent an avalanche. We know that the snow cover is layered and that some layers are weaker than others. During periods of snowfall or blowing snow, or both, an additional load, or weight, is being applied to the snow in the starting zone, the snow is creeping faster, and the new stresses are beginning to approach the strength of the weakest layers. What finally happens to set the avalanche in motion? The weakest layer must also have a weakest point some-

3.17 An avalanche path has three parts — starting zone, track and runout zone (B. Armstrong photo)

where within its continuous structure. If the stresses, caused by the load of the new snow or the weight of a skier, reach the level where they equal the strength of the weakest point, the snow fails completely at that point. This means that the strength at that point immediately goes to zero. This is analogous to what would happen if someone on your team in a tug-of-war let go of the rope. If the remainder of your team is strong enough to make up for the lost member, then not much changes, at least not immediately (though your team might tire more rapidly and suffer the consequences later). The same situation exists with the snow cover. If the surrounding snow has sufficient strength to make up for the fact that the strength at the weakest point has now gone to zero, then nothing much happens beyond perhaps a local move-

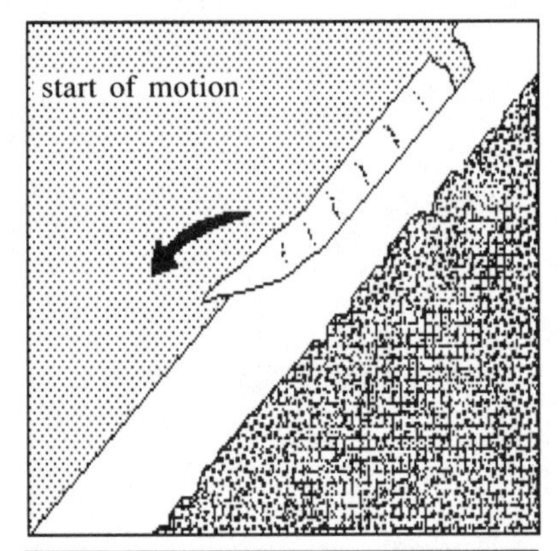

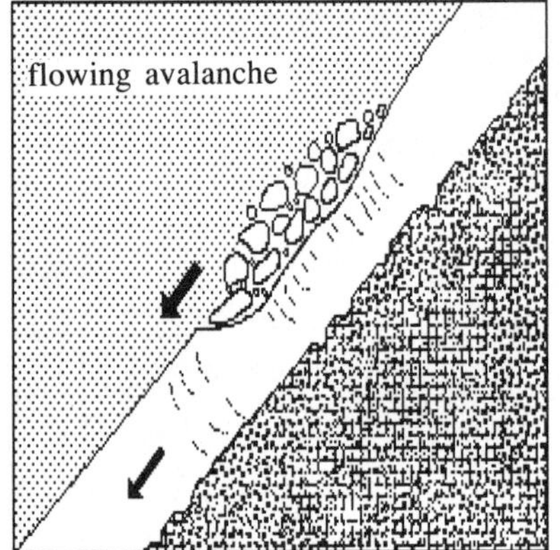

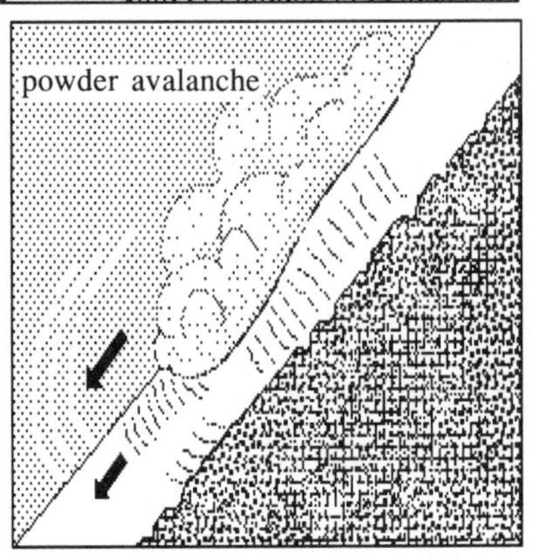

3.18 A dry snow avalanche may have a flowing motion and travel near the surface or, with lower density snow and higher velocities, the turbulent dust cloud of the powder avalanche develops.

ment or settlement in the snow. If, however, the surrounding snow is not capable of doing this, the area of snow next to the initial weak point fails, and then the area next to it and the chain reaction begins. Again, similar to the tug-of-war team, if you lost one, two, and three members, the fate of your team would be clear.

In order to understand clearly what is happening, we must remember the elastic component in the snow cover. As the initial crack forms in the now unstable snow, this elastic energy is released, which in turn drives the crack further, releasing more elastic energy, and so forth. The ability of the snow to store elastic energy has a lot to do with the mechanism of avalanche release, and is essentially what allows large slab avalanches to occur. As long as the snow properties are similar across the avalanche starting zone, the crack will continue to propagate, thus allowing entire basins, many acres in area, to be set in motion within a very few seconds. The snow slab in this situation is reacting like a pane of glass; once the crack begins it often continues across the entire pane to the edge of the glass.

The Effect of Temperature on the Mechanical Properties

Earlier in this chapter we discussed the role of temperature in snow metamorphism. The processes involved occurred over a period of days, weeks, and even months. In terms of the influence of temperature on the mechanical state of the snow cover, the changes frequently occur on the order of minutes to hours. The actual effect of temperature is not always easy to interpret. One might hear a knowledgeable person state that an increase in temperature has contributed to the stabilization of the snow cover, while at another time they might well state that an increase in temperature has led to avalanche activity. At different times both statements may be correct, but the exact mechanism must be understood in order to appreciate how this could be.

There are several situations where an increase in temperature clearly produces an increase in the avalanche potential. In general, these include a rise in temperature during a storm or immediately after a storm, or a prolonged period of warm, fair weather such as would occur with spring conditions. The first example may occur following an overnight snowstorm which did not produce an avalanche on the slope of interest. By morning the precipitation has stopped and clear skies allow the morning sun to shine directly on the slopes which face generally northeast. From what we have already learned about snow mechanics, it is easy to imagine what happens. The sun rapidly warms the cold, low density, new snow which then begins to deform and creep downslope. The new snow layer is settling, densifying, and thus gaining in strength. However, at the same time, it is being stretched downhill and some of the bonds between the grains are being pulled apart, and thus the snow layer is also becoming weaker. If more bonds are broken due to the stretching than are formed from the settlement, there is not enough strength to hold the snow on the slope, and an avalanche occurs.

In the second example, the temperatures at the beginning of snowfall are well below freezing, but as the storm progresses the trend is for the temperature to increase. As a result, the initial layers of new snow will be light, fluffy, low-density snow which are relatively low in strength, while the later layers which accumulate on top of this layer will be warmer, denser, and stiffer (Figure 3.14). Thus the essential ingredients for a slab avalanche have been provided within the new snow layers of the storm — a cohesive slab resting on a weak layer. If the temperature continues to rise, the falling snow will turn to rain, a situation not all that uncommon in lower elevation coastal mountain ranges. Once this happens avalanches are almost certain because as the rain falls, additional weight is added to the avalanche slope but no additional strength is provided, as is the case whenever a layer of snow accumulates.

In the first example, the complete snow cover remained at temperatures below freezing, while the second example involved perhaps a small amount of melting in the near-surface snow layers. The third example occurs when a substantial amount of the winter's snow cover is warmed to the melting point. During winter, sun angles are low, days are short, and air temperatures are cold enough so that the small amount of heat that is gained by the snow cover during the day is lost again during the long cold nights. As spring approaches this pattern obviously changes and eventually there is enough heat available at the snow surface during the day to cause some melt. This melt layer will refreeze again that night, but the next day more heat may be available so that eventually a substantial amount of melting occurs and melt water begins to move down through the snow cover. As this melt water percolates or moves slowly downward, it tends to melt the bonds which hold the snow grains together and the strength of the

3.19 The large powder cloud associated with a fast-moving dry snow avalanche (R. Armstrong photo)

layers decreases. At first only the near-surface layers are affected, with the midday melt reaching only as far as the uppermost few inches, and there is little or no increase in the avalanche hazard. However, if the warm weather continues, the melt layer becomes thicker and the potential for wet snow avalanches increases. The conditions most favorable for wet slab avalanches occur when the snow structure provides the necessary layering. Experience has shown that when the melt water encounters an ice layer or impermeable crust, or in some cases a layer of weak depth hoar, wet slab avalanches are often occur.

AVALANCHE DYNAMICS

The topic of avalanche dynamics includes how avalanches move, how fast they move, and just how far and with how much destructive power they will travel. The science of avalanche dynamics is not well advanced, although much has been learned in the past few decades. Perhaps the main reason that the problems have not been solved is the lack of measured data for avalanche velocity and impact pressure. While any environmental measurement presents its own set of problems, it is obvious that making measurements inside a moving avalanche presents some extreme limitations.

Although avalanche paths exist in a variety of sizes and shapes, they all have three distinct parts with respect to dynamics (Figure 3.17). In the starting zone, usually the steepest part of the path, the avalanche breaks away, accelerates down the slope and picks up additional snow as it moves. From the starting zone the avalanche moves into the track ,where velocity generally remains constant and little or no additional snow is added to the moving avalanche; the average slope angle has become less steep and often the snow cover is more stable than in the starting zone. (Small avalanches often stop in the track.) After traveling down the track it reaches the runout zone. Here the avalanche motion ends, either slowly as it decelerates across a gradual slope such as an alluvial fan, or abruptly as it crashes into the bottom of a gorge or ravine. As a general rule, the slope angle of starting zones is in the 30 to 45 degrees, the track is 20 to 30 degrees, and the runout zones are less than 20 degrees.

As we noted above, there have not been many actual measurements of avalanche velocities but enough data have been obtained to provide some typical values with respect to avalanche type. For the highly turbulent drypowder avalanches, the velocities are commonly in the 75 to 100 miles per hour range with rare examples being higher, perhaps in the 150 to 200 miles per hour range. Such speeds are possible only for powder avalanches because the entrainment of large amounts of air in the moving snow greatly reduces the forces resulting from internal friction. As the snow in the starting zone becomes more dense or wet or both, movement becomes less turbulent and a more flowing type of motion reduces typical velocities to the 50 to 75 miles per hour range. During spring conditions when the snow contains large amounts of liquid water, speeds may reach only about 25 miles per hour (Figure 3.18).

In most cases the avalanche simply follows a path down the steepest route on the slope while being guided or chanelled by terrain features. However, with the very high speeds of powder avalanches, the avalanche may deviate from this path. Terrain features, such as the side walls of a gully, which would normally direct the flow of the avalanche around a bend, may be overridden by a high-velocity powder avalanche (Figure 3.19). The slower-moving avalanches, which travel near the ground, tend to consistantly follow these terrain features, giving them a somewhat predictable course. The fastest-moving powder avalanches, however, may follow a direct path down the slope which is barely influenced by terrain features.

Because avalanches can travel at very high speeds, the resultant impact pressures can be significant. Smaller- and medium-sized events have the potential to heavily damage wood frame structures (impact pressures of 1 to 15 pounds per square inch). But on the other end of the scale, extremely large snow avalanches possess the force to uproot mature forests and even destroy structures built of concrete (impact pressures of more than 150 pounds per square inch). Actual destruction would, of course, occur only when such an avalanche came in contact with some type of structure — which represents just a very small fraction of the total avalanche events.

Some reports of avalanche damage describe circumstances which cannot be easily explained simply by the impact of large amounts of fast-moving dense snow. Some observers note that as the avalanche passes, some buildings actually explode, perhaps resulting from some form of vacuum created by the fast-moving snow. Other reports indicate that a structure was destroyed by the "air blast" preceding the avalanche, because there was no evidence of large amounts of avalanche debris in the area; however, this is more likely to be damage resulting from the powder cloud, which, although when it comes to rest and settles to the ground may only comprise a few inches of snow, can contribute significantly to the total impact force. A powder cloud may not seem like much of a factor, but the presence of the snow crystals in the air can increase the density of the air by a factor of three. This means that a powder cloud traveling at a moderate dry avalanche speed of 60 miles per hour would have the impact force of a 180 miles per hour wind, or well beyond the destructive capacity of a hurricane.

One of the most practical aspects of avalanche dynamics is the effort to predict just how far an avalanche will continue to travel after it has reached the runout zone. Runout zones often look like good building site: road access is easy along the valley floor, there may be water nearby and often the site is located in a forest clearing allowing good exposure to the sun. Unfortunately, the forest clearing also allows good exposure to avalanches — and, in fact, an avalanche very likely could have created the clearing in the first place. Methods to predict avalanche velocity, runout distance, and associated impact force were first developed in Switzerland about 30 years ago. Because initially there was little experimental or historical data available, early methods were highly theoretical and tended to treat the avalanche as a fast-moving fluid. Over the past decade some very large data samples have been collected, mostly from Switzerland and Norway, which have provided many hundreds of cases where the actual maximum known avalanche runout distance was located on the ground. The overall accuracy of the original methods has been greatly improved through the combination of the theory, the maximum observed runout data, and the specific terrain features and snow cover conditions of a given location. While the current methods are far from perfect, they can provide land-use planners with excellent guidelines and in many cases offer a reasonable set of probabilities regarding potential hazard in a given location.

The lofty domain of Mt. Rainier, Washington, where snowfields, glaciers, and winter storms conspire to produce a world of challenge to mountaineers (National Park Service photo)

4 BUILDING UP TO A DOWNFALL

AVALANCHE TERRAIN

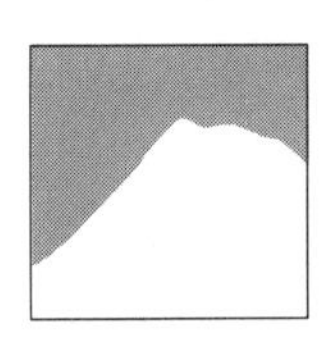

MOUNTAINS PROVIDE THE REAL estate on which avalanches are built. Characteristics like elevation, slope profiles, and weather determine whether a mountain can produce avalanches. The ingredients of an avalanche — snow and a steep enough slope — are so simple that any mountain can produce one avalanche if conditions are exactly right. But to be a consistent producer of avalanches, and a threat, a mountain and its weather must work in harmony.

Elevation

In an earlier discussion in Chapter 1 of mountains in general and the mountains of America in particular, the point was made that mountains had to be at high enough latitudes and high enough in elevation to build up and sustain a winter snow cover before their slopes could become avalanche threats. Elevation is a foremost factor, for temperature drops steadily with elevation. On the one hand, this has the obvious effect of allowing snow to build up deeper and remain longer at higher elevations before melting depletes the snow cover. On the other hand, a less obvious effect of the temperature and elevation relationship upon avalanche formation is the demarcation called timberline. This is the level above which the combined effects of low temperature, strong winds, and heavy snowfall prevent tree growth.

No snowflake in an avalanche ever feels responsible.
STANISLAW JERZY LEC

The terrain lying above timberline is called tundra. (Climatologists define timberline as being that elevation at which the average temperature of the warmest month is 50 degrees Fahrenheit.) Timberline can be quite variable in any mountain range, depending on the microclimates that exist. For example, on a single mountain, timberline is generally higher on south slopes than on north slopes (at least in the Northern Hemisphere), because more sunshine leads to warmer average temperatures on southern exposures. The latitudinal variation in the elevation of timberline ranges from sea level in northern Alaska to almost 12,000 feet in the Sierra of southern California and the Rockies of New Mexico.

The point we wish to make about timberline is that mountains that rise above this level are more likely to produce avalanches. Dense timber anchors the snowpack, so that avalanches can seldom start. Below treeline, avalanches can start on slopes having no trees or only scattered trees — a circumstance arising either from natural causes such as a streambed or rockslide area, or from man-made causes such as a clearcut. Above treeline, avalanches are free to start, and once set in motion, they can easily cut a swath through the trees below. The classic avalanche path is one having a steep bowl above timberline to catch the snow and a track extending below treeline. Avalanches run repeatedly down the track and ravage whatever vegetation grows there, leaving a scar with only small or stunted trees that cuts through larger trees on either side.

Steepness

How steep must a slope be to produce an avalanche? In snow that is thoroughly saturated with water so that a slush mixture is formed, the slope needs only to have a slight tilt. There is the story of a wet-snow avalanche in Japan releasing on a beginners' slope at a ski area. The slope was only 10 degrees, but the avalanche was big enough to kill seven skiers. Surely this shallow grade is the extreme and could apply only to a water-logged snowpack, which would behave more like a liquid than a solid.

4.1 Avalanches start most frequently on slopes of 30 to 45 degrees but can also initiate on steeper and more shallow slopes.

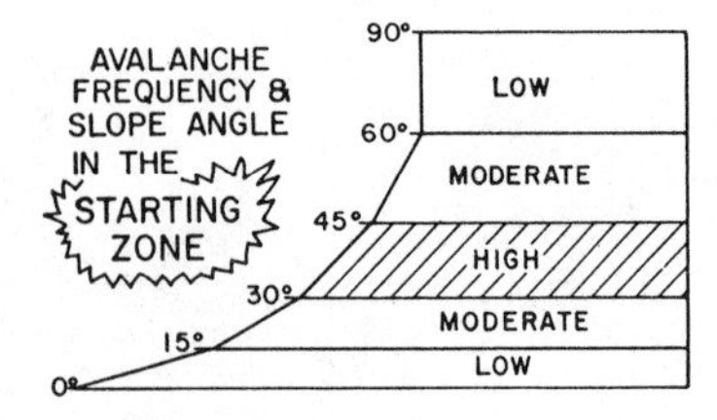

A more realistic number is 22 degrees, for it is at this pitch that we find the "angle of repose" for such granular substances such as sand and dry, unbonded snow. Round grains will not stack up in a pile having sides much steeper than 22 degrees, before gravity rearranges the pile. Indeed, dry-snow avalanches have been observed releasing on slopes of, say, 22 to 25 degrees. These, though, are rare events, for snow grains are seldom round and they seldom touch one another without forming bonds. A useful minimum steepness for producing avalanches is 30 degrees. It is at this angle and above that we see most avalanche releases. In fact, avalanches occur with the greatest frequency on slopes of 30 to 50 degrees. These are the steepnesses in which the balance between strength (the bonding of the snow trying to hold it in place) and stress (the force of gravity trying to pull it loose) are most critical. On even steeper slopes, the force of gravity wins; snow continually rolls or sluffs off, preventing the buildup of deep snowpacks. Exceptions exist, of course, one being the example of damp snow plastered to an extra-steep slope by strong winds.

Orientation

Avalanches can and do fall down slopes facing every point of the compass. Certainly steep slopes have no preference of, say, east over west, or north over south. There are factors, however, that cause more avalanches to fall on slopes facing north, northeast, and east than those facing south through west. These have to do with the slope orientation with respect to the sun and wind. Consider first the sun angle, which in northern winters causes south slopes to get much more sunshine and heating than north slopes. This frequently leads to a radically different snow cover on the two slopes. North slopes have a deeper and colder snow cover, and one that often has a substantial layer of depth hoar near the ground. South slopes usually carry a shallower and warmer snow cover, and one that is laced with multiple ice layers formed on warm days between storms. Avalanches fall more frequently from the snowpacks on the north slopes. (Also most ski areas are built on predominantly north-facing slopes to take advantage of the deeper and longer-lasting snow cover.) At high latitudes such as in Alaska, however, the winter sun is so low on the horizon and the heat input to south slopes is so puny that we seldom see big differences in the snow covers of north and south slopes.

Next consider the effect of the prevailing west wind at mid-latitudes. Storms most often move west to east, and storm winds are most frequently from the western quadrant — southwest, west, or northwest. The effect is to pick up fallen snow and redeposit it on slopes facing away from the wind; that is, onto northeast, east, and southeast slopes. These are the slopes most often overburdened with fresh pillows of wind-drifted snow at the tops of avalanche paths.

The net effect of sun and wind is to cause more avalanches to fall down north through east-facing slopes. However, there is one important exception that is worth noting. When dawn breaks clear and sunny the day following a storm that has brought a fresh load of snow to south and southeast slopes (a storm with prevailing northwest winds), there is an excellent chance of seeing avalanches release on those south and southeast slopes during the morning hours. What happens is that the sun initially weakens the snow by warming it and causing the top layer to creep downhill, thereby increasing the stress and the avalanche danger. But after a few hours of sunshine, the new snow begins to densify and strengthen, and the danger begins to ebb.

Shape of Terrain

Avalanche paths come in all shapes and sizes. Some are open slopes, while others are narrow gullies. Some are straight shots that maintain a constant pitch from top to bottom. Some have a vertical profile that shows a convex curvature in the upper portion, a rollover that starts out gentle but steepens dramatically to a pitch of 45 degrees or steeper. Others show that opposite vertical curvature, a concave shape, when viewed from the side. These sometimes start at the base of cliffs.

The frequency with which a path produces avalanches depends on a number of factors. One path might produce 10 slides a winter, another might spawn one a winter, and yet another might set loose only one every 10 years. What separates the productivity of these paths is their ability, first, to collect snow, and, second, to create stress much greater than the snow can stand. The easiest way to create high stress is to increase the slope angle: gravity will work that much harder to stretch the snow out and rip it from its underpinnings. A slope of 45 degrees will spawn many more avalanches than one of 30 degrees, if all other things are equal.

A broad slope that is curved into a bowl shape and a narrow one that is confined to a gully will both be more efficient at collecting snow than slopes that face a single direction and are open on the sides. Those having a curved horizontal profile, such as a bowl or gully, trap blowing snow coming from several directions; the snow drifts over the top and settles into a deep, deadly pillow. On the other hand, the horizontally straight slope collects snow efficiently only if it is being blown directly from behind. A side wind scours the straight slope more than it loads it.

A particularly dangerous type of avalanche is one that releases its snow in a piecemeal fashion. The danger, of course, comes from a first avalanche creating one problem — such as blocking a highway or burying a skier — and a second avalanche threatening a work or rescue party below. (Remember the example given in Chapter 1 of the East Riverside avalanche on Red Mountain Pass, Colorado, that did exactly this?)

Two types of path configuration lend themselves to this sort of harrowing possibility. First is the large bowl-shaped starting zone in which a section of snow pulls out and slides away, thereby removing support from the adjacent sections in which stress increases by the minute and hour until these sections can no longer support themselves and they too break loose. Second is the path that consists of several gullies that feed into a common track lower down. One gully might turn loose its load of snow before the others had quite reached that point of readiness, but they remain poised to dump their loads at the slightest provocation.

Ground Cover and Roughness

The surface conditions of a starting zone often dictate the size and type of avalanches produced. A particularly rough ground surface such as a jumbled boulder field will not usually produce avalanches early in the winter, for it takes considerable snowfall to cover the ground anchors. Once most of the rocks are covered, avalanches will then pull out in sections, with the area between two exposed rocks running one time, and the area between two other rocks running another. A smooth rock face or a slope of grass provides a surface that is too slick for the snow to grip. Therefore, full-depth avalanches are distinctly possible: if the avalanche does not run during the winter, it is almost guaranteed to run to ground in the spring, once melt water percolates through the snow and lubricates the ground surface.

Vegetation has a mixed effect on avalanche releases. Bushes provide anchoring support until they become totally covered; but at that point they may actually provide weak points in the snow cover, for air circulates well around the branches, twigs, and needles of the bush, providing an ideal habitat for the growth of depth hoar. It is common to view the fracture line of an avalanche and see that it has run from a rock to a tree to a bush, all of which are places of healthy depth-hoar growth.

A dense stand of trees can easily provide enough anchors to prevent avalanches from releasing. Indeed, reforestation of slopes devoid of trees because of logging, fire, or avalanche is an effective means of avalanche control. Scattered trees on a gladed slope, however, offer little, if any, support to hold the snow in place. In fact, isolated trees may do more harm than good by providing concentrated weak points on the slope.

Lightly timbered slopes have been the sites of numerous serious, and occasionally fatal, accidents. One such slope having a deadly history is the Floral Park avalanche on Berthoud Pass, Colorado. This slope is right on the highway — sometimes literally on it, for about once every two winters the avalanche buries the roadway. Floral Park is steep — about 38 degrees — and is studded with large trees spaced at 10- to 15-foot intervals — easy enough to turn skis between but not close enough to anchor the snow. Skiers have made thousands of safe ski passes down Floral Park, but several have been buried here and one has died. It was on February 13, 1960, that a 34-year-old man was buried and killed in an avalanche here — while his wife, waiting in their car to pick him up, watched in helpless horror.

A WEATHER PRIMER

What comes to mind when you think of the rainiest and snowiest places on earth? Maybe tropical rain forests, maybe monsoon downpours, maybe cold climates where winter storms roll across the snowscape one after another, seemingly without end. Certainly you're on the right track with these visions. But did you think about mountains? All of the wettest spots on earth, from the rains of Cherrapunji, India, to the snows of Mount Rainier, Washington, have one thing in common — mountains. But we're getting ahead of ourselves. Before we talk about the influence of mountains on weather, we need to lay out some basics.

What makes it snow? Water is always present in the atmosphere, and it can exist in three states; solid, liquid, and invisible vapor. The air around us always contains some amount of water vapor in addition to the oxygen, nitrogen, and other gases that make up the atmosphere. The amount of water vapor varies from near zero percent in cold deserts to about four percent in the hottest, most humid jungles. Despite its small percentage, water vapor is a necessary constituent, but it is also an exciting one, for without it there would be no clouds, no rain, no snow.

To form a cloud, the air must first become saturated. By saturated, we mean that the water vapor is the greatest it can possibly be at a given temperature. If additional water vapor forms, the excess moisture would be condensed out into tiny liquid water droplets, forming a cloud. This represents a change that we can see, from invisible water vapor molecules in the air to a visible cloud of water droplets.

There is another way of making the air saturated, a way

much different from adding more water vapor, and that is to cool the air. One of the basic properties of the atmosphere is that "warm air can hold more water vapor than cold air." Stated in more scientific terms, the moisture capacity of the air depends on the temperature: as the temperature increases, the moisture capacity increases; as the temperature decreases, the moisture capacity decreases.

Relative humidity is a term that we are all familiar with; it is commonly used because it is very useful. The relative humidity is the amount of water vapor the air is holding, expressed as a percentage of the amount the air could hold at that particular temperature. Remember that warm air can hold more vapor than cold air. So when we cool air that has a fixed amount of water vapor, its relative humidity goes up. If we cool it far enough, the relative humidity will reach 100 percent. At this point, the air is saturated, and if it is cooled further, the relative humidity remains at 100 percent, but the excess vapor condenses into droplets forming a cloud.

The relative humidity (RH) is useful because it tells us how close the air is to being saturated. A relative humidity of 50 percent is halfway there, one of 75 percent is three-quarters the way there, and so on. Air that is saturated (100% RH) is said to have reached its moisture capacity, and if forced to try to hold more vapor, it will condense the excess into liquid drops.

Have you ever spent time watching the sky and observing how clouds sometimes form in one part of the sky and disappear in another? If so, you were watching air become saturated (100% RH) where the clouds formed and become unsaturated (perhaps 99% RH) where they dissipated. (Ninety-nine percent RH is very moist, but it's not saturated.)

There are two ways to get the air saturated. First, simply add more water vapor. This happens regularly near large moisture sources, where water evaporates into the air from the ocean, lakes, and snowfields.The second way is to cool the air. One way of doing this, obviously, is to mix in colder air. This happens all the time in day-to-day weather with the passage of cold fronts. But there is another, highly efficient way to cool air, and that is to lift it. Let's look at this process to see how it works.

Air pressure decreases rapidly with altitude. This is because the higher one goes, fewer molecules of air exist. In other words, the air gets thinner with elevation. To put this in perspective, at 5,000 feet (the elevation of Denver), there is only 85 percent as much air as at sea level; at 10,000 feet (the elevation of Leadville, Colorado), there is only 70 percent as much air as at sea level; and at 18,000 feet, there is only half as much air as at sea level. A practical consideration of all this would be that a mountain climber at the 18,000-foot level of Mount McKinley would have to take twice as many breaths to get the same amount of oxygen as at sea level.

What happens then to a parcel of air that gets shoved upward from sea level? It encounters lower pressure as it goes up, so it expands. Expansion is a cooling process, so as the parcel rises, it gets larger and its temperature drops. Thus, lifting becomes a cooling process. If the parcel of air rises high enough, it will cool until it reaches saturation, and condensation will form a cloud.

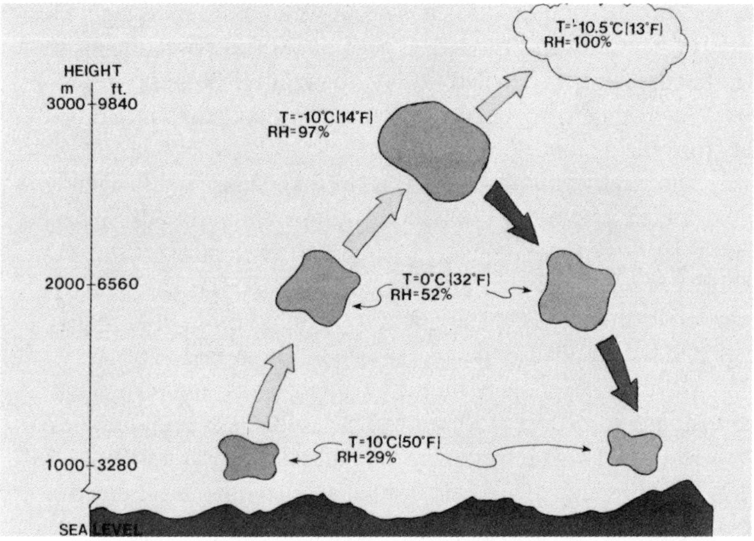

4.2 When a parcel of air (indicated by the shaded, irregular shapes) is lifted, it expands, its temperature (T) decreases, and its relative humidity (RH) increases. The opposite effects occur when the parcel sinks.

The atmosphere knows four ways to lift air. These are *convection, cyclonic lifting, frontal lifting,* and *orographic lifting.* We have already alluded to convection, for that is exactly what happened with our parcel of air. In nature, the sun heats the earth's surface unevenly so that thermals tend to rise in the atmosphere over the hot spots. Thermals, or convective updrafts, are rising columns of air that have been heated more than the surrounding air and therefore have buoyancy. Convection forms cumulus clouds, which grow into thunderstorms when the atmosphere is particularly turbulent.

Cyclonic lifting is the upward push of air around low-pressure systems. Weather maps are highlighted with highs and lows, with fair weather accompanying the highs and stormy weather accompanying the lows. Air flows counterclockwise around a low, and it also spirals inward, converging on the center. The air cannot simply pile up at the center, so it is forced upward, resulting in cooling, condensation, cloud formation, and frequently precipitation.

Fronts occur wherever one air mass butts against another. A mass of cold air will not readily mix with a mass of warm air. Rather, the cold air, being denser, will slide underneath the warm air and lift it off the ground. This is called frontal lifting. (We've all experienced cold fronts on a small scale when we've been sitting in a warm room on a winter's day; if someone opens the door and lets in a rush of cold air, it flows across the floor chilling our feet first before eventually mixing with the air in the room. That's a mini-cold front.) Warm and cold fronts are features on a weather map that weathercasters love, for the passage of a front means a change of air mass and usually turbulent weather for a day or two. At the boundary of, say, an advancing cold front, the cold air wedges under the warm, moist air to force it upward and form clouds and precipitation.

Orographic lifting is the forced lifting of air up and over a mountain barrier. When wind speeds are strong, this is a very powerful lifting mechanism. (On a smaller scale, updrafts in powerful thunderstorms can reach 80 miles per hour.) Maximum lifting occurs when the wind speeds are strong and the wind direction is perpendicular to the mountain barrier. In mountainous areas, this lifting effect is often added to the effects initiated by convective, cyclonic, and frontal lifting. The cumulative effect is to make the windward sides of mountain barriers some of the wettest places on earth. For example, the world record for rainfall in one year is 905 inches at Cherrapunji, India, in the foothills of the Himalayas; and the equivalent records for snowfall is 1,122 inches at Paradise, Mount Rainier, Washington. Clearly, mountainous regions have an advantage in producing precipitation — regions such as the Great Plains cannot compete.

SNOW

We see ice in our atmosphere in a variety of forms. Some of it falls as snow, sleet, or hail; while at other times, varieties such as frost, rime, and glaze can form on or cover all exposed surfaces. Of these forms, it is snow that we find the most intricate, beautiful, and fascinating.

When a snow crystal forms, it does so in a shape that shows a six-sided pattern — a hexagon. (It is only in the solid

4.3 Stellar snow crystal (R Armstrong photo).

state that crystalline shapes emerge.) To understand the reason for this, we must look at one, and then many, water molecules. Two hydrogen atoms are joined to one oxygen atom by strong attractions called hydrogen bonds. The angle between the oxygen atom and the hydrogen atoms is 120 degrees, such that when many molecules of water join together in a lattice to form a single ice crystal, the result is a hexagonal pattern. But the variety of shapes that a hexagonal pattern can take on is virtually limitless, so that the often-heard claim that no two snowflakes are exactly alike just might be right. (Of course, it's also easy to argue that this is a foolish claim to make, since the number of ice crystals viewed beneath a microscope is absurdly small compared to the number that have fallen over the millennia.) Ice crystals grow into basic shapes of flat plates, pointy stellars, thin columns, and thinner needles, and then form all sorts of permutations on these basic shapes (see Figure 3.1).

The condensation of water vapor into droplets and the freezing of droplets into crystals requires outside help. The help comes in the form of microscopic dust, smoke, salt, and pollition particles in the air. These provide what are called *condensation* and *freezing nuclei,* which become the catalyst for forming the droplets or crystal.

Almost any minute particles work fine as condensation nuclei, so there is never a problem forming water droplets in the atmosphere. Ice crystals, however, are another matter. Freezing nuclei are much rarer, because ice will not form on just any speck of dust, but rather on one with a crystalline structure similar to that of ice. Whereas there might be as many as 10,000 condensation nuclei in a cubic centimeter of air, there may be as few as 10 freezing nuclei. The lack of appropriate freezing nuclei causes an interesting occurrence in the atmosphere: water droplets are frequently cooled to temperatures well below freezing, and these remain in a liquid state. These are called *supercooled droplets,* and they are a very common constituent of cold clouds, coexisting in the midst of ice crystals that have already undergone the freezing transition. Several things can happen to a supercooled droplet: it will instantly freeze into a crystal upon contacting a freezing nucleus; it will spontaneously freeze upon reaching a temperature of minus 40 degrees, even if it does not contact a nucleus; it will freeze to the surface of an ice crystal if the two collide; it will evaporate, with its molecules contributing to the growth of larger ice crystals; or it will strike an object on the ground such as a tree and spontaneously freeze into a white, feathery substance called *rime.*

In order for droplets to fall as rain or crystals to fall as snow, the droplets and crystals must attain a size large enough to fall. For each cloud that produces rain or snow, there are many clouds that produce neither. This means that, more often than not, the particles making up a cloud stay so small that they remain suspended and don't fall as precipitation. In the case of ice crystals, growth to a size large enough to fall as snow is done in three ways. First, crystals can collide with other crystals to form clusters which fall as snowflakes. Second, crystals can collide with supercooled droplets, which freeze to the crystals, forming coatings of rime, which then fall from the cloud in soft pellets called *graupel.* Third, crystals can rob droplets of their molecules, causing the crystals to grow at the expense of the droplets. (This happens because the vapor pressure over the crystal is lower than that over the droplet, and molecules are drawn toward low pressure.) The method of growth determines the type of crystals that form, but regardless of the method, once the crystals are large enough to overcome updrafts in the cloud, they fall from the skies as snow.

As a final note in our discourse on snow, we should mention cloud seeding. When meteorologists discovered that all too often there were too few natural freezing nuclei in the air, the theory was born that more ice crystals could be formed if suitable nuclei could be injected into the cloud. The nuclei had to have a crystalline form similar to ice, and they take effect at temperatures just a few degrees below freezing. Silver iodide was found to be the most suitable agent: AgI is burned in generators on the ground or in aircraft that send the seeding agent into the clouds to do its stuff. That's the theory and the method, but the results are far from being clear-cut. The best experiments hint that effective seeding augments natural precipitation by 10 to 15 percent.

HOW MOUNTAINS AFFECT — AND CREATE — WEATHER

Precipitation effects

By virtue of their air-mass lifting capabilities, mountains can create weather. They can turn fair skies into stormy skies and small storms into respectable ones. In doing this year after year, they create climates. We have seen that the upwind sides of mountain ranges are where extra rain and snow fall, and if the mountain barrier stands in the way of an exceptionally strong prevailing storm track, it produces some of the wettest climates on earth.

Downwind of major mountain ranges, however, are some of the drier areas of the globe. The rain and snow that fall on the ride up the mountains mean less moisture for the other side. But the problem is more complicated than that. If rising air cools and becomes more humid, then sinking air warms and becomes drier. So not only is there less moisture to begin with, there is also less likelihood that the moisture will form clouds, because the relative humidity decreases with every foot the air slides down the mountain. Two factors have created the desert country of the American Southwest. One is the dominance of the Pacific High, a semi-permanent high-pressure cell. The other is the Sierra Nevada range, which places Nevada and Utah in a regime of sinking air in the lee of the mountains. Eastern Oregon and Washington, lying in the lee of the Cascades, have dry climates, but not nearly so severe as that of Nevada, because they are situated north of the influence of the Pacific High. Similarly, the Great Plains, lying leeward of the Rocky Mountains, are semi-arid. Were it not for moisture pumped northward from the Gulf of Mexico, much of the Great Plains would resemble a desert.

A few weather "stats" might help focus on the profound effect of mountains on snowfall. We've previously mentioned that Mount Rainier, Washington, holds the world record for snowfall in one winter: 1,122 inches in 1971-72. In fact, Mount Rainier has made a habit of breaking its own world record: for years it stood at 1,000.5 inches; then in 1970-71, it recorded 1,029 inches, only to break this record the very next winter. The Sierra Nevada has had many banner years of snowfall. The seasonal record for California is held by the long-abandoned site of Tamarack, which received 884 inches in 1906-07. Donner Summit, California, recently set a new record for its own snowfall with 793 inches in 1982-83. The world record for greatest depth of seasonal snowcover on the ground is also held by Tamarack: 451 inches on March 11, 1911.

The Wasatch Range makes an abrupt jump from the desert of Utah at 4,500 feet to peaks over 11,000 feet. It is one of the most imposing orographic barriers of the West, a fact reflected in the snowfall and avalanche history of the mining town turned ski resort of Alta. Snowfall records for the six months of November through April began in 1944. In 1983-84, Alta set a new record with 750 inches of snow for the six month; 247 inches fell in December 1983 alone.

The snowfall record in Colorado is held by Wolf Creek Pass with 837 inches in 1978-79. Wolf Creek is perfectly situated in the San Juan Mountains to catch moisture-laden storms from the central Pacific. Although the San Juans lie 650 miles from the ocean, no other mountain barriers stand in their way.

Another world record, that for the most snow in 24 hours, is held by another Colorado mountain site. On April 14-15, 1921, 76 inches of snow fell at Silver Lake, a spot high on the east slope of the Front Range west of Denver. A storm with east winds, termed an "upslope" by Coloradans, zeroed in on this spot and buried almost everything.

Wind Effects

Mountains jut well into the zone of strong winds that circle the globe. Like a rock in a river, the mountain disturbs the flow, not only at the spot but also for a great distance downstream. They block, split, deflect, channel, accelerate, and slow the flow. An excellent example of blocking is the way the Cascades protect Seattle and the Puget Sound region from outbreaks of arctic air sliding out of Canada. Similarly, there are many winter days when arctic air masses get bottled up on the east slope of the Rockies, putting Denver in a gloomy deep freeze while the ski resorts of the western slope bask in sunshine and temperatures 30 degrees warmer.

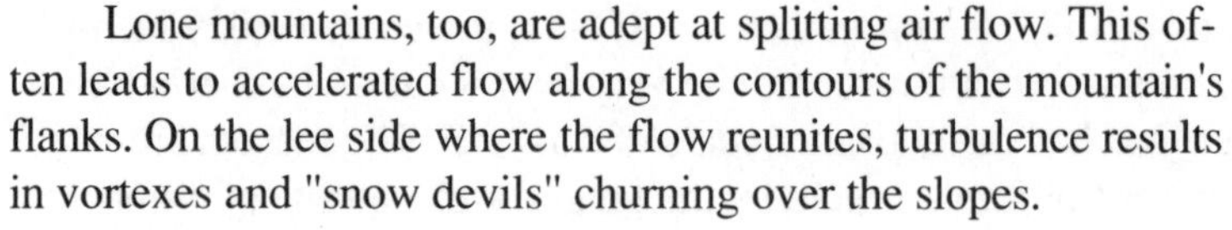

Lone mountains, too, are adept at splitting air flow. This often leads to accelerated flow along the contours of the mountain's flanks. On the lee side where the flow reunites, turbulence results in vortexes and "snow devils" churning over the slopes.

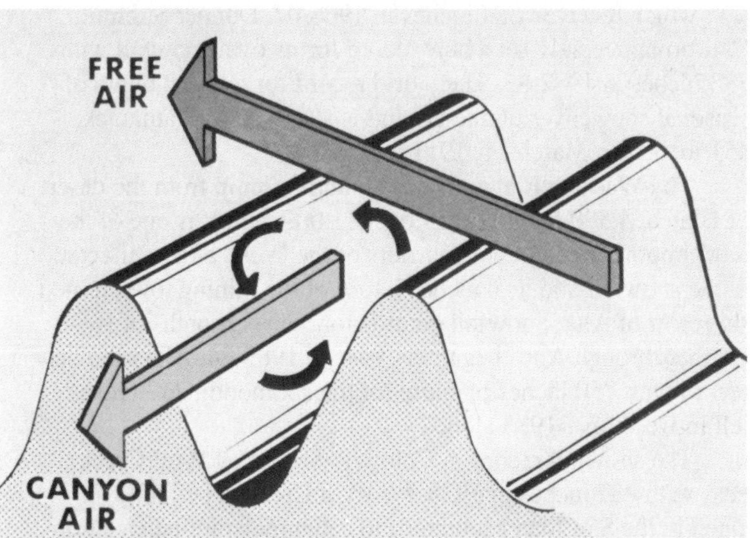

4.4 Mountains deflect free air flow into turbulent canyon flows.

Mountains commonly deflect winds from their original directions, so that flow is aligned up and down canyons rather than across them. Canyon flow usually is turbulent because of the drag along the rough terrain; the winds typically become so twisted by the terrain that they bear little resemblance to the prevailing winds at ridgetop level. Canyon winds also are routinely squeezed through narrow gaps, causing dramatic accelerations in the speed. A good example of this effect is what happens in Boulder, Colorado, several times a winter. Strong winds, which are initially intercepted along the Continental Divide west of Boulder, are deflected and accelerated down narrow Boulder Canyon, which has a straight shot into the city. The winds emerge from the canyon in gusts that sometimes top 100 miles per hour. The strongest gust recorded in Boulder was 147 miles per hour on January 25, 1971. Needless to say, these unwelcome blasts cause considerable damage.

The "bane of Boulder" is an extreme example of a chinook. Chinooks are downslope winds that accelerate on their downhill runs, are warmed by compression, and therefore have exceptionally low relative humidities. Called "snow eaters" in some Indian tongues, they can evaporate snow from the ground and ice from frozen lakes as if by magic. Chinooks do their best magic in the

4.5 Mountain winds form when strong winds blow perpendicular to mountain ranges.

Great Plains east of the Rockies, where some of the fastest warm-ups on earth have taken place. The most dramatic case occurred on January 22, 1943, in Spearfish, South Dakota, when the onset of a chinook caused the temperature to rise from minus 4 degrees Farenheit to 45 degrees Farenheit in two minutes!

A frequent visitor to the mountain scene is the appearance of wave clouds hovering over and downwind of the higher peaks. Most often these appear as curved stacks of thin laminar clouds that stay in one place for hours at a time. For this reason, mountain wave clouds are accurately referred to as standing lenticular clouds. The explanation for their behavior is simple. The mountain creates a wave pattern in a fast-moving air current, just like a submerged rock does in a river. The peaks of the waves remain fixed as long as the air flow stays constant. On the ride up a wave, the air cools and condenses into a cloud; on the ride down the other side of the wave, the air warms and the cloud evaporates. The air flows through the waves but is saturated only at the peaks, so the clouds stand in place. A most spectacular sunset fires Colorado skies when bands of arched red-orange wave clouds stretch toward the eastern horizon.

Temperature Effects

Mountain terrain guarantees a complex pattern of differential heating from the sun, what with the variety of slope aspects, steepnesses, and elevations. We've already discussed the general trend of colder temperatures with higher elevations. Certainly this is true but the coldest temperatures do not occur on the peaks but rather at night in high-elevation valleys. This is where cold air pools, stagnates, and chills further through nighttime radiation losses. The coldest temperature recorded in Colorado — a numbing 61 degrees Farenheit below zero — was set on February 1, 1985, at Maybell, when a massive icebox inversion settled in.

CONTRIBUTORY FACTORS TO AVALANCHE FORMATION

Understanding mountain weather is a first step to understanding avalanches. The factors that make avalanches are part terrain, part weather, and part snowpack. Putting the pieces of the puzzle together is not easy, but this is what avalanche forecasters must do every day of the winter, and every day they are dealt a new set of pieces. Let's look over the forecaster's shoulder at the factors that play a part in evaluating the avalanche hazard.

The terrain factors are fixed — slope orientation, steepness, and roughness, which we've already discussed, certainly play a role in avalanche release, but they need not be re-evaluated daily. The state of the weather and snowpack, however, changes daily, even hourly. Precipitation, wind, and temperature factors, and snow depth, snow surface, weak layers, and settlement factors, if properly weighed, help answer the question, Will it slide? That these factors are interrelated makes the evaluation process that much tougher.

Snowfall

Snow, of course, is the *sine qua non* of all the contributory factors, for it is literally the stuff of avalanches. New snowfall is the event that leads to most avalanches; more than 80 percent of all avalanches fall during or just after a storm. Fresh snowfall provides extra weight to the existing snow cover, and if the snow cover can neither absorb the extra weight nor bond it in place, avalanche releases will occur.

The size of the avalanche is roughly related to the amount of new snow. Snowfalls of less than six inches seldom produce avalanches. Snows of six to 12 inches usually produce a few small slides, and certainly some of these could cause harm to skiers who release them. Snows of one to two feet produce avalanches of larger size that present considerable threat to skiers and pose closure problems for highways and railways. Snows of two to four feet are that much more dangerous, and snowfalls greater than four feet produce major avalanches thundering to the valley floors and threatening everything within reach with destruction.

These figures are merely guidelines based on many years' data and experience. Certainly they must be used with other factors to arrive at the true hazard. For example, a snowfall of 10 inches whipped by strong winds will be more serious than the guidelines; a fall of two feet of feather-light snow will likely produce no avalanches at all.

Snowfall Intensity

The rate at which snowfall accumulates is almost as important as the amount of snow itself. A snowfall of three feet in one day is far more hazardous than three feet in three days. Snow is a visco-elastic material. (Remember Chapter 3?) That is, under a slow load, the snow can absorb the load by changing its shape with a slow deformation or compression. This is snow as a flowing or viscous material. Under a rapid load, there is less time for the snow to absorb the weight by changing its shape, it is much more likely to crack under the strain, which is how avalanches begin. This is snow as a brittle or elastic material.

A snowfall rate of one inch per hour or greater that is sustained for 10 hours or more is generally a red flag indicating danger. The danger worsens even further if the snowfall is accompanied by wind.

Rain

Light rain falling on a cold snowpack invariably freezes into an ice crust, which adds strength to the snow cover. (At a later time, however, the smooth crust could become a sliding layer beneath the new fall of snow.) Heavy rain (usually an inch or more), though, greatly weakens the snow cover — in two ways. First, it adds weight. An inch of rain is the equivalent in weight to 10 to 12 inches of snow. Second, it adds no internal strength of its own (in the form of a feathery skeleton of ice — as new snow would), while at the same time it dissolves bonds between snow grains as it percolates through the top snow layers, thus reducing strength even further.

Many serious accidents can be attributed to a snowpack weakened by rain. These are most apt to occur in the Cascade Range or Sierra Nevada, which are susceptible to occasional heavy rains. A classic case involved a party of snowshoers at Stevens Pass, Washington, on January 20, 1979. It was not a good day for a tour; when the group headed out at 10:30 a.m., it had been raining for five hours and the top six inches of the snowpack was thoroughly saturated. Natural wet, loose avalanches were running on all steep slopes. An hour into the tour, a natural wet slide broke loose above the group of eight. Three were caught, and 23-year-old Sherrie Clark was tumbled off the trail and totally buried. Two and a half hours later, her body was pulled from beneath five feet of wet snow. Death was from suffocation. A victim buried beneath five feet of dry snow has a slim chance of surviving; beneath five feet of crushing wet snow, the chance is almost none.

New Snow Density and Crystal Type

As we already know from Chapter 3, a layer of fresh snow contains only a small amount of solid material (ice); the large majority of the volume is occupied by air. It is convenient to refer to snow density as a percentage of the volume occupied by ice. New snow densities usually range from 7 to 12 percent. In the high elevations of Colorado, 7 percent is the average value; in the more maritime climates of the Sierra and Cascades, 12 percent would be a typical value. Density becomes an important factor in avalanche formation when it varies from these average values.

Wet snowfalls or falls of heavily rimed crystals, such as graupel, may have densities of 20 percent or greater. A layer of heavier-than-normal snow presents a danger because of its excess weight. But snowfall that is much lighter than normal — 2 to 4 percent for example — can present a dangerous situation also. If this low-density layer quickly becomes buried by further snowfall of normal or high density, a weak layer has been introduced into the snowpack. By virtue of its low density, the weak layer has marginal ability to withstand the weight of layers above, making it susceptible to collapse. Storms which begin with cold temperatures, but during their course become many degrees warmer, are the ones most responsible for laying down a profile for lightweight snow beneath heavyweight snow.

Crystal type is closely linked to density. Snowfalls consisting of graupel, fine needles, and columns can descend at high densities. Snowfalls of plates, stellars, and dendritic forms which barely cling to others of their kind and fall as feathery flakes account for most of the light densities. *Wild snow* is the name given to extreme low density snows. It is great fun to walk in wild snow, for the barest shuffling of your feet sends the stuff flying. And to clear it from your windshield is a breeze, literally one puff and the windshield is clean.

Wind Speed and Direction

If snowfall is the principal architect of avalanches, then wind is surely the sculptor. For it is the wind that drives the fallen snow into the rolls and pillows from which avalanches begin. Winds pick up snow from exposed slopes and drive it swirling and drifting onto new slopes, where it is deposited into the hollows and gullies protected from the wind. The lee slope is indeed the lair of avalanches.

Wind direction makes slopes facing the wind the sources of blowing snow, and slopes facing away, the collectors. Winds accelerate on windward slopes and attain the ability to strip snow from the surface. On leeward slopes, winds slow down and the suspended snow falls back to the surface.

If wind direction selects the targets, then wind speed loads the targets. Speeds of 15 miles per hour are sufficient to pick up freshly fallen snow. Higher speeds are required to dislodge older snow. Speeds of 20 to 50 miles per hour are the most efficient in transporting snow into avalanche starting zones. Speeds greater than 50 miles per hour can create spectacular banners of snow streaming from high peaks but much of this snow is lost to evaporation in the air or is deposited far down the slope, never to end up in starting zones.

Winds actually do double duty when blowing snow, and both effects lead to worsened avalanche conditions. First, the wind scours snow from a large area (of a windward slope) and deposits it in a smaller area (of a starting zone). Wind can turn a one-foot snowfall into a three-foot drift in a starting zone. The rate of which blowing snow collects in bowls and gullies can be impressive: in one test at Berthoud Pass, Colorado, the wind deposited snow in a gully at a rate of 18 inches per hour. The second effect is that blowing snow is more dense after deposit than before. This is because the snow grains are subjected to harsh treatment on their travels; each collision with another grain knocks off arms and sharp angles, reducing the grain size and allowing the pieces to settle into a denser pillow. The net result of wind on snow is to fill avalanche starting zones with much more and heavier snow than if the wind had not blown.

Temperature

While it's easy to understand the contributions of snowfall and wind to avalanches, the effects of temperature are more elusive. Temperature affects almost everything that goes on with snow, from the type of crystals that form inside clouds to the densities of newly fallen snow, from the types and rates of metamorphism inside the snowpack to the bonding and densifying of the top layers after a new snow, and finally to the melting and freezing cycles of springtime. It remains less clear, though, what the real effects of temperature are on avalanche release. One thing that is understood, however, is that strong temperature changes or rapid changes are often more important than absolute values.

Let's look at static temperature situations first. Sustained, very cold temperatures (below zero Farenheit readings) pretty much bring things to a standstill — similar to what happens to people, as well. The stability of the snowpack is going to change oh so slowly. There will be no settlement or sintering, but in a shallow snow cover, temperature-gradient metamorphism can progress slowly but steadily. Temperatures in the teens are good for growing TG grains in shallow snow areas, but don't cause much else that's remarkable. Warmer temperatures (in the 20s and approaching 32 degrees) promote rapid settlement and sintering, which stabilize the snow cover.

Temperatures above freezing are easy to diagnose. They cause melt-freeze metamorphism, settlement, and wet-snow avalanches. The stress caused by fallen and wind-driven snow is the greatest cause of avalanches, but certainly in second place is the weakening created by thaw.

Large changes in air temperature make their presence felt inside the snowpack. The key to how effective a temperature change is in creating snowpack stability changes is the duration of the temperature change. Sudden changes, or those lasting only a few minutes, can have little effect, for snow is such a good insulator that the temperature change cannot work more than a few inches into the pack in so short a time. An example of a sudden temperature change is the rolling back of shadows in the morning and the reappearance of shadows in late afternoon. Snow stability is changing, but not enough to cause releases within a minute or so of the sun striking or leaving a slope. (We make this statement despite some interesting stories we've heard and read of avalanches releasing one after another as evening shadows crawl up the slopes. We know of no reliable observations to substantiate these claims, so for now we'll file such tales as interesting talk over a few beers, but nothing else.)

There is no doubt, though, that a temperature rise which casts its effect on the snow pack for several hours can lead to important stability changes. We have previously mentioned the case of freshly fallen snow being stressed by a few hours of sun. The temperature rise increases the creep rate of the surface layers, making the snow unstable for several hours. If an avalanche does not release, eventually the instability subsides as the snow becomes less brittle and more pliable, so that settlement relieves stress.

The passage of a warm front is an event that has often been observed to cause avalanche releases. This often happens in the Cascades and the Sierra along the Pacific coast. Frontal passage can increase temperatures 20 to 30 degrees Farenheit in a short time, which destroys the strength of the upper snow layers. Often the warm-up is accompanied by rain, which makes the situation worse. Some of the largest avalanche cycles of the maritime mountain ranges have been precipitated by warm fronts.

Depth of Snow Cover

Of the snowpack factors contributing to avalanche formation, this is the most basic. When the early-winter snowpack covers the natural anchors such as rocks and bushes, the start of the avalanche season is at hand. North-facing slopes are usually covered before other slopes. A scan of the terrain will usually suffice in weighing this clue, but another method can be used to determine the time of the first significant avalanches. Long-term studies show a relationship between snow depth at a study site of avalanche activity. For example, along Red Mountain Pass, Colorado, it is unlikely that an avalanche large enough to reach the highway will run until close to three feet of snow covers the ground at the University of Colorado's snow study site. At Alta, Utah, once 52 inches of snowpack has built up, the first avaanche to cover the road leading from Salt Lake City can be expected to run during the next storm or two.

Nature of the Snow Surface

How well new snow bonds to the old snow surface is a key factor in judging whether avalanches will run only in the layer of new snow, or whether something else, possibly more serious, might happen. A poor bond — usually new snow resting on a smooth, cold surface — with snowfalls of a foot or more will almost always produce new-snow avalanches. A strong bond — usually onto a warm, soft, or rough surface — may produce nothing at all, or if weaknesses lie at deeper layers of the snow cover, a large snowfall will cause avalanches to pull out older layers of snow in addition to the new snow layer. These avalanches have more potential for deadliness and destruction.

A cold, hard snow surface offers little grip to fresh, cold snow. Ice crusts are commonly observed to be avalanche-sliding surfaces. The crust could be a sun crust, a rain crust, or a hardened layer of firn snow that has survived the summer. Firn layers are especially dangerous in early winter when first snows start flying. Two young climbers from Boulder, Colorado, found out just how deadly this combination can be. On October 13, 1973, David Emerick, 23, and Robert Hritz, 19, signed out at Rocky Mountain National Park headquarters for a climb of Powell Peak. Their planned route was up a very steep (65 degrees at the top) ice-filled couloir that Hritz had successfully climbed twice during the preceding two weeks. But on this day a foot of fresh snow from the season's first storm lay tenuously on the firn. Emerick and Hritz never made it to the top. At some point in their climb they triggered loose the snow, which broke only six to 12 inches deep to the firn. The two men were roped together and were either not on belay or the belay failed. The wounds suffered in the fall down the couloir were fatal to both.

Weak Layers

Any layer susceptible to collapse or failure because of the weight of the overburden is the weak link in the chain. Of the several snowpack contributory factors, this is the most important, for a weak layer is one ingredient that every avalanche must have. This layer, when indeed an avalanche runs, is called the failure plane, sliding surface, or bed surface (see Figure 3.16).

We've just mentioned one common weak layer, and that is an old snow surface that offers a meager bond for new snow. Another weak layer that forms on the snow surface is hoar frost, or surface hoar. This is the solid equivalent of dew, and it forms — on clear, clam nights — a layer of feathery, sparkling flakes which grow on the snow surface. The layer can be one-eighth to three-quarters of an inch thick, and make a delightful hissing sound when skied over, but can be deadly when buried by a snowfall. Many avalanches have been known to release on a buried layer of surface hoar, sometimes a layer that is more than a month old and six feet or more below the surface.

A weak layer that is almost always found in the snowpacks that blanket the Rocky Mountains and occasionally in the Cascades and Sierra Nevada — and which is discussed in detail in Chapter 3 — is temperature-gradient snow, or depth hoar. These weak grains are so common and widespread in cold, shallow snowpacks that it is sometimes a wonder that any of the snow cover can hold itself on steep mountainsides. The key to deciding whether a TG layer is near its collapse point is in measuring the strength of the overlying layers and the support provided around the edges of the slope. This is no easy task, and no rules of thumb have any validity here. One test is to try jumping on your skies while standing on a shallow slope. A collapse here is a good indication that a similar snow cover on a steeper slope will produce an avalanche. Often skiers and climbers cause inadvertent collapses while skiing or walking on a depth-hoar-riddled snowpack. The resulting "whoomf" sound is usually so startling that the fright sends an icy chill and adrenaline rush ripping through the body. It is always an unforgettable experience.

Another notable weak layer is a thin layer of TG snow that forms near the very top of the snow cover during extreme cold snaps. The weather causes a strong temperature gradient to form in the top few inches, and small grains develop in a day or two. This layer can sometimes hold its weakness when buried under new snowfalls and become a danger, similar to a layer of buried surface hoar. A more subtle weakness is a layer of low-density snow usually deposited during cold temperatures or deposited without wind which then gets covered by higher-density snow. Finally, a weak layer can be created within the snow cover when surface melting or rain cause water to percolate into the snow and then fan out on an impervious layer, thereby lubricating that layer and destroying its shear strength.

Combining what we know of the contributory factors on a day-by-day basis is the avalanche forecaster's art. Every avalanche must have a weak layer to release on, so knowledge of snow stratigraphy or layering and what sort of applied load would cause a layer to fail is the essence of forecasting — and of survival, if risk-taking is your game. Natural avalanche releases caused by excessive loads of snow, or man-made releases caused perhaps by the carving turns of a skier or the rumbling traverse of a snowmobile, all happen because some combination of contributory factors exist in precarious harmony.

Cardiac Pass, Alta, Utah. This photo was taken after both avalanches had run and rescue described on page 115 had been completed (from The Snowy Torrents III)

5 THE RIGHT CHOICE

DECISION-MAKING: GENERALLY SPEAKING

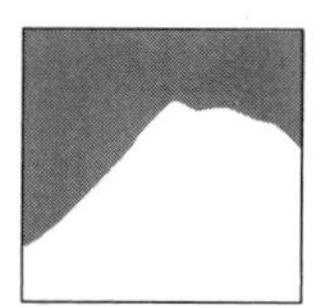

IN THIS CHAPTER WE ARE GOING to talk about making choices — specifically about decision-making and risk-taking in avalanche terrain. Proper decision-making requires the application of many of the ideas we've brought up in previous chapters — things such as avalanche path recognition, contributory factors to avalanche formation, and personal skills on snow.

When we are children, most of our decisions are made for us. But once we have emerged from adolescence and are presumably responsible for leading our own lives, we constantly face choices and challenges. These range from the trivial (Shall I get another beer?) to the serious (Shall I go skydiving?). Certainly a knowledge of what is involved, and the consequences, is required to make rational decisions. Many of our choices involve risk. Crossing the street is one example of an everyday situation with an element of risk; we use common sense to get us through this one. Other decisions which occur less often but are still risky might be making investments or falling in love; common sense may be of no value in doing these right.

Just because risk is involved is no reason not to try something. The rewards of success, whether spiritual, physical, or monetary, are usually enough to make us try. Surely, though, we must assess our skills and resources to judge the chance of success. The consequences of failure must also be figured in before leaping at the challenge. Risk must always be balanced against benefits to arrive at a rational decision of go or no go. It helps to have experience on our side.

I give myself very good advice, but I very seldom follow it.
ALICE, WALT DISNEY'S *ALICE IN WONDERLAND*

DECISION-MAKING: AVOIDING OR RISKING AVALANCHES

The first major decision often faced in backcountry situations is whether to avoid or to confront avalanches. Usually this can be resolved by asking the question, Why am I here? A group that is touring with no particular goal in mind, other than a fun day, will likely not challenge avalanches. At the first sign of worsening weather or questionable terrain, they might call it a day. A second group might have a plan in mind, such as completing a particular tour or climbing a peak. They probably already know that they must negotiate avalanche slopes along the way, but they plan to assess conditions as they travel. A third group, such as a mountaineering expedition, has a specific goal in mind, and is willing to wait out a dangerous period or take severe risks to succeed. They plan on using their equipment, skills, and route-finding abilities to avoid serious confrontation.

The decision to travel in avalanche terrain requires special preparations, including an avalanche education and possession of certain safety and rescue equipment. The group should have the skills required to answer two big questions: Will it slide, and What will happen to me if it does? More on this shortly, but first we want to look at the safer alternative of avoiding avalanches altogether. We can divide this option into three skills: recognizing avalanche terrain, route-finding, and selecting safe campsites.

Recognizing Avalanche Terrain

This is probably the single most important factor in avalanche safety, for avalanche encounters occur only when people enter the avalanche domain. Remember that the criteria for avalanche slopes are pretty simple: a snow cover, and a slope steep enough to allow it to slide. Any slope having a pitch of 30 degrees or greater must be viewed suspiciously, for under the right conditions it could produce an avalanche. Remember also that most avalanches release on slopes of 30 to 45 degrees of pitch. This makes judging the steepness of a slope a prime skill in recognizing potential avalanche areas.

An inclinometer is an instrument used for measuring slope angles; it is worth owning one if you frequent the haunts of avalanches. A compass also can be used for the same purpose; in addition to the designed use of measuring direction, the graduations in degrees can be used to measure slope angles. This is done best by sighting across a slope, but also can be done by sighting up or down. Even a ski pole can also be useful in judging the steepness of the slope you are on: by dangling a pole by its strap, it becomes a plumb line from which the slope angle can be eye-balled.

There are clues other than steepness that identify avalanche slopes. The best is presence of fracture lines and the rubble of avalanche snow on the slope or at the bottom of it. This is the "smoking gun" of evidence. Other clues are just about as good. Where avalanches run to treeline, look for a swath of missing trees or trees that are bent downhill or damaged, especially with the uphill branches removed. Above treeline, steep bowls and gullies are almost always capable of producing avalanches. In the timber, trees can anchor the snow only if they are closely spaced. The rule is that a slope having trees so close together that they are annoying — making it a nuisance to try to ski down or traverse — will generally not avalanche. If the trees offer openings large enough to easily turn skis in, it is not safe from avalanches.

Finally, remember that a slope need not be large to produce a fatal avalanche. If it meets any of the above criteria, recognize it as an avalanche area.

Route-Finding

Good route-finding techniques can mean safe travel in terrain that you recognize as having avalanche dangers. A background can be gained from reading, but as with almost everything associated with avalanches, proficiency in route-finding can be achieved only by doing it. This means going out with experienced (and sane) tourers until you yourself become proficient at decision-making.

The object of a good route in avalanche country is more than avoiding avalanches. It should also be efficient. This means taking into account the abilities and desires of your group to lead them on a route that is not overly technical, tiresome, or time consuming. This can be quite a juggling act when the going gets rough, and the leader must keep the tour within the original plans and not extend it beyond a point of diminishing returns for the individuals. Never be afraid to turn back when the terrain becomes too tough, the weather turns sour, or the group loses its zest for continuing.

The safest way to avoid avalanches is to travel above them or below and well away from them. When taking the high road, choose a ridge line that puts you above the avalanche starting zones. It is safest to travel the windward side of the ridge; the snow cover is usually thinner and windpacked, with rocks sticking through — not the most pleasant skiing, but safe. Don't get too near the edge, though, because cornices present a very real hazard. Either a fall off a cornice or a cornice caused to collapse are recipes for disaster. Avoid them at all costs by staying on the roughened snow more to windward.

When taking the low road in the valley, don't linger in the runouts of avalanche paths. Even though it is most unlikely that you could be the trigger of an avalanche while traveling the valley, you should not boost the odds of getting caught by one releasing by natural forces far above. In other words, don't increase your chances of being the victim of a freak accident by being in the wrong place at the wrong time.

When traveling in between, avoid slopes of 30 degrees or more. If you do your climbing, descending, and traversing in gentle terrain only, you will be out of harm's way. A word of caution, however: be leery of gentle terrain with a steep bank or slope rising above it. The cut made by a summer road is a good example. Skiers or snowmobilers traveling the road might bring avalanches down on themselves. Exactly such an incident happened near Aspen, Colorado, on January 15, 1975. Tom Worth, age 15, was ski touring with his father and another man on a logging road above Castle Creek. The weather was exceptionally fine, but the snowpack throughout the Colorado Rockies was riddled with depth hoar and was especially weak. When Worth was crossing Sawyer Creek Gulch, his weight and sliding skis were enough to cause a collapse of the snow cover. A fracture broke loose an avalanche on the steep gully wall above him. The father yelled a warning, but the youth had no chance of escape. The avalanche swept him off the road and into the gully. An hour and a half later, Mr. Worth helped dig out his son from under four feet of snow. The teenage boy was already dead from suffocation.

Selecting Safe Campsites

Winter campsites are occasionally cozy, but more often they offer only marginal comfort from the cold that brings out the masochistic tendencies within us. They should at least be pitched in sites safe from avalanches. The mountains, however, sometimes offer no sites that are totally risk free. In Chapter 1, we told you of the Mount St. Helens tragedy, when an avalanche rumbled through a camp and killed five. There have been other incidents.

On March 21, 1975, an avalanche of ice and snow overran the campsite of two mountaineers — Jim Carlson and Doug Buchanan, both 27 — on the McGinnis Glacier near Big Delta, Alaska. The men had established camp in this location after viewing several ice avalanches that had stopped well short of the site; the one that got them, however, was much larger. The avalanche obliterated the camp and killed Carlson. Buchanan escaped with his life when the avalanche buried him only to his chest.

Another incident ended no less tragically less than a year later in Colorado. It was January 17, 1976, and 11 members of the Colorado Mountain Club were participating in a winter camping course on Berthoud Pass. On skis and snowshoes, they traveled several miles to the site, where they unshouldered their packs to dig snow caves for their overnight shelter. They chose the base of a steep, convex slope to tunnel into. Campers digging snow caves prefer a slope over level terrain because it makes their task easier, but in this case their slope was ill-chosen — it was too steep. Two hours of digging had resulted in several nice caves, but it had also undermined the slope. Sixty feet above, it avalanched four feet deep and flowed over all 11 campers. Two were buried inside their caves. Fifteen minutes later, Jerry Hasmer popped out of the snow: his cave had not collapsed and he had his shovel, so he dug his way out. After another 50 minutes, the lifeless body of Christina Hahn, 28, was pulled from the snow. She had suffocated in her collapsed snow cave.

Accidents teach lessons, and here the lesson is obvious: make camp in avalanche-free areas. You are going to be there a good many hours, so don't expose yourself to that much risk.

EVALUATING AVALANCHE RISK

Avalanche risk-taking means exposing oneself to the chance of injury or death. Risk can be involuntary, in which someone is exposed to danger through no choice of their own — for example, a motorist stalled under an avalanche path — or it can be voluntary, in which someone knowingly exposes himself or herself to risk. The majority of avalanche encounters in the United States have occurred because somebody voluntarily took a risk.

Most recreation involves some risk, but recreating in avalanche terrain carries risk to a high degree. In order to determine acceptable risk, recreationists must evaluate the risk in proportion to the benefits: the greater the benefits, the greater the risk acceptable. For example, a group of tired, cold ski tourers near the end of the day may have to decide if the benefits of a shortcut through avalanche-prone terrain (which would get them to warmth and shelter much faster than the longer, safer route) is worth the risk. At the other extreme, expedition climbers often accept the risks of high altitude, storms, and avalanches for the personal benefits gained in pitting skills and endurance against formidable mountains.

A willingness to take risk, and to enjoy the success or endure the failure, is usually healthy and productive. Recreationists must weigh not only the benefits but also the potential loss in time, money, injury, or life itself. When injury or life is at stake, rational people will attempt to minimize risk. Of course, every individual uses his or her own value system, training, and experience to evaluate risk. Differing perceptions of risk may cause dissension, and group leaders, whether on short tours, expeditions, or rescue missions, must be prepared to make final decisions based on the group's best interest. A reasonable philosophy is that an individual should have the freedom to take risks as long as the lives of others are not endangered.

There are, however, the adrenaline addicts who live — and die — by the credo, "no risk, no gusto," or the macho tag, "ski to die." A rational approach to risk-taking does not apply here.

We have spent many hours reading avalanche accident reports with the intent of using these incidents of one person's misfortune to teach safety to others. We discovered that avalanche victims could be categorized into three broad groups according to their ability to assess risk.

First, there are those who were totally unaware that an avalanche hazard existed and that they were at risk. They willingly put themselves into the recreational situation, but their lack of avalanche awareness led them into traps that more experienced skiers or mountaineers would have recognized and avoided. Several brief examples should give you an idea of what we mean.

On December 30, 1973, 10 members of the youth group of an Anchorage, Alaska, church decided to make a Sunday evening climb of Flattop Mountain in Chugach State Park. They made the summit at 5 p.m. and sang songs and admired the lights of Anchorage. For their descent, they decided it would be fun to slide on their backs down the snow in the west gully. All 10 were in the gully when it avalanched. Amazingly, only one died.

Four weeks later on Sunday morning, January 27, 1974, six members of two Seattle families headed off on a snowshoe tour at Source Lake, Washington. This area has a long history of avalanches, and the trailhead is posted with a large warning sign. The hazard was posted as high on this Sunday. At 2 p.m., a large natural avalanche peeled off the steep slopes of Chair Peak. Two young girls, ages 10 and 13, were directly in its path. The older brother of one of the girls described what happened: "We saw them running, then they were swallowed up in the snow. They were holding hands as they ran." This massive avalanche was taking no prisoners: it buried the girls under 30 feet of snow. Their bodies were recovered seven months later.

On December 15, 1974, three novice cross-country skiers left the highway on Monarch Pass, Colorado, for a short tour on the slopes within sight of the road. None had skied more than five times, and one, a 20-year-old woman who was the fiancee of the group leader and who was to become the avalanche victim, had taken up the sport less than a month earlier. None knew anything about avalanches. Their ascent up a short, steep slope was in the safety of trees, but this was only to avoid putting tracks on the open slope they wished to descend. Part way up, though, the woman ventured on a traverse that took her out of the trees and into the open. While she and her fiance discussed the situation — she wanted to continue in the open because it was easier, and he wanted a slope without tracks — the avalanche released. She yelled his name and instantly disappeared in the flowing snow. An hour and twenty minutes later, she was pulled from two feet of snow. Resuscitation efforts failed; she died a victim of suffocation.

The second category is those who were aware of and accepted the risk of their sport but who lacked the experience to properly evaluate the conditions. This group, armed with only a little knowledge, found themselves in avalanche terrain, whether by accident or design, and were forced to make decisions and take risks without full awareness of the possible consequences. Again, some examples.

On March 24, 1977, Steve Karl, 23, and Bill Ford, 25, both from Salt Lake City, Utah, headed into the Gros Ventre Mountains east of Jackson, Wyoming, for several days of ski touring. Both men were accomplished skiers, but this tour took them into unfamiliar terrain. Their destination was a ski cabin, where they spent the night. They spent the next day skiing gentle terrain in the trees. The following day, March 26, two local skiers arrived, and the four men skied together. When Karl and Ford wanted to ski steeper slopes, the local men warned of the avalanche danger and declined. Karl and Ford went their own way, and minutes later Karl triggered a sluff, which he skied out of. The two parties again came together, and again the local skiers warned the Salt Lake City skiers of the avalanche danger. The locals returned to the cabin while the visitors sought steeper slopes. A short time later, they triggered a slide that broke two to four feet deep and 100 feet across. Both men took a harrowing ride through scattered timber, and when the slide stopped, Ford was buried to the neck, and Karl was buried eight feet and killed. Ford, unable to dig himself out, shouted on and off for five hours before the men at the cabin heard him and came to his aid. So at least one man survived this incident of poor risk evaluation.

A second example occurred on November 4, 1979, at Mammoth Mountain, California. The ski area had not yet opened, but early snows left a good snow cover on the upper mountain. Carrying their skis, Briant Wells, 22, and Steve Ryan, 28, began the long hike to the top, with anticipation of a powder run in 18 inches of new snow as their reward. Wells had these thoughts: "Most of the bowls and chutes had already slid. Cornice Bowl, moderately pitched compared to the others, was the only slope that hadn't slid yet. The Cornice would be our bowl. It looked good, almost too good. Steve and I didn't really talk too much about the avalanche conditions. We were willing to take the chance." (Powder Magazine, December 1980) They never reached the top. The bowl avalanched 600 feet wide, and swallowed up the two men. Wells came to rest with only his head out; other skiers on the ridge came to his rescue. Ryan was buried three feet for five hours — before an avalanche rescue dog sniffed him out. He did not survive.

A few weeks later on November 22, Michael Croonquist, 25, died in an avalanche he triggered near Telluride, Colorado. Croonquist had attended at least one avalanche clinic and had skied in this area for the two previous winters. On this day he was tutoring Barton Coffman, 21 and a novice skier, on the ways of avalanches. They dug several snowpits and found considerable depth hoar, which prompted Croonquist to mention how easily an avalanche could start where they were skiing. We'll never know the reason for Croonquist's next move, for he let out a whoop and skied diagonally onto a steep slope. It fractured all around him, knocked him down, and flowed over him. Other skiers in the area began probing with ski poles, but it was an hour later that they struck the victim's body under four feet of snow. Croonquist had correctly evaluated the hazard, but took a foolhardy action under the circumstances.

The third category is comprised of thoroughly skilled and experienced skiers or mountaineers capable of evaluating conditions, examining alternatives, and judging consequences to arrive at a well-considered decision. They were able to decide if the benefits justified the risk, and if the risk was small enough to be accepted comfortably. Unfortunately, avalanches are capricious, and even the most experienced will sometimes err when predicting stability. One very good example is the accident of March 4, 1979, on Mount Rainier, Washington, that claimed the lives of Willi Unsoeld and one of his students, an accident discussed in Chapter 1. But other good examples abound.

Mike Covington and Duncan Ferguson are mountaineers who have climbed the world over and know mountains and snow as well as anyone. They survived a scary incident in Rocky Mountain National Park, Colorado, on November 27, 1975. Their intent that day was a Thanksgiving ice climb, but before reaching their objective, they had to negotiate a steep snow slope. Covington began climbing in firm snow. He had gained 100 feet when the snow around him fractured but did not slide. Cautiously, he retreated in his footsteps, and both men knew it was past time that they should leave. Before they could get off the bench that was their refuge, a second avalanche broke above them. It knocked Covington over a 50-foot cliff and carried Ferguson on a 300-foot ride. Feeling lucky to be in one piece, they abandoned the climb.

Another instructive incident occurred on December 2, 1977, in Big Cottonwood Canyon, Utah. Larry Daum, 26, Joe Holland, 25, and Allan Murphy, 24, were expert skiers, knew the terrain well, and on this day were "thinking avalanche." They all carried shovels and rescue beacons. After the long hike up, they dug a snowpit on the slope they intended to ski. They studied the various layers, which altogether appeared stable enough to ski. But after all three had descended well down the slope, the whole bowl fractured across the top. Murphy, on the edge, was pinned against a tree but not hurt. Holland was in the center of the slope and found himself in a fight for his life. His thoughts: "The slide engulfed me completely. I knew it was a big avalanche. The last thing I remember, before I blacked out, was the avalanche stopping and my trying to get to the surface. But I couldn't move!" Daum tried to bear-hug a tree, but the avalanche yanked him off it and buried him. The skill of Murphy using his rescue beacon saved his friends' lives, although Holland suffered a badly broken ankle. The moral to this story: totally trusting what you read in a snowpit can be hazardous to your health.

Some thoughts on traveling alone. We have no real quarrel with those who like to travel alone in the backcountry. In fact, Thoreau made a very good point when he so eloquently stated, "I never found the companion that was so companionable as solitude." But we would be remiss if we did not point out that traveling alone increases risk significantly. A person buried while alone must rely on self-rescue, and damn few victims totally buried dig themselves out. The case books are filled with needless tragedies, and the saddest are those who died alone in a shallow burial with a ski tip, pole, or hand on the surface.

Laine McMurray, age 22, died exactly this way. On December 24, 1979, while touring near his home at Taos, New Mexico, with only his two dogs as companions, he skied off an avalanche which buried him completely save for one ski tip protruding from the snow. Two days later a search team located his body easily: the ski was sticking out of the snow and his dog Wizard was right there. The other dog was 30 feet away, barking at the group. The dogs had uncovered part of McMurray's arm and leg.

Enough said on traveling alone.

IMPROVING THE ODDS IN AVALANCHE TERRAIN

If you feel you have the experience and skills to go into the domain of avalanches, to assess the risk, and to make the right decisions to minimize that risk, then we support you. After all, the thrill of a successful climb or tour gives a strong sense of accomplishment. But before we say, "Go for it," we want to offer a few more words of caution, and words of advice on the topics of safety equipment, stability evaluation, and travel techniques.

The words of caution are these: Avoiding avalanches is easier than surviving them. Confronting avalanches is a little like playing with snakes and swimming with sharks: if you do it long enough, you are going to get bit. Keep that in mind, no matter how skilled and experienced you are.

Now for our survival advice.

Safety Equipment

There are available pieces of avalanche safety equipment that easily fit into a backpack that could save your life or that of a friend. A shovel is one piece of equipment that we recommend everyone carry, even if you don't plan on going into steep terrain. There are several types of folding plastic or aluminum shovels that will do. A shovel is useful for so many things — digging a snowpit, scooping out snow for a dry place to sit, digging a snow cave, or setting up a camp kitchen. We'll limit this discussion, though, to the value of a shovel in digging out avalanche victims.

There are several ways of locating a buried victim, and we'll talk much more about this later. But speed is critical in digging out the victim. Your hands, skis, and poles make lousy tools for digging in avalanches. Avalanche debris sets up hard, many times harder than the powder you may have been skiing before the avalanche. There's really no substitute for a strong shovel. Here's a story that should get the point across.

A number of years ago the Swiss conducted a test. A group of people was assembled at a mound of fresh avalanche debris and instructed to excavate a one-cubic-meter hole (1m x 1m x 1m). The first time, they did it using only hands, skis, and poles; it took the average person 45 minutes. The second time, they used a shovel; it took an average of eight minutes. The difference — 37 minutes — is literally a lifetime to a buried victim.

Many real-life dramas have shown the value of a shovel. Just a few pages back, in the incident in Big Cottonwood Canyon in December 1977, Joe Holland would not have survived had Allan Murphy and Larry Daum not had shovels. On December 24, 1982, at Big Sky, Montana, a life was lost for want of a shovel. Ski patroller David Stutzman, 31, took a free run with a friend into a permanently closed area. They wore rescue beacons but no shovels. Stutzman triggered a slide and was totally buried except for a boot heel. His companion found him but was unable to dig with her hands in the hard snow. By the time she notified rescuers and they dug Stutzman out, he had died of suffocation.

There are several pieces of equipment designed specifically for finding buried avalanche victims. The first is a collapsible probe pole. Organized rescue teams keep rigid poles in 10- or 12-foot lengths as part of their rescue caches. For the recreationist, you can buy probe poles of tubular steel that come in two-foot sections which fit together to make a full-length probe. Also on the market are ski poles, with removable grips and baskets, which can be screwed together to make an avalanche probe. Survivors of an incident use the probes to feel for buried victims.

An avalanche cord is a 50-foot length of thin rope, colored

orange or red, that can be coiled and attached to a belt. Before crossing an avalanche area, a skier, climber, or snowmobiler strings the cord out behind. The idea is that if an avalanche releases and the victim is buried, the cord will float and some portion of it will come to rest on the surface. Rescuers will be able to pull the cord, or probe in the immediate area, to locate the victim.

We're not true believers in avalanche cords. Indeed they have saved lives, as have ropes attached to buried climbers. But tests done in the early 1970s by the International Vanni Eigenmann Foundation of Milan, Italy, showed that avalanche cords were only marginally effective. The test was performed by attaching an avalanche cord to a sandbag dummy, which was tossed onto an avalanche path and the avalanche then released with explosives. The results were that a portion of the avalanche cord remained on the surface only 40 percent of the time. The other 60 percent, the length of the cord was buried along with the dummy.

While the observable benefits of an avalanche cord are dubious, the psychological benefits are positive. By stringing out his cord, the user is putting him or herself into a positive frame of mind by "thinking avalanche." This behavior generally leads to safer decision-making and route selection. The popularity of avalanche cords has waned considerably, however, since the invention of avalanche rescue beacons.

5.1 An avalanche rescue beacon and a shovel are lifesaving equipment for backcountry travelers (K. Williams photo)

Avalanche rescue beacons, or transceivers, have become the most-used personal rescue devices worldwide, and for good reason: when used properly, there is no faster or more effective way of locating buried avalanche victims. In the United States, these have become standard issue for all ski-area patrollers and heli-ski guides and clients. They are also commonly used by highway departments, search and rescue teams, and an ever-increasing number of winter recreationists. Since the introduction of beacons into the United States around 1970, at least 17 lives have been saved by these units.

Costing from $80 to $180 per unit (at least two are needed to make them work), transceivers act as transmitters that emit a signal on a frequency of 2275 Hz or 457 kHz. A buried victim emits this signal, while the rescuers turn their units to receive to pick up the signal. The signal carries about 100 feet, and once picked up, searchers can home in on the buried unit.

There are four brands of beacons sold in the United States (Skadi, Pieps, Echo, and Ortovox), and all use the 2275 Hz frequency and so are compatible with one another. In other countries, there have been instances in which incompatible units operating on different frequencies were used in rescues — with predictably fatal results.

Merely possessing a beacon does not assure its life-saving capability. Frequent practice is required to master them, for unfortunately their use is not straightforward. Skilled practitioners can always find a buried unit in less than five minutes, once they pick up the signal. Since speed is of the essence in avalanche rescues, beacons are obvious lifesavers. The best safety equipment you can carry is a beacon for a quick find and a shovel for a quick recovery.

Stability Evaluation

Stability evaluation is the process of deciding the likelihood of avalanche releases. It combines the skills of terrain recognition and the application of the contributory factors to avalanche release. At best, it is an imperfect science (and so might better be called an art). This is because the snowpack is a delicate skeleton of ice, with air and sometimes water as companions. The snowpack exists near its melting point, which adds to the complication. The vagaries of changeable weather play on the snowpack to cause major variations over short distances or short time spans. A snowpit dug in one spot may have no truth a snowball's throw away. It is a science (or art) with only crude guidelines and no strict rules of thumb.

How about rules of thumb? Everyone likes to use them, but in the avalanche game, there really are no rules of thumb — which is itself a very good rule to remember. Oh sure, there are rules that are right far more often than wrong, but in this game, exceptions kill.

How do you learn this difficult art? By reading and going often into the field with people more experienced than yourself. And by making your mistakes in relatively safe areas — short slopes with easy escape routes, for example. This is not like learning to play tennis, where after making the same mistake a hundred times, you get it right and you're a better player for it. The avalanche game is not so forgiving. For the very unfortunate, one mistake can be fatal. Of course, the vast majority of us get to make more than one mistake, but we quickly learn to make them in non-fatal circumstances.

While you read about stability evaluation, try to put yourself in a backcountry setting in which you must decide what the avalanche potential is, and how this decision affects your route or actions. An estimate of low hazard would normally allow you to proceed; moderate hazard, proceed with great caution and perhaps alter your planned route; high hazard, contemplate life after this tour and alter your route to encompass only the safest terrain, or abandon the trip. Low- and moderate-hazard situations require you to reappraise the hazard often, to prevent rude awakenings.

As you travel, apply your knowledge of the contributory factors by keeping one eye on the terrain, one on the weather, and one on the snowpack (yes, three eyes are better than two), and by asking yourself the right questions. For example, asking "Is the slope steep enough to slide?" will keep you from unknowingly entering an avalanche slope. When in doubt about steepness, measure it.

Asking "Are there any weather factors that could warn me of danger?" will make you appraise recent and ongoing weather happenings. Some more specific questions to ask: "How much new snow has fallen? Is it a dangerous amount? Did it fall in a short time? How strong have the winds been? What was the direction? Which slopes are scoured and which are loaded? How much snow has drifted onto lee slopes? Is there anything in the temperature trend — such as a rapid rise — that could worsen hazards?"

Similar questions will allow you to appraise the state of the snowpack: "What is the snow surface like beneath the new snow? Will it provide a good bond or a poor one? What is the layering like? Are there weak layers that could slip or collapse? How much depth hoar is present? Will the snow support my weight?"

There are tests that you can do to help answer some of these questions. First, you should be observing all along how the snow feels, sounds, and acts beneath your feet or skis. How soft, firm, crusty, or damp is it? Has it changed from firm to soft, or the other way around? Are your skis sinking in deeper, or shallower? Has it changed from dry to damp? All of these things indicate a change of snow texture in the surface layers, and this could mean a change in strength and stability.

Take notice also of whether the snow is merely being mashed down by your skis, or whether small cracks are shooting out or small blocks are shearing off. Cracking or shearing snow indicates slab, a more hazardous situation. Slab can also be determined by the way the snow sounds as you travel over it. Hollow sounds from underneath tell you that a hard slab has bridged over an air space, leaving a hollow layer that can collapse. A booming or "whoompf" sound tells you that you have indeed caused a collapse. This sound is sometimes followed instantly by long cracks shooting through the snow. This, in turn, is usually followed by a sudden adrenalin rush and a little voice inside your head saying "Please, Mister Custer, I don't want to go." Cracking and settling snow are excellent clues of a dangerous snowpack.

If you can find a small slope that is not too steep (and therefore will not avalanche), you can try a ski test. Run your skis on a shallow traverse, then set them in a hard check. Any cracks or settlement noises that occur are telling you that the same slope, if steeper, would have probably avalanched — and being steeper, it would have taken less weight or a jolt to cause the avalanche.

Another test is to push a ski pole into the snow, handle end first. This helps you feel the major layering of the snowpack. You normally can feel the layer of new snow, mid-pack stronger layers, and depth-hoar layers, if the pole is long enough. Hard-snow layers and ice lenses will resist penetration altogether. This test will only bring out the gross layers: thin weak layers, such as buried surface hoar or a poor bond between any two layers, cannot be detected. Thus, the ski-pole test is of limited value.

A much better way to observe and test snowpack layers is to dig a hasty snowpit. (This is one good use for that shovel you've been carrying in your pack.) Now you can look at and feel the layers of snow. You can see where the new snow touches the layer beneath. You can poke the pit wall with your finger to test hardness. You can brush the pit wall with a paint brush to see which layers are soft and fall away, and which are hard and stay in place after being brushed. You can grab a handful of depth hoar to see how large the grains are and how poorly they stick together. You can perform a shovel shear test to gauge the shear strength between layers. This is done by inserting the sho-

5.2 Snowpit tests reveal much about the strength and layering. On the left, the strokes of a brush remove soft layers more easily them hard layers. On the right, the shovel shear test shows how well bonded the layers are (K. Williams photos)

vel vertically into the snow about eight to 10 inches behind the pit wall, then pushing the shovel down several inches and prying forward, pushing down and prying forward, all the while watching for a layer that shears loose from the layer below. The easier a layer shears off, the easier it would be to release an avalanche. You can use this test to find thin, weak layers that cannot be detected by any other method. A layer that pops loose easily every time you do the test must be viewed as a sign of danger: one that says "Avalanche danger. Proceed at your own risk."

Unfortunately, snowpits do not always tell the whole truth, as shown by an accident recounted earlier in this chapter. To be effective, snowpits should be dug frequently to keep up with the changeable snow cover. The bottom line is to not trust your life to a snowpit showing an innocent-looking profile. If you do, sooner or later you are bound to get caught.

In addition to these various stability tests, there are visual clues that warn specifically of avalanche hazard. The best is seeing fresh avalanches. There is no better indicator that one slope may be near failure than to see other slopes that have already failed. Another clue is one that we already mentioned as a test: that is snow that cracks or noisily collapses beneath your feet. Such snow is primed to avalanche. Cracking and collapsing snow are a warning, much like the rattling of a rattlesnake's tail.

SAFE TRAVEL IN AVALANCHE TERRAIN

Travel through avalanche country always involves risk, but there are travel techniques that can minimize that risk. Proper travel techniques might not prevent an avalanche from being released, but they can improve the odds of surviving the avalanche. We have already told you how to avoid avalanches by staying on valley floors, gentle slopes, ridge tops, or in dense timber; but what about when you want to climb, traverse, or descend (e.g., ski down) an avalanche slope? Here's what you need to know.

Avalanches and Storms

Foremost, remember that most avalanches run during and just after storms. The timing of your trip can have a lot to do with its safety. If you can wait a full day after a storm has ended, you will improve your odds by giving the snowpack a chance to react to the new snow load and gain strength. It is the powder hounds who often become avalanche victims during storms. To them, the lure of fresh powder is a powerful narcotic, but it is an unfortunate truth that powder skiing and avalanches go hand in hand.

Method of Travel

Avalanches have trapped victims in all modes of over-snow travel — on foot, snowshoes, downhill skis, cross-country skis, and snowmobiles. When entering avalanche terrain, you should choose the method of travel with which you are most competent, or in other words, the method with which you are least likely to fall down. There are many instances in which a skier did fine descending a slope until he or she fell. The jolt of that impact was enough to cause the avalanche. There have been cases where snowmobilers caused avalanches only after their machines became stuck; then the thrashing about trying to get unstuck triggered the slide.

Crossing Avalanche Slopes

Before crossing, you need to get your personal gear in order. Tighten up your clothing — zip up zippers, put on hat, gloves, and goggles. The reason: you want to be padded and insulated if trapped. If carrying a heavy mountaineering pack, loosen the straps or sling it over one shoulder only. The reason: you want to be rid of the pack if knocked down. A heavy pack makes you top-heavy, making it difficult to swim with the avalanche. This precaution is not necessary if carrying a small day pack. If on skis, remove pole wrist straps and ski runaway straps. The reason: poles and skis attached to a victim hinder swimming motions and serve only to drag the victim under. Finally, if wearing a rescue beacon, be certain it is transmitting. Now you are ready to cross.

If possible, cross low on the slope, in the runout zone. It is rare that your crossing will cause a release in the starting zone far above. Your greatest risk is getting hit by an untimely natural release from above.

If you must cross high and cannot get to the safety of the ridge, traverse the starting zone absolutely as high as you can. This means as close to rocks, cliff, or cornice as possible. Should the slope fracture, most of the sliding snow will be below you; you may take a scary and dangerous fall down the avalanche path, but with most of the avalanching snow below you, you have a better chance of staying on the surface. There have been dozens of avalanche accidents involving two or more people on a slope. Invariably, the person highest on the slope runs the least risk of being buried, while the person lowest runs the greatest risk.

An accident that exemplifies this perfectly happened at Sun Valley, Idaho, on February 5, 1975. This was the first sunny day after five days of snowfall. The powder hounds were out in force. By noon, all available powder had been skied out, and the bolder (and more reckless) skiers began heading out of bounds. A group of four skiers ducked under the boundary ropes to ski the "back side," an infrequent avalanche area. When they reached a steep, lightly-timbered slope, three skiers stopped at the top while one continued 100 feet downslope before stopping. A moment later, the slope fractured under the weight of the four skiers. At the top, one was right at the fracture and was able to fall uphill out of danger; another grabbed a tree and held on as the snow slid past; and the third was at one edge and escaped to the side. The fourth man, well below the fracture and in the center of the slope, was swallowed up by the avalanche. Two hours later, rescuers pulled his lifeless body from four feet of avalanche snow. Skiing powder out of bounds at a ski area is inherently more dangerous than in bounds because of the absence of compaction and control.

If an avalanche path must be climbed or descended, you should keep far to the sides. Should the slope fracture, you have a better chance of surviving by bailing out to the side. Being in the center of a bowl or gully takes away this chance.

5.3 A good example of bad travel technique. The rules are to avoid the center of avalanche-prone bowls and to expoise only one person at a time to danger (from Avalanche Handbook*)*

Only one person at a time should cross, climb, or descan avalanche slope; all other members should watch from a safe location. Two common-sense principles lie behind this advice: first, only one group member is exposed to the hazard, leaving the others available as rescuers; and second, less weight is being put on the snow. If the slope is especially wide, traversing members should space themselves several hundred feet apart. This helps insure that only one person will be caught. All persons should traverse in the same track. This of course reduces the amount of work required, but more important it disturbs less snow, which statistically lowers the chance of avalanche release.

Finally, never drop your guard when on an avalanche slope. This means you should not stop in the middle of a slope (to rest or take a picture, for example); stop only at the edge or beneath a point of protection, such as a rock outcropping. Also remember that it is not uncommon for the second, third, or even tenth person traversing or skiing down a slope to be the one to trigger the avalanche. We repeat: never drop your guard, always anticipate trouble, and have an escape route in mind, such as getting out to the side or grabbing a tree.

Our advice will not keep you out of trouble, but it will help your odds when trouble happens (as it eventually does to all risk-takers.) Let's analyze one more accident that includes most of the ideas we've talked about in this chapter — decision-making, risk-taking, and safe traveling in avalanche terrain.

The date was February 27, 1972; the place, Alta, Utah. Nine members of the Wasatch Mountain Club departed Alta for a Sunday ski tour over Cardiac Pass. The tour would test them with a strenuous climb then reward them with an exhilarating powder run down the other side on more gentle slopes. Before they got their reward, though, they had to negotiate some pretty hairy avalanche terrain.

The group knew the area — and the risks — well. But on this day the stakes were higher: the Forest Service snow rangers at Alta felt the danger was too great and recommended the group not make the tour. The group conferred, weighing risks against benefits, and decided to go ahead.

The climb to Cardiff Pass went without incident. From there, they had to ascend the steep cirque below Cardiac Ridge. This was the dangerous slope they had been warned about (and one they knew was treacherous because of previous accidents on it). They found the new-snow deposition in the cirque considerably deeper than at Alta. They decided to zigzag up the left side of the bowl then traverse the full width of the bowl just beneath the cliffs to reach Cardiac Pass. For safety on the traverse, they spread out to keep 50 yards between skiers.

Four skiers reached the pass, and the fifth in line, Gail Dick, was just yards away when a fracture line suddenly split the slope directly along the ski track. Dick felt the snow shudder, and watched as a three-foot fracture shot 75 yards along the track and an avalanche rushed down the cirque for a quarter mile, sending a giant powder cloud into the air. The snow dropped out from un der Dick's skis, but he was not caught. He hastened to the safety of the pass.

5.4 A single frame from Dave Hanscom's movie taken from Cardiac Pass, Alta, Utah. The first avalanche has just run, triggered by Gale Dick, walking on the bed surface. Next in line are Wayne Slagle and Marge Yerbury who were caught when the second avalanche released seconds later (from The Snowy Torrents III)

Next in line were Wayne Slagle, Marge Yerbury, and two others, all spaced about 50 yards apart. The fracture split the snow directly beneath the skis of Slagle and Yerbury, but the snow stayed in place. Slagle described his uneasy predicament:

I was in a very bad position right in the middle of the danger area. I was calm but struck with indecision as to what action to take. After a few moments hesitation, I recalled from recent training I'd had that I should pull my skis off. This I did, then moved a few steps above the fracture and yelled to the pass for advice.

(Removing skis is a safety measure that allows a victim much more freedom to swim with an avalanche if swept down-hill. A victim almost never has the opportunity to remove skis.)

The group leader urged Slagle to put his skis back on and

move cautiously to the pass. Slagle followed the instructions, but he had taken only two steps when a second avalanche released. Again in Slagle's words:

"About a minute after the first slide, a second fracture occurred that encompassed the entire area of the first and more, running 15 yards above me very near the rock outcroppings. The snow around me gained its speed almost instantly. I fell up the hill and fought desperately to stay on the surface. The force of the snow swung me around quickly so that I was on my stomach with my head downhill. I was fighting with all my power to stay up and breathe. After a few moments, my worst fears had occurred. I was submerged. Each breath was extremely difficult. I was taking in a lot of snow. My depth varied several times. At times it felt like I was deep in the snow because of the pressure and complete helplessness. I rolled with the snow, completely out of control. On one or two occasions after submerging, I could feel myself near the surface. A most vivid memory is wishing the motion would stop, but down again I would go. Panic occurred for the first time when, without any advance warning that I could detect, I came to a stop. My mouth was wide open gasping for air which did not come. My mouth and throat were packed firmly with snow. My face was toward the surface, but I could move no part of my submerged body. The panic was momentary. I happily discovered my right hand was above the snow. I felt sure then that I would not die. I dug desperately with the free hand until I found my face about eight inches under the snow. I gouged my mouth free of snow and cleared my throat and breathed again with great pleasure but still with some difficulty due to exhaustion and pressure of the snow on my chest. I lay quietly and waited for my companions to rescue me."

Indeed, Slagle was rescued, as was Yerbury who too had been caught at the edge of the avalanche. She was only shallowly and partly buried, and managed to dig herself out. This encounter is a study in risk-taking and decision-making. The group had avalanche training and knew the terrain well. They knew (and were warned that) the hazard was high. Nonetheless, they decided that with good travel technique they could minimize the risks and reap the rewards of a stimulating tour. They were, indeed, following two good safety measures: they were well-spaced, and they crossed high on the starting zone. However, they were not spaced quite far enough apart, nor quite high enough. Still, though, they were "thinking avalanche" every step of the way, and this greatly improved their odds. The tour was a failure, but it was not a tragedy.

Mammoth Mountain, California. An aerial view of this large, early-winter avalanche. Two probe lines are looking for victims as other rescuers search the avalanche area (from The Snowy Torrents III)

6 WHEN THINGS GO WRONG

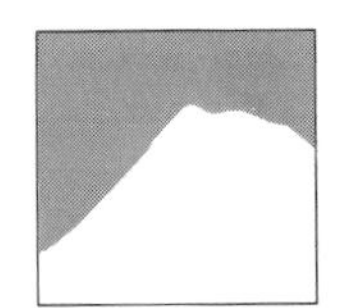

WE SPENT THE BETTER PART OF THE previous chapter telling you how to avoid avalanches. But suppose you don't. Suppose you are one of the ski tourers involved in the Cardiac accident discussed at the end of that chapter. What would you do if you were one of the victims? One of the survivors?

It's time we talked more about surviving avalanches. Is there really anything that you can do for yourself if trapped? Or if someone else is trapped? You bet there is. Most people actually survive avalanche mishaps. In fact, nine out of every ten people caught by avalanches survive. That's because most victims are not buried in their ordeal. That's the good news. The bad news is that only one out of four victims totally buried, with no clues on the surface, survive. The key to survival is to reach or to get a clue to the surface. We'll talk about ways of doing this — or at least ways that others have used to survive. And we'll talk about what eyewitnesses or survivors can do to save a life.

THE MODERN AVALANCHE VICTIM

We have met the enemy and they are us.
POGO GOOD NEWS AND BAD NEWS

We have kept close tabs on avalanche accidents in recent decades. This was all part of a research effort to stem the rising trend in avalanche deaths. In pre-historic America, there were no doubt many avalanche victims among native American Indians, explorers, mountain men, and the like. When gold lured prospectors and miners into the mountain West, many who searched for a rainbow found the white death instead. The modern era of avalanche victims is marked by the coming of the tourist, an era that began in the 1940's. We can use statistics from 1950 to 1985 to paint a portrait of the modern avalanche victim.

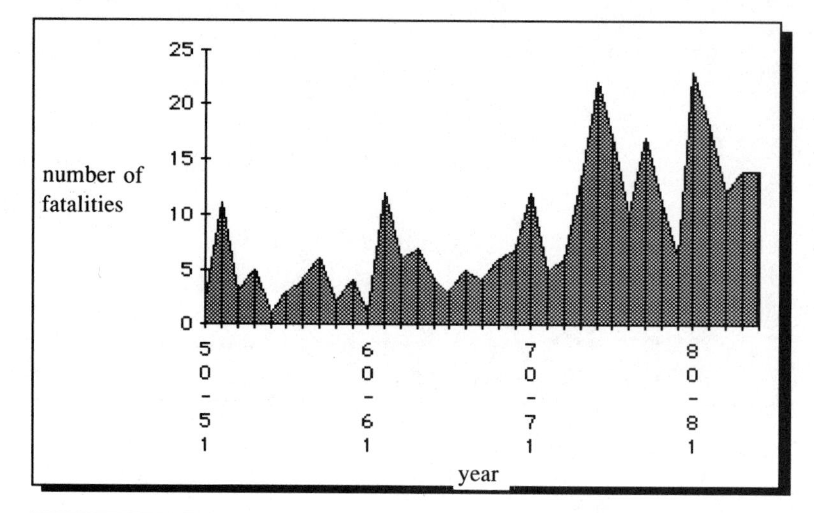

6.1 Annual avalanche fatalities in the United States (1950-51 through 1984-85)

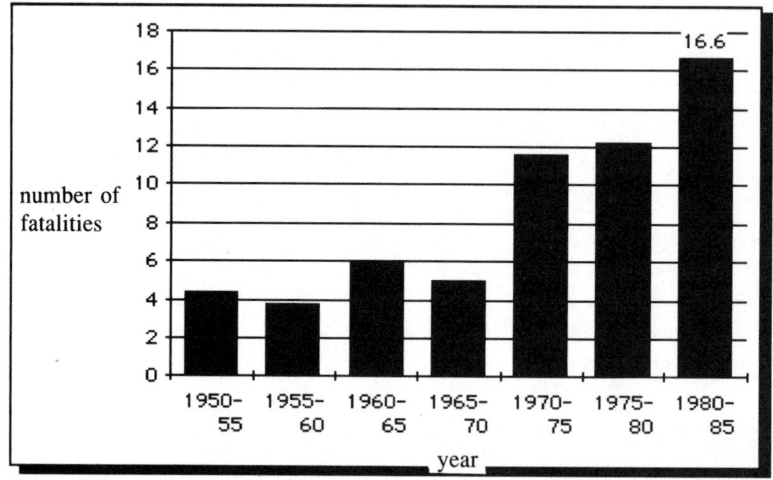

6.2 Avalanche fatalities in the United States, five-year averages (1950-51 through 1984-85)

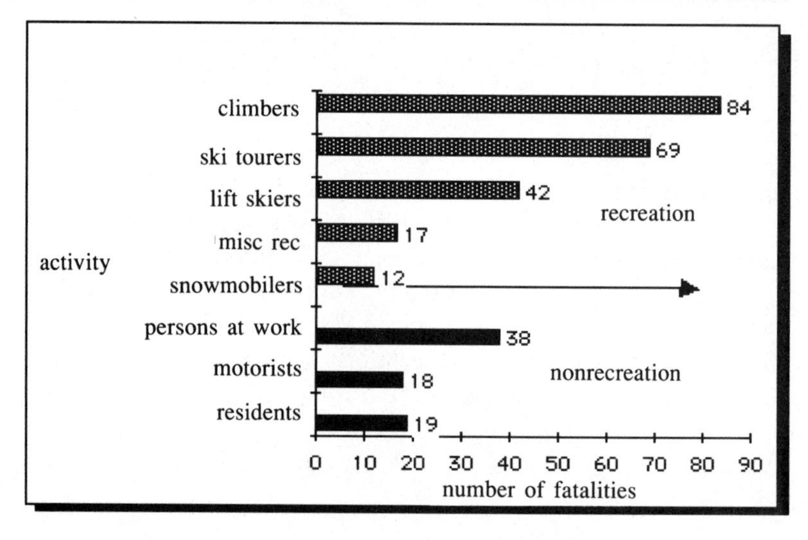

*6.3 Avalanche fatalities by activity category (*1950-51 *through 1984-85)*

Avalanche deaths have been on the rise in the United States in every decade since 1950. Figure 6.1 shows annual deaths, while figure 6.2 shows these numbers when averaged over five-year periods. The trend is clearly upward: in the 1950s, an average of four people a year died by avalanche; in the 1960s, this figure increased to about six people a year; in the 1970s, it doubled to 12 a year; and thus far in the 1980s, it stands at almost 17 a year. In the 35 winters beginning in 1950, 298 people have died by avalanche. Of these, 257 (86 percent) were men, and 41 (14 percent) were women. The average age of all victims was 27 years. The youngest was seven; the oldest, 66.

Take a look now at figure 6.3, which shows the activity groups for the victims. Most victims (76 percent) were pursuing some form of recreation at the time of their fatal encounter. Climbers, ski tourers, and lift skiers head the list. The distinction between ski tourers and lift skiers is that lift skiers rely on lifts to get them up the hill, even though they then might head beyond the ski-area boundary to find trouble. Ski tourers — which include ski mountaineers, helicopter and snowcat skiers, and snowshoers — take their pleasure in the backcountry, often far from developed areas. Among the non-recreation groups, the persons-at-work category includes ski patrollers, highway personnel, and others who were on the job when the avalanche struck.

Where do the accidents occur? Since 1950, 14 states have registered avalanche fatalities, with Colorado having the dubious distinction of leading the list (figure 6.4). And when do they occur? As figure 6.5 shows us, certainly they are mainly a wintertime threat, with the majority of accidents falling in January, February, and March — but they are not exclusively a winter event. Fatal accidents have occurred in every month of the year. Most of the summer incidents involve climbers. For example, the only fatal accident to occur in July took the life of a climber in Rocky Mountain National Park, Colorado. On July 4, 1976, James Boicourt, 29, attempted a solo climb of the Y Couloir on Mount Ypsilon, perhaps to celebrate our nation's bicentennial in his own special way. We really don't know what went wrong, but he either triggered or was hit by a natural avalanche of the previous winter's snow cover. He suffered fatal injuries when the slide swept him down the steep, rocky couloir.

THE DEADLY STATISTICS OF AVALANCHE BURIALS

Numerous factors affect a buried victim's chances for survival — time buried, depth buried, clues on the surface, safety

6.4 Avalanche fatalities by state (1950-51 through 1984-85)

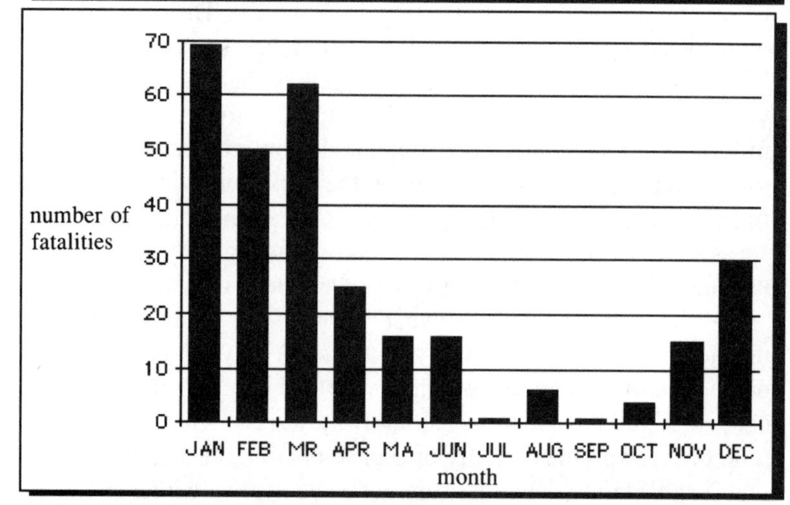

6.5 Avalanche fatalities by month (1950-51 through 1984-85)

equipment, injury, ability to swim with the avalanche, body position, snow density, presence of airspace, size of airspace, and so on. A victim who is uninjured and able to fight and swim on the downhill ride usually has a better chance of ending up only partly buried, or if completely buried, a better chance of creating an airspace for breathing. A victim who is severely injured or knocked unconscious is like a ragdoll being rolled, flipped, and twisted by a merciless demon. Being trapped in an avalanche becomes literally a life and death struggle, with the upper hand going to those who fight the hardest.

Avalanches kill in two ways. First, serious injury is always possible in a tumble down an avalanche path. Trees, rocks, cliffs, and the wrenching action of snow in motion can do horrible things to the human body. About one-third of all avalanche deaths are attributable to trauma, especially to the head and neck. Second, snow is a suffocating environment when buried in it: two-thirds of avalanche deaths are due to suffocation. The problem of breathing in an avalanche, of course, does not start with being buried. A victim being carried down in the churning maelstrom of snow has an extraordinarily hard time breathing. Every breath is apt to inhale snow which clogs the mouth and nose; suffocation comes very fast if the victim is buried with airways already blocked. In addition, the snow that was light and airy when a skier carved turns in it becomes viselike when buried in it. Whereas the snow might have been 80 percent air to begin with, it might become less than 50 percent air after an avalanche. Thus the snow is much less permeable to airflow, making it harder to get oxygen.

That's not all. The snow sets up very hard and solid after an avalanche. This means it's almost impossible to dig yourself out, even if buried less than a foot deep. The hard debris also makes rescue from the outside a losing proposition in the absence of a sturdy shovel.

But wait. It gets even worse. The pressure of the snow in a burial of several feet sometimes is so great that the victim is unable to even expand his or her chest to draw a breath. Even if you are able to breathe, a sinister change can take place around you: the warm breath that you exhale begins to freeze on the snow around your face, eventually forming an ice mask that cuts off all airflow. It takes longer than snow-clogged airways, but the result is the same — death by suffocation. No wonder the odds are stacked so heavily against the completely buried victim, and why speed is so essential in avalanche rescues.

We'll now look at some statistics on survival that are derived from a large number of avalanche burials. In compiling these figures, we have included only persons who were totally buried in direct contact with the snow. Meaning that we have not included victims buried in the wreckage of buildings or vehicles, for such victims can be shielded from the snow to allow sizable airspaces. Under favorable circumstances such as this, some victims have been able to live for days. Indeed, Anna Conrad lived for five days at Alpine Meadows, California, in 1982 in a demolished building — the longest survival on record in the United States. Her legs were pinned (she would lose one to amputation later), and she was immobile, but she survived by eaing snow.

Survival Versus Burial Depth

Figure 6.6 shows how the chance of survival varies with depth. In burials of less than a foot, there is a good chance of living because, first, you have a shot at digging yourself out; second, it is easier for rescuers to find you; and third, you have a good chance of breathing. That's the end of the good news, though. At burials of little more than a foot, your odds are only slightly greater than fifty-fifty, and they drop steadily from there. No one (at least in the United States) has survived a burial of seven feet or more. The reasons are obvious: the snow is tightly packed at such depths, the victim cannot expand his chest against the compressive weight of the snow, and it takes so much more time for rescuers to pinpoint and dig down to the victim.

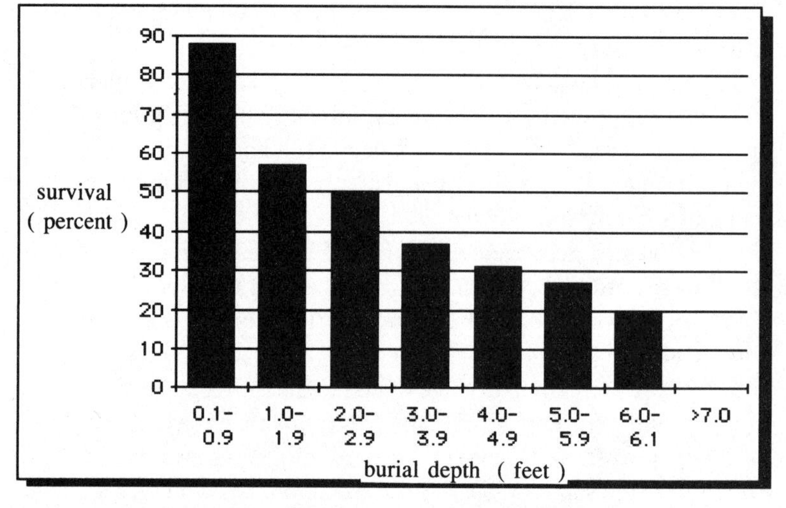

6.6 Percent survival as a function of depth of burial (1950-51 through 1984-85). Only those buried in direct contact with the snow, not in a vehicle or building, are included.

Survival Versus Time Buried

Figure 6.7 shows how the chance of survival varies with elapsed time of burial. Note that the 50 percent survival time is about 30 minutes. In other words, after a burial of 30 minutes, only half of all victims can be expected to survive. The numbers get grimmer as the clock ticks: only one in three victims will survive after one hour, one in six after two hours, and one in 10 after three hours. The message is obvious: time kills.

These statistics put enormous pressure on rescuers. Organized rescue teams, such as ski patrollers, must be highly practiced. They must have adequate training, manpower, and equipment to perform a hasty search and probe of likely burial spots within a minimum time span. And for backcountry rescues, the message is clear and blunt: virtually the only way a buried victim

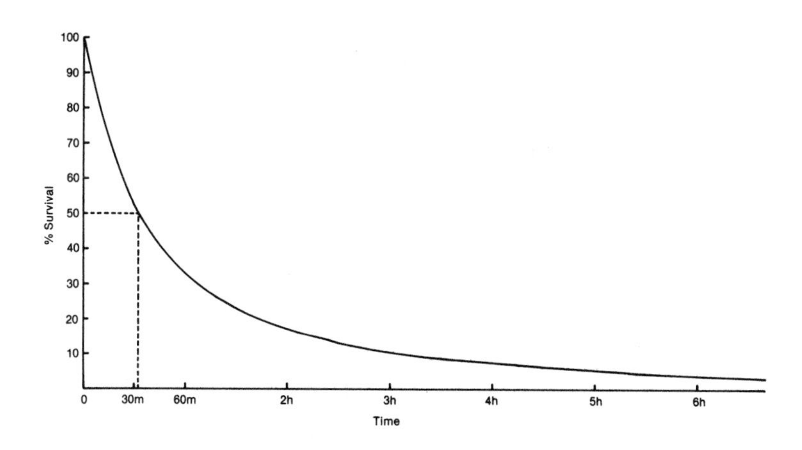

6.7 Percent survival as a ***function of length of time buried (1950-51 through*** *1984-85). Only those buried in direct contact with the snow, not in a vehicle or building, are included.*

will survive is to be found by his or her companions. The need to seek outside rescue units practically assures a body-recovery mission only.

No doubt these are pretty depressing statistics. But a word of encouragement. We are looking at average statistics from a large number of incidents. In individual incidents, favorable circumstances have allowed some victims to survive many hours under the snow. This can happen when the snow does not pack tightly around the victim's face. This could be because of good luck — blocks of snow leaving open spaces in between, for example — or because the victim was able to get his hands in front of his face. Either way, a life-extending airspace was formed.

The point is that rescuers should not become dejected after half an hour or even an hour has passed. The search must go on. One out of 30 or 40 victims will still be alive after six hours, and in the United States the record for survival is nine hours (again, we are talking about people buried in direct contact with the snow). In Canada, the record is an amazing 25-1/2 hours. This remarkable case took place in January 1960 near Invermore, British Columbia. James Duke, 59, working for the Department of Highways, was swept away and buried while acting as an avalanche lookout for a work crew. Searching into the next day, rescuers scratched, probed, and dug in the avalanche and eventually found their man beneath five feet of snow. They were stunned to find him alive and well. Duke owed his life to a natural airspace that he described as being the "size of a washtub."

SURVIVAL, IF YOU ARE THE VICTIM

Escape to the Side

The moment a slope begins to crumble around you, you

have a split second to make a decision or make a move. Whether on foot, skis, or snowmobile, first try to escape to the side of the avalanche or try to grab onto a tree. Do what you can to stay on your feet or machine, for this gives some control and it keeps your head up. Escaping to the side is effective if you can do it. This maneuver either gets you out altogether or gets you to where the forces and speeds are less, which helps your chances of surviving. Turning your skis or machine downhill in an effort to outrun the avalanche is a bad move, for the avalanche invariably overtakes its victims.

Shout, then shut your mouth. Make a shout so your companions are sure to see what's happening. (If you have been following our safety rules, you are the only person caught, and your friends are watching from safe havens.) Then clamp your mouth shut and breath through your nose. If you can do this — admittedly easier said than done in a panic situation — you will not inhale a mouthful of snow, and that's good.

Swim!

If knocked off your feet, put all your effort into swimming with the avalanche. Rid yourself of cumbersome or heavy gear. This means toss your ski poles and hope the avalanche strips away your skis; get away from your snow machine; and try to shed a heavy pack before it drags you down. Doing these things gives you the freedom to swim, the freedom to maneuver your body with swimming motions with your arms and kicking with your legs. What you are trying to do is get to the edge of the flowing snow or maintain a position near the surface. Any swimming motions will do, but if you have been thrown forward and are being carried headfirst downhill, a breast stroke with the arms has worked for some victims (similar to body surfing); if you are being carried down feetfirst, try to roll onto your back and attempt to "tread water" with your arms and legs.

The avalanche annals include many testimonials to the effectiveness of swimming. In one case in December 1973, ski patroller Rod Levinson was caught while protective skiing at Mount Hood Meadows, Oregon. He tried to ski out of it but was tumbled downhill instead. He lost poles but not his skis, which pulled off but remained attached by the safety straps. He slid in a head-uphill position on his back and began a backstroke swimming motion with his arms until the snow stopped. He wound up buried hip deep. In another case in January 1974 in Grand Teton

National Park, Wyoming, Wes Krause, 20, was trapped along with six companions in a large slide while touring. Krause saved himself by ridding himself of his pack, poles, and one ski, and swimming with the snow to stay on top. Three others died in this avalanche. In January 1976, Roger Wilkinson, 25, managed to swim in a slide that caught him on Chittenden Mountain, Colorado — despite breaking a leg in that accident. He feels swimming saved his life.

Nothing is so instructive — and moving — as the first-person accounts of survivors. On February 15, 1968, Bill Flanagan survived a large avalanche in Highlands Bowl at Aspen Highlands, Colorado. Highlands Bowl is an enormous, open bowl that is closed to skiing because it can — and does — produce avalanches that fall nearly 4,000 feet in elevation. (It was the site in March 1984 of a giant avalanche that killed three ski patrollers while they were running an out-of-bounds control route.) On this day in February, Flanagan, a patroller, threw several hand charges but got no releases. He and Matt Wells then skied the deep powder. In Flanagan's words:

I had made about three turns when I fell. I started to sit up when it broke. Matt recalls that it fractured just below him. I recall that the snow seemed to suddenly settle, and I noticed several whirlpool effects in the snow surface around and above me. I was rolled under almost immediately, and breathing hard as a result of the deep-powder skiing, my mouth immediately filled with snow. Try as I did, it was absolutely impossible to expel the snow from my mouth. The ball of snow simply packed harder each time I tried to gulp air around it. I recall I was able to swim and did so as naturally as one would were he trying to surface in a pool of water. There was only a "whooshing" sound of sorts and it gained speed incredibly fast. I knew where the top was because there was always a lighter side. I can't recall when I lost my poles. But a terrific drag suddenly built up on my right leg and was just as suddenly relieved when the ski tore off. I remember realizing this even as it happened, and I know that this is the important reason for my surviving this horror. Once free of that ski, I started rolling again and was again able to swim, or at least move my arms. It slowed down and stopped very quickly. It felt lighter above my shoulders, and I struggled my arms loose and broke through to daylight. The ball in my mouth was so big and hard that I was unable to get it out from behind my teeth. I was able to crush it bit by bit with my front teeth and finally reduced it to a size I could at last spit out. I dug my legs free, released my left ski, and stood up. My throat was so sore that taking a breath actually burned, and for a good half-hour I couldn't draw a full breath. I figured that I was still in plenty of trouble. I had no poles and only one ski, with several miles of chest-deep, untracked snow to negotiate down to the road. Then I spotted Matt high up on the rim of the bowl. Until then I wasn't completely sure that he hadn't been caught and carried down too. Matt managed to get down to me. He gave me his poles, and after many hours of agonizing effort, we made it out to the road.

Listen to another survivor's tale, this one from an avalanche at Breckenridge, Colorado, on December 25, 1969. Jim Hagemeier, a Forest Service landscape architect, had gone to the ski area for a day of skiing; but once up the mountain, he had been invited to go with the snow ranger and several patrollers to inspect a fracture line that had been released with explosives several hours earlier. Here was Hagemeier's experience, in his words:

Everyone put on his orange avalanche cord except me. Mine, unfortunately, was down in the car. We traversed out onto the slide area, directly beneath the four-foot fracture line. I was apprehensive about staying there, especially since I was the only one without an avalanche cord. The rest of the people had moved out away from me, and we were all about 50 feet apart. I thought I should be going back and turned to look for a safe way out. At this time I heard a sharp sound, like a clap of thunder, similar to a charge going off in the snow. My first reaction was that a charge had been set off, but as I looked upslope, I could see a new fracture line going across the top of the slope and the snow starting to move! Since the big load was still above us, there was not an immediate movement of the snow under my skis. I immediately turned my skis downhill into a schuss, thinking that I could reach a rock outcropping and possibly outski the slide. I had skied a second or two when the major impact hit me, tossing me into the air and completely engulfing me. At this time I lost my poles and had a terrible feeling of panic. Several thoughts ran through my mind: first, I was a damn fool for coming here; and second, I fully realized the size of the slide and was certain I would die. The feeling was like being dunked under water, as the impact took my breath away. For some reason, when I started to move with the slide, I could breathe much easier. I thought about the fact that I didn't have an avalanche cord and that it was up to me to get myself out. My right leg was being bent behind me by the pressure on the ski, which then released. Neither of my arlberg straps had been taken off; I am not certain this was a hindrance to me, though this thought occurred to me as I was engulfed in the slide. As it was, I got a good belt on the shins from one of my skis. The sensation of speed was fantastic. I had put my skis into a schuss on a 30-degree slope and was engulfed immediately. I remember the speed increasing as I went down the slope. The ride was very rough, and I was being tossed around quite a bit. It seemed as though I was in a big flume of water, where I was occasionally able to get a breath of air, but most of the time I was overwhelmed by snow. Later, people asked me if I had a sensation of which way was up or down. I can truthfully say that I was aware of up and down, at least after the initial shock of the slide hitting me. Initially, when the full blast of the slide struck me, I had no idea which way was which. As I moved downhill faster, I was able to orientate myself fairly well with the movement of the snow. I worked myself into a sitting position with my feet downhill and tried to swim as if treading water. This seemed to work, and I instantly started to rise in the snow. I kept doing this as I sped down the hill and increased the swimming motion as the slide began to slow down a little. Actually, it was not a fast decrease; it was just going very fast, then it started to stop slowly. I swam until I could feel the slide coming to a stop. I was still buried at this time. How deep I didn't know, but it seemed deep! I pulled my arms in near to my head; at that second the slide came to a rather abrupt halt, and I found my head and hands sticking out of the snow. The snow was still moving very slightly, and I was able to work my body out to where I was sitting on the surface. As far as injuries go, I was perfectly okay, though later in the evening and the next morning, I felt as though I had played football all day.

All four men had been caught. One, a patroller, was near the edge and managed to ski out to the side. Another rode it out, swam, and wound up partly buried. The fourth man was totally buried, but his avalanche cord was on the surface. In Hagemeier's words: "Looking uphill, I spotted a piece of orange cord protruding from the snow. I ran to the cord and used it to pull myself up the snow to where it disappeared into the snow. I made one swipe with my hand, a little ahead of the cord, knowing it was tied around his waist. The second swipe hit something, and I was able to dig out Al's head. He was still conscious." An avalanche cord and quick action saved a life.

In retrospect, Hagemeier had some final thoughts on the outcome of this accident:

Looking back on this whole operation, we can no doubt say we were extremely fortunate not to have anybody killed. Personally, I feel extremely lucky not to be dead at this time. It was an awful incident, and one which we need not have experienced had we used a little sense. However, it is worthwhile to pass this experience on to others. In conclusion, I might say that it was the best Christmas gift I have ever had in my life to end up sitting on top of the slide.

Reach the Surface

Avalanches come to a stop when they flow onto flatter terrain. You, as a victim, will have a second, or two or three, when you feel the sensation of slowing down. This is a crucial point in your ordeal, for your best chance to reach the surface, or stay on it, is right now. Thrust upward with your swimming motions;

try to burst through to the surface. Unless you are very deeply buried at this time, yes, you will know which way is up. Go for it with all your strength. Get your head, a hand, or an arm above the surface. That's where life is!

Even if you can't get your head out, being near the surface greatly improves your odds. And if you get any clue to the surface, it gives your rescuers something to see, rather than feeling their way over a sea of white.

Create a Breathing Space

When you feel the avalanche stopping and you have no sensation of being near the surface or no idea which way to thrust with your swimming motions, try to make an airspace in front of your face. Do anything to keep the snow from packing in tightly. You might do this by getting one or both hands in front of your face, by tucking your chin and mouth inside the collar of your parka, by getting your face in the crook of your elbow, or by shaking your head — anything to create space. This can be extremely hard to do, for avalanche debris, as we've said many times, is dense and unyielding; but if done, it can be a lifesaver.

Snow Ranger Robert Cooper was caught in a slide at his home area of White Pass, Washington, in December 1973 while running an avalanche route. The snow crumbled all around Cooper, and he remembered, "The snow pulled unbelievably hard on my skis. My right ski finally came off, and I felt as though I were going down an elevator. My other ski was torn off as I went down. Luckily, my head was uphill, and I was able to get my hand to my mouth and created an airspace. It took all my strength to move one hand underneath the wet snowpack." Others had watched Cooper's descent and knew his approximate location. Within six minutes, they had dug him out, shaken but uninjured, from three feet of snow.

In an earlier incident on January 1967 at Jackson Hole ski area, Wyoming, patroller Richard Porter was running an avalanche control route with two other patrollers when he made a slip that almost cost him his life. A first-person account of Porter's ordeal, taken from Western Skier magazine (January 1968), reveals his thoughts of being caught and then buried:

I looked uphill and saw the snow hurtling toward me. There was no chance to outski the slide; I was knocked down almost immediately. I dropped my poles and began swimming with it in an effort to stay on top of the snow. I finally came to a stop lying on my side, twisted round so that my feet were higher than my head. As the snow from above buried me, I managed to move my head around enough to form a small air pocket. The avalanche ended as quickly as it had begun. I could hear the muffled crunch above as the snow settled around me. It was solid, like being in a bag of wet cement. I couldn't move at all, but I wasn't uncomfortable. Oddly enough, I felt no sensations of cold, pressure, or even fear — just a cozy feeling of being all covered up with a thick, soundproof quilt. Even though I concentrated on breathing slowly to conserve the limited air supply, I soon lapsed into unconsciousness.

This was in the days before rescue beacons, which if in use would have led to a recovery within 10 minutes. As it was, a probe line struck Porter on the second pass, and he was dug out from a five-foot burial. Altogether he was buried 65 minutes, and he was pulled out gray, unconscious, and not breathing — but alive. This was an exceedingly close call: only the small air space Porter managed to create, and his ability to stay calm and conserve air (when further struggle was futile) tipped the scales in his favor.

Remain Calm

When you find yourself completely buried and unable to move, as in Porter's case, try to remain calm. You have fought the avalanche tooth and nail, but it still buried you. Struggling and shouting at this point will not help. It's time to calm your panic, relax, and conserve your air supply. Rescue is already under way (You weren't skiing alone, were you?), so give yourself the best chance, and that is to preserve your precious oxygen and extend the time for the rescuers to find you.

There is a time for shouting, however, and that is if you hear rescuers working overhead. You should be aware of a particularly cruel fact, though: it is always easier for buried victims to hear their rescuers than for victims to be heard. In other words, your shouts may not make it out of the snow. Do it anyway; it's well worth a try.

RESCUE, IF YOU ARE THE SURVIVOR

Mark the Last-Seen Point

As a survivor or eyewitness to an accident, you need to act quickly and positively. Your actions over the next several minutes may mean the difference between life and death for the victim. First, fix the victim's last-seen point and mark the spot with a piece of equipment, clothing, tree branch, or anything that you will be able to look back and see on your search farther downslope. It is most often safe to move out onto the bed surface of the avalanche. One dangerous situation, though, would be when the fracture line has broken at mid-slope, leaving a large mass of snow still hanging above the fracture. This is what happened in the aforementioned accident at Breckenridge, Colorado, that was such a close call for Jim Hagemeier and two of his friends.

Search for Clues

Search the fall line below the last-seen point for any clues of the victim. Scuff the snow by kicking and turning over loose chunks of snow. You are looking for a ski tip or pole, a gloved hand barely breaking the surface, pieces of clothing or equipment such as a hat or pack — anything that might be attached to the victim or that will give the victim's trajectory and narrow the search area. Even blood on the snow, although not a good sign, can be a useful clue.

Make shallow probes into likely burial spots by using an avalanche probe, ski, ski pole, or tree limb. Likely spots are the uphill sides of trees and rocks, benches or bends in the slope where snow piles up, or depressions which have filled with snow. Search the very toe of the debris thoroughly; many victims are found in this area.

Rescue Beacons

If your group was using beacons, all survivors must immediately switch their units to receive mode. While you are making the fast scuff-search for visual clues, you are at the same time covering the debris, listening for the beeping sound coming from the buried beacon. When you pick up the signal, you will be able to narrow the search area quickly, and if you are practiced in this kind of search, you will pinpoint the burial site in minutes.

Avalanche Guard

If yours is a large party and the threat of a second avalanche exists, place one person in a safe location who can shout out a warning. This gives the searchers a few seconds to flee to safety. Rescues are often carried out in some pretty risky situations, and looking out for your own neck should be one of your major considerations.

Going for Help

A tough question often comes up in rescues, and that is when to go for outside help. The circumstances usually dictate the answer. If the accident occurs in or very near a ski area and there are several rescuers, send one person to notify the ski patrol immediately while the rest search. If you are the only rescuer, the right choice becomes harder. The best advice is to search the surface hastily but thoroughly for clues before leaving to notify the patrol. One exception to this advice would be to notify the patrol if a patrol phone were seconds away, after which you could return immediately to begin the search. So you see, there is no pat answer: the right choice will vary depending on the circumstances, but try to choose the one that gives your buried friend the best chance.

If the avalanche occurred in the backcountry far from any organized body of rescuers, all party members should search, scuff, and probe the area thoroughly, with concentration on the most likely burial sites based on last-seen point and any other clues. If that fails, do it again. And again. Because you know the statistics — the ones that tell you that time kills. The guiding principle in backcountry rescues is that survivors search until they cannot or should not continue. Eventually, the decision to stop can properly be made when the group becomes exhausted and endangered from hypothermia, darkness, deteriorating weather, or another avalanche. To end a search in which no more can be done with the people and equipment on hand, and in order not to lose any more lives, is certainly the right decision.

There is one exception to our rule of all party members staying to search. That would be when there are a large number of survivors — at least ten. Then you can send two people out to secure help and still have a sizable rescue force on hand.

Let's end this sober discussion of backcountry rescues by looking at one more real-life drama, this one with a happy ending. The date was March 1, 1976; the place, Hailey, Idaho. Neil Patterson and Mike Dunn, both 16, had hopped on their snowmobiles and headed up a narrow canyon east of town, to a slope where they had played on their machines before. The two boys had zoomed up and down the slope once or twice, when both became stuck in the soft snow. Patterson was digging out his machine when he heard a rumble and looked up to see a wall of snow rushing toward him. He jumped up and ran a short distance downhill before the snow clubbed him from behind and knocked him down.

Patterson was scared, but he remembered a life-saving tip he had learned from an avalanche film he had seen just a few weeks earlier — swim! So swim he did, and he managed to stay near the surface in his 200-foot ride. Patterson soon felt the avalanche coming to a stop. He had one arm near his face and could move his head slightly. Again, advice from the avalanche film came to him, and he was able to push out a small air pocket before the snow set up. He was buried under two feet of snow and was pinned in an awkward position. He could see light barely filtering through the snow, so he knew which way was up, but there was no way he could move as much as a finger to dig. Just before he lost consciousness, he wondered if his friend had also been buried.

Mike Dunn had not been buried. He watched as the avalanche swallowed up Patterson, then finished digging out his machine. A quick search revealed nothing, so Dunn buzzed down the canyon and stopped at the first house he came to. A phone call to the county search-and-rescue team, and then an alert sent over CB radio for rescuers to meet on the east side of town, set the search in motion. They obtained metal conduit from an electrical supply shop to use as probes, and then headed to the site with Dunn.

Fifteen minutes into the search, the probe line struck Patterson. He was uncovered from two feet of snow, face up, unconscious, but breathing. He soon regained consciousness, and after spending the night in the hospital, he was released in fine condition. Patterson had beaten some tough odds by surviving a burial of one and one half hours, but he had helped himself by swimming and creating an airspace. Although he was totally buried, it was a fairly shallow burial, which allowed enough air for survival. Compare this to the missing snowmobile, which was found several days later under ten feet of snow.

Leadership

Ski patrols and search-and-rescue teams are trained in the ways of avalanche rescue, and when the alarm is sounded, they are prepared and equipped to respond quickly and efficiently. All rescues are chaotic to some degree, so the first thing an organized team must do is to turn chaos into order. This is best done by establishing firm leadership. The rescue leader is the overall coordinator of the operation. He or she may be at the accident site, but more often would be located at the staging area for sending rescuers to the site. The site commander is in radio contact with the rescue leader and decides where to search, how to use his manpower, and how to coordinate the different types of search, such as probe lines and avalanche dogs. The site commander must also make decisions that affect the safety of the rescuers — whether to post an avalanche guard, whether to do explosive control, whether to pull out the rescuers because of hazard, and when to abandon the mission. Column leaders are those who lead groups of five to ten rescuers to the site, using a safe route, and then are responsible for keeping the group together and working efficiently at whatever task they are assigned by the site commander.

Three-Staged Rescue

A full-blown operation is divided into three stages. The first stage is the hasty-search column. This group, composed of as many people as are on hand, heads swiftly to the site carrying probes, shovels, and first-aid equipment. It is their job to scuff the avalanche for clues and probe likely areas with hopes of making a quick find. The person reporting the avalanche often accompanies this column back to the site.

The second stage brings the main body of rescuers, traveling in columns, to the site. They are carrying the bulkier equipment needed for search, resuscitation, and evacuation — more probes and shovels, toboggans, sleeping bags, resuscitation equipment, medical supplies, and a trained avalanche dog and handler, if available. Ideally, stage two should begin to arrive 10 to 15 minutes behind stage one.

The third stage brings in support for stages one and two, in the case of a prolonged rescue. Included in stage three are fresh manpower to take over for cold and tired searchers, hot food and drink, tents, warm clothing, and lighting equipment. Avalanche dogs and handlers can be ferried or flown in for additional searching power. Most rescues are concluded before a third stage is needed.

Methods of Rescue

Almost all rescues begin with the surface search or scuff. More victims have been rescued alive by this method than by any other. Of course, for this to be effective, the victim must have gotten a hand, ski tip, or other attached object to the surface, either by design or by luck. Only when the victim is wearing a rescue beacon (and the rescuers too have beacons) can a thorough surface search be short-circuited. Rescuers should still use their eyes to pick up clues, but they should be concentrating on listening for the victim, for they will usually pick up the beacon signal long before they see a small clue on the surface.

We have mentioned a fact about beacons before, and we shall do so again here: their effective use requires a little training and a lot of practice. Most successful beacon rescues have involved professional ski patrollers and heli-ski guides — people who train regularly with these units. There have also been several beacon rescues involving backcountry skiers. Let's look at one accident that shows the effectiveness and the problems of beacons.

It was April 2, 1979, when seven men headed out on a tour in Big Cottonwood Canyon, Utah. They all were experienced skiers, carried rescue transceivers and shovels, and wore touring skis. They made five descents on moderately steep, gladed slopes, but their sixth found them at the top of a steeper, open slope that some of the skiers thought was dangerous. And that is exactly what it was: when the third skier started down, a fracture two feet deep and 300 feet wide broke across the top. The avalanche set the whole slope in motion and swallowed up all three skiers. Two were totally and deeply buried; one would survive and one would not.

The survivor, 24-year-old David Carter, recalls the slope cracking and seeing ripples in the snow on all sides. The slide quickly knocked him down. He tried to swim, but his boots stayed firmly attached in his three-pin bindings, and his skis pulled him down and frustrated his swimming motions. When he sensed the slide slowing down, he tried but could not get his hands in front of his face. He wound up buried on his side in a fetal position five feet deep. He could hear his beacon beeping, and that was reassuring. He meditated to help stay calm and conserve his air.

Gregory McIntyre, 28, did not survive. He was low on the slope when the avalanche broke and tried to out-ski it. He made it to the top of a rock outcrop, when the slide caught him. There a wall of snow knocked him off the rock into a 10-foot fall to the slope below. He was buried four feet at the foot of the rocks.

Four party members were not caught and one was partly buried and able to dig himself out. These five immediately began a beacon search, but one of the five — the partly buried victim — forgot to turn his transceiver to receive mode and therefore was still transmitting. The error was not discovered until quite a few confusing minutes had passed. Once corrected, the rescuers were able to work on the problem of isolating one buried signal from the other. They uncovered McIntyre in 20 minutes, but he showed no life signs and could not be revived; they found Carter five minutes later, and he did respond quickly once uncovered. So beacons saved one out of two. Did the delay caused by confusion in using the beacons cost a life? Perhaps not, but this incident does show that even experienced people can have problems with beacons.

There have been several recent efforts at inventing alternative personal rescue devices. One idea is a balloon that inflates upon impact in an avalanche and floats in the air attached to the victim by a cord. Another is a vest that inflates on impact much like air bags in automobiles; the idea is to provide protection and flotation for the victim. A third attempt is a diode inserted permanently into ski boots; the location can be picked up by a radar-like device carried by rescuers. These are all experimental devices, none of which has yet gained practical application.

More victims, dead and alive, have been found by probe lines than by any other method. A probe line is comprised of up to a dozen rescuers with avalanche probes, or sounding rods, who stand elbow to elbow on the avalanche debris. Upon commands from the leader, they probe down, lift, step forward, probe, lift, step, and so on until the leader stops the line and moves it to another area. This method gives about a 70 percent chance of finding the victim, if indeed the line passes over the burial spot. Once the whole area is probed without a find, the proper decision is to do it again. In rescues with enough manpower, shovelers are standing nearby to check out any possible strike. The line does not stop in such an event but continues to march forward with its methodical "down, up, step" cadence.

The use of trained avalanche dogs is slowly becoming more widespread in the United States. With their keen sense of smell, dogs trained to sniff out victims buried beneath the snow have been quite effective in avalanche rescues. The problem, though, is the invariably long burial times once the dogs have been brought to the avalanche site, a problem which almost inevitably makes for an unsatisfactory outcome: the recovery of a dead victim. In 1982, however, in the Alpine Meadows disaster, a dog made the first live recovery of an avalanche victim in the United States when Anna Conrad was pulled from a demolished building after five days' burial. As more ski areas begin to have trained dogs on the site, we have real hope that the number of live recoveries will increase.

6.8 An avalanche dog, working a search and rescue mission with its master (from the Snowy Torrents III)

A recent rescue device that simulates the ability of dogs has been invented and is in limited use in Europe. This is a probing device that senses carbon dioxide levels, and when inserted into the snow, it can literally sniff out the location of a buried victim. Tabbed a snuffler, it can be thought of as a mechanical avalanche dog. The jury is still out on its usefulness.

AVALANCHE FIRST AID

Stage two of a rescue should include a doctor or emergency medical technician (EMT) trained to handle avalanche emergencies. The first task of rescuers upon uncovering a victim is to restore breathing. Sometimes a victim will spontaneously start breathing once a plug of snow is removed from around the mouth and nose. Often, mouth-to mouth resuscitation and cardio-pulmonary resuscitation (CPR) are required, if the victim is neither breathing nor a pulse can be felt. Of course, rescuers must check the victim carefully for neck injuries before starting resuscitation.

In the final stages of digging out a victim, be careful not to inflict injury with the shovel. The victim should be treated immediately for serious bleeding, if necessary at the same time as other rescuers may be trying to restore breathing. Broken bones can be attended to after the immediate attention to breathing and bleeding is accomplished.

A victim should be pulled from the snow as gently as possible and placed in a toboggan equally gently. If breathing has been restored, any bleeding stemmed, and suspected broken bones immobilized, then treat for shock and hypothermia. Basically this means warming the core (chest and abdomen). Warming the extremities first (arms and legs) could possibly cause death by causing cold blood to flow from the extremities to the core. Transporting the victim by toboggan or any other means should be done smoothly without jars and jolts to prevent further injury. Also during transport, the victim should be checked every few minutes for breathing and heartbeat.

The severity of avalanche emergencies do not favor the victim: more buried victims will die than will live. The key to saving lives lies much more in education and prevention of accidents than in improved rescue techniques. No rescue method or device will ever be a substitute for proper decision-making and route-finding.

A snowshed partly covered by avalanche debris on Maria's Pass, Montana. This shed protects the Burlington Northern Railroad (Don Bachman photo)

7 GETTING THINGS UNDER CONTROL

TO A LARGE DEGREE, AVALANCHES can be controlled, by either of two wholly different approaches. One is to attack a slope to cause it to slide when we want it to and when it can do no harm. The other is to defend against avalanches; that is, to prevent a slope from sliding, or if it does, to channel the avalanche out of harm's way or stop it before it can do damage.

TWO APPROACHES: ATTACK OR DEFEND

We use the term active control to refer to the attack on a slope, usually done with explosives. The idea is to test the stability of the snow by giving it a massive jolt. This is done at a time when ski trails are closed to the public, when highway traffic is temporarily held at a safe roadblock, or when buildings of a village or work site are evacuated. As you might expect, this often results in an avalanche release. Then again, it often does not; when this is the case, it is not necessarily a negative result — the blasters have at least learned something about the snow stability. Active control is most commonly used in ski areas and along highways. More on this later.

We use the term passive control to refer to the use of structures built to control avalanches. Avalanche defense structures are of three general types. There are those built in the starting zone of an avalanche path; these are designed to hold the snow in place, to prevent an avalanche from ever occurring. There are those built in the track or runout of an avalanche path; these are designed to divert an avalanche or to dissipate its force. And there are those built above an avalanche path, either on the opposite (and windward) slope or on the ridge itself; these are designed to alter snow deposition patterns.

Make the avalanche run to the tune of artillery.
FROM THE BBC FILM *AVALANCHE*

Avalanche defense structures are expensive. To justify the expense of construction and maintenance, they must protect something which, if destroyed, would mean a dear loss in property or human lives. Therefore, their use is restricted to the protection of villages, industrial sites, and major highways.

There is actually another kind of passive control, one used frequently in ski areas, and that is the use of closures. Areas of a ski mountain can be temporarily, or even permanently, closed because of avalanche danger. We'll look at this in more detail a little later on.

EARLY EFFORTS AT AVALANCHE CONTROL

The earliest recorded attempts at avalanche control came, not surprisingly, from Europe. Colin Fraser, in his book Avalanches and Snow Safety, makes mention of some of these efforts. The first known reference appears in a French document dated 1323. Written by a forestry inspector, the text states that if the cutting of the wood behind Le Bourg d'Oisons (Dauphine region) continued, the town would be menaced by avalanches. Fraser speculates that the first defense structure may have been a deflection wall built above the Swiss village of Leukerbad, following a devastating avalanche in 1518 that killed 61 villagers. During the next several centuries, a village here or there would undertake the construction of a defense structure, but it was not until the mid- to late-1800s that widespread building of avalanche defenses in the Alps was done.

Similarly, active methods to trigger avalanches are mostly a recent practice. Fraser makes reference, however, to a very early effort. In 1438 a Spaniard named Pero Tafur led a party on a crossing of the Alps. Before passing any area they judged avalanche-prone, they discharged their firearms in an attempt to release them. Pero Tafur does not tell whether they brought any down, but Fraser doubts (as do we) that they did, given what we know today about what it takes to accomplish this.

The modern era of avalanche control by explosives began in Europe in the 1930s. At least this was when military weapons were first used for avalanche protection. Some 20 years earlier in World War I, weapons had been used to release avalanches as instruments of death. During the fighting in the Alps, armies aimed their cannons not on the opposing armies but on the slopes above them, and avalanches rained down in torrents of death. The losses were staggering: estimates of lives lost range from 40,000 to 80,000 troops.

In the United States, it was during the mining era of the late 1800s that the first attempts to control avalanches were noted. Mining towns like Alta, Utah, and Silverton, Colorado, sat in the shadows of some of the worst avalanche country imaginable; every winter brought the very real threat of death by avalanche to those who wintered over. It was in February 1879 that an avalanche buried and killed two miners at the Highland Mary Mine near Silverton. While attempting to locate the buried men, two of the rescuers were swept away and killed. The risky business of locating the victims and reopening the mine led to the first mention of using dynamite to set off avalanches. In its February 15, 1879, edition, the LaPlata *Miner* reported: "An effort is to be made today, with giant powder, to start the dangerous drifts that obstruct the trail."

It seems, though, that early experience at controlling avalanches with explosives came about as much by accident as by design. The February 3, 1883, edition of the LaPlata *Miner* noted that a snowslide was started by a blast inside the tunnel of the Little Charlie Mine, killing one of the two men waiting outside. And as reported in the March 22, 1919, edition of the Silverton *Standard*, two miners were killed and one injured when a slide was released by the concussion of the blasting inside the Sunnyside Mine.

The men toiling for riches in this area of Colorado did not rely on explosives alone for avalanche protection. One need only to walk among the long-abandoned mines to see evidence of other methods used in their battles against avalanches. Some of the most impressive are the splitting wedges built above the towers of aerial tramways that were used for hauling ore. These wedges, often constructed of logs and stone, were meant to protect the towers by dividing the avalanche. Also apparent in several sites are mounds of dirt upslope from mine buildings, designed to stop snowslides. Many of these were quite effective, as proven by the ruins of mine buildings that have been destroyed by age and not by avalanche.

MODERN METHODS OF AVALANCHE DEFENSE

Passive avalanche control can be accomplished in several ways. Let's look at the methods in use today: the three categories of structures, plus reforestation and closure. These provide protection for projects as varied as dwellings, industrial sites, highways and railroads, and ski areas.

7.1 Snow bridges in the starting zone of an avalanche path in Switzerland (E. Wengi photo, from Avalanche Protection in Switzerland)

Supporting Structures in the Starting Zone

Designed to anchor the snow in place, these are most often heavy, rigid structures built of wood, steel, aluminum, concrete, or a combination of these materials. They are built in parallel lines stretching along the contours of the starting zone. There are two types of rigid support structures: those having horizontal bars, called snow bridges; and those having vertical bars, called snow rakes. There is also a third type of support structure: snow nets are flexible supports consisting of nets of steel cables hung on tubular steel posts.

Supporting structures are costly to build and maintain. Much of the expense goes into the cost of the materials, mostly steel and concrete. But labor costs can also be high because of the difficult terrain where these must be located. In the Alps it is not unusual for millions of dollars to be invested in supporting structures for a single starting zone, when that avalanche threatens the homes and buildings of a town. In the United States, supporting structures are not widely used because so far we have been able to build away from threatening avalanches.

Deflecting and Dissipating Structures in the Track and Runout Zone

This kind of defense is designed to divert, retard, or stop a moving avalanche from reaching valuable objects. Since they must withstand huge dynamic forces, these are usually massive structures made of earth, rock, or concrete.

Earthen and stone dams and dykes are built in the track of an avalanche path to divert the moving snow away from its normal path. The deflection angle should not exceed 15 or 20 degrees; walls built at sharper angles to the flow will likely be overrun by fast-moving masses of dry snow. Indeed, villages of the Alps have suffered more because of walls built at too sharp an angle to the avalanche. Massive snowslides are capable of jumping these walls, and once airborne, are capable of more destruction by descending onto the roofs of houses in crushing torrents.

Several types of structures can be built in the lower track and runout of a path to retard the advance of an avalanche and dissipate its force. Earthen cone-shaped mounds are frequently built for this purpose. These are inexpensive to construct and

7.2 Deflecting walls of back-filled masonry built in an avalanche track to protect a village in Switzerland (E. Wengi photo, from Avalanche Protection in Switzerland)

maintain. Simlarly, concrete or masonry walls backfilled with earth will do the same job. Once such protection has effectively stopped an avalanche, it is necessary to bulldoze the snow from around the mounds to make them effective for stopping subsequent avalanches.

Structures can also be built directly uphill of, or as an integral part of, a building or tower in need of protection. We have previously mentioned splitting wedges as an example of protective structures built to protect mining interests in the San Juan Mountains of Colorado. Several ski areas of the western United States have built concrete splitting wedges to protect ski-lift towers. It is in the Alps, though, where you will find many wedges (and ramps) incorporated into the design of buildings. One of the most impressive is the church at Davos-Frauenkirch, Switzerland, of which the back wall is a giant wedge pointing up the hill like a ship's prow.

7.3 The east snowshed on Interstate 90, Snoqualmie Pass, Washington. Eastbound traffic can be struck by avalanches running over the shed (from The Snowy Torrents III)

Along mountain highways and railways, avalanche sheds or galleries can be built to protect from avalanches that intersect the right of way. Avalanche sheds are merely roofs built at the same angle as the slope that allow avalanches to cross over without interrupting traffic. Sheds are expensive, costing a minimum of $4,000 per foot (over a two-lane road; much more for four lanes). This means that a 1,000-foot shed would cost no less than $4 million.

Sheds, when built properly, always do the job as planned, but problems have arisen when the shed was built too short, allowing avalanches to spill onto the road or rail at either end, or when it has been built to cover only two lanes of a four-lane road, leaving the outside lanes totally exposed and even providing a nice ramp for the snow to hurtle unimpeded onto the road. One such example exists on Interstate 90, which winds over 3,004-foot Snoqualmie Pass in the Cascade Mountains of Washington. Two serious accidents have occurred at the snowshed several miles east of the summit, a shed which shields only the inside lanes from a frequent-running avalanche path. In January 1971 a small avalanche ran over the shed during the night and trapped a passing motorist. A short time later, moments after a wrecker had pulled the stranded car out, a second slide came flying over the shed. The motorist, standing by his car, was totally buried alongside his car as avalanche snow suddenly piled up on the road. Highway personnel were already at the site, but it still took one hour to find the victim who, buried beneath 10 feet of crushing snow, did not survive.

A second incident at exactly the same spot took place in March 1972. Three school teachers were returning late one night to their homes in eastern Washington, but their timing could not have been worse. As they passed the snowshed, an avalanche poured over the shed and onto the road and the car. The driver, Ralph McEwen, recalled, "The last thing I saw was a big blob of snow come over the top and hit us. The car came to a stop like hitting a wall." The snow had buried the car beneath six feet of snow and had broken the front and rear windshields. Although some snow had poured in through the broken windows, the three trapped victims had plenty of room inside the car. One and a half hours later, one of nine probers sounding the avalanche shouted out that he had hit what he thought was the roof of a car. From inside the car, the victims could hear the rescuers overhead. Suddenly a probe pole poked through the broken windshield. McEwen grabbed it and jerked it downward. "I wanted to make sure those people knew we were down here," he said later. The rescuer was equally startled. "Someone's pulling my probe back down!" he shouted. This happy result led to a most remarkable rescue.

Structures Built Above the Starting Zone

It is possible to use structures to alter snow deposition patterns and to reduce deposits in the starting zone. The intent is to reduce the number and size of avalanches that can run. Two types of structures help accomplish this. Snow fences can be erected on the windward slope upstream from a starting zone to cause large drifts of snow to form behind the fence, snow which ultimately is kept out of the starting zone. Also there are structures that can be built right on the ridge line. One interesting design is the jet roof. This structure consists of a sloping roof supported on posts above the ground. Wind coming over the ridge to hit the underside of the roof and be deflected and accelerated downward. The result is a wind that scours snow from the lee slope, preventing cornice formation and deep drifting in the upper starting zone. Vertical eddy panels erected along the ridge act similarly by disrupting the flow and preventing cornice growth.

Reforestation

Dense stands of timber in a potential starting zone act as anchors to prevent avalanche releases. Worldwide there have been many projects undertaken to replant native vegetation in existing avalanche paths. The planting is almost always done in conjunction with supporting structures, which provide protection for the growing trees until they become large enough to protect themselves. Frequently it is necessary to contour the slope into terraces to prevent snow creep from ripping out the newly planted stock. If successful, a forested slope offers better avalanche protection, and far better aesthetics, than one studded with structures.

Closures

Passive avalanche control within ski areas can be accompished with the judicious use of area closures. These may be temporary closures, for hours or up to several days, until active control measures, or the passage of time, have relieved a serious avalanche threat. Or they might be permanent closures, where no amount of control offers a significant improvement in safety. Many ski areas have chutes, gullies, or depressions that represent deadly traps and are, therefore, permanently closed. These are always thoroughly signed and roped to prevent skiers from entering by mistake. Still, accidents have happened.

One textbook example of a permanent avalanche closure is the Snake Pit at Alta, Utah — a slope seemingly designed to be a killer. To those with a trained avalanche eye, the Snake Pit looks as sinister as it sounds; it is a cup-shaped depression with steep walls on three sides. When the snow breaks loose from these walls, it falls about 100 feet and piles up deeply in the pit. In January 1976, a 26-year-old skier became separated from three companions — separated by the Snake Pit. Rather than climb up and around, he ducked under the ropes and died. The avalanche he triggered was not deep, only about 18 inches, but it buried him 10 feet under. An hour and 45 minutes later, rescuers pulled his lifeless body from the snow.

Overall, passive defenses provide a good measure of protection for buildings and other installations. Often, a combination of several types of structures provides the best defense. For example, supporting structures in the starting zone might well be backed up with a diversion dam or mound field in the runout. There are many avalanche problems, however, for which structures are not the answer. These cases call for active measures.

MODERN METHODS OF ACTIVE AVALANCHE CONTROL

Control Skiing

Ski patrollers and heli-ski guides often use the method of control skiing, or protective skiing, to cut potential avalanche starting zones. The control team skis cautiously, one at a time, across the starting zone on a traverse or making a sweeping turn to chop the zone into small segments to break slab cohesion. Other team members follow when the first has reached a safe observation point.

Control skiing is quite similar to test skiing, which is the deliberate cutting of a starting zone, bouncing and thrusting the tails of the skis, to see how the snow reacts to this assault. Control skiing and test skiing, both, are risky business and should be done (as a first measure) only on small avalanche areas; larger avalanche areas should first be hit with explosives and then ski cut. Every year dozens of patrollers take scary rides when they have miscalculated the risk. Fortunately, these incidents have seldom resulted in serious injury or death, owing mostly to the patrollers skills and training. They constantly anticipate trouble so that they usually can react fast enough to avoid the worst, by escaping to the side or grabbing a tree.

Hand Charges

The most common form of explosive avalanche control is the use of hand charges tossed into avalanche zones by ski patrollers and other avalanche technicians, like heli-ski guides. Explosives are one of the most important tools in avalanche work and are used routinely to test and control slopes in ski areas. Every winter something more than 100,000 hand charges are used for avalanche control in the United States. Areas such as Alpine Meadows, Squaw Valley, Alta, Snowbird, Jackson Hole, and Bridger Bowl will throw 5,000 to 10,000 charges yearly. We should emphasize here that explosive control is never done when the skiing public is in the vicinity.

The purpose of using explosives, of course, is to release avalanches by hitting the snow with a massive jolt, or to gain further knowledge of snow stability when slides do not release. When a charge goes off, it blows a large crater in the snow and sends cracks radiating out from there. The fracturing of the snow caused by the blast is reinforced by stress waves that travel through the snow, the air, and the ground. The snow wave is actually the weakest, and wet snow can quickly absorb the energy of a propagating stress wave so that the effective diameter of the blast might be only 25 or 30 feet. Since air and ground waves are more efficient in transmitting the blast energy, special techniques of control are sometimes used to take advantage of this. One such technique is to suspend charges over the snow on bamboo poles, or on specially designed cable systems, all in an effort to maximize the effective blast area. A cable system consists of a cable strung above a starting zone so that a blaster can prepare a charge, run it a desired distance out the cable, and lower it to within three to six feet above the snow before it detonates. These systems are widely used in the Alps, and there is also one in place at Bridger Bowl, Montana.

Two types of hand charges are commonly used for avalanche control: sticks of 80 percent gelatin dynamite, and blocks of TNT cast into cylindrical cannisters designed especially for avalanche work. Two-pound charges are the standard size. The charges are armed with blasting cap and safety fuse, lit by the blaster with a pull-wire igniter, and heaved into the avalanche

7.4 Tramway designed to transport explosives to avalanche starting zones (Joel Juergens photo)

path. Fuses are usually cut in two-minute lengths to allow a safety margin for the blaster, if he needs to retreat to a safer location. Some ski patrols are using homemade slingshots — made of a pouch, elastic straps, and ski poles — to double or triple the distance that they can hurl a two-, four-, or six-pound charge.

Hand charges were first used in the United States in the 1940s by Monty Atwater at Alta, Utah. In his book *The Avalanche Hunters*, Atwater describes in exquisite prose those pioneering days of forecasting and control. Since then, avalanche workers have thrown several million charges and have an excellent safety record to show for it. Only two blemishes mar an otherwise perfect record, and both came at Mammoth Mountain, California, within one month of each other. On December 13, 1973, a charge blew up in the hands of a patroller; he was killed instantly. On January 1, 1974, a patroller temporarily laid a charge on the snow and moments later, just as he was reaching for it, it exploded. Amazingly, this man survived but suffered severe damage of the hand and arm nearest the blast. The causes of the accidents were never determined for certain. Some people have speculated that static electricity was the cause, that the discharge of static buildup on clothing or the snow had spontaneously detonated the charges. We suspect, though, that improper procedures in handling the charges were the cause; and that, were this an airline accident, the cause would be listed as pilot error.

In addition to avalanche control, hand charges have found widespread application in cornice control. Cornices are monstrous formations of wind-driven snow that develop along exposed ridgelines, and are an integral part of the mountain environment. They grow by a succession of layers of wind-hardened snow in which each layer grows out farther than the layer underneath, creating an overhanging and unstable profile. A fully mature cornice might be 1,000 feet long, 30 feet high, and overhang by 10 feet. In ski areas, cornices are bad news, for they are hazardous because of their tendency to break off, and they deny access to ski runs from the ridge. (Cornices do, however, provide launches for daring — and demented — skiers who want to see who can survive the free fall onto the run below.)

Cornice control can be done by stomping off, while wearing skis, small chunks of new growth. To keep this from becoming dangerous, it must be done daily. The standard control for larger cornices is explosives. The job requires a team of people — one to work on the cornice, one to prepare charges, one or more to act as spotters and guards, and several to belay those on the cornice. The man on the cornice drills holes in the snow, drops charges into the holes, and links all the charges together using detonating cord. "Det cord" is an explosive shaped just like a rope, so that many charges can be tied together in a long line, and they can be set off all at once. A typical cornice operation will use 50 to 100 pounds of explosives; when this goes off, an awesome blast peels off a large piece of the cornice which then tumbles in jagged blocks down the slope, sometimes triggering an avalanche in the process.

Cornice control is one of the riskier jobs that an avalanche blaster must do. There have been several accidents associated with cornice work, and all occurred because the cornice broke while a worker was on top drilling holes or loading them with charges. In March 1976, a Bureau of Reclamation employee was killed on Mount Nast, Colorado, when the cornice he was working on collapsed. He was not on belay at the time.

In an earlier incident in April 1967, Ron Perla was nearly killed during a cornice blasting operation at Alta, Utah. Perla was on the cornice drilling holes; he became alarmed when his drill punched all the way through the cornice and he could see light through the hole. Nevertheless, the team leader instructed him to continue. Moments later the cornice broke. Perla fell into space, his belay rope pulled taut, and then it snapped in half! Perla was off on a 1,500-foot fall down a steep chute, all in the midst of large chunks of cornice and the churning snow of an avalanche that the cornice fall had released. In Perla's words:

"The rope broke and I was on my way. I knew it was a large avalanche. I tried to make swimming motions. The force of the snow against my face closed by eyes. I sensed the snow coming to rest. Next, I thought only of the snow piling on top of me, and the amount would determine my survival chances. I was face up, and I tried to place my left hand over my face, but the piling up snow forced it away. But before the snow set up, I got my right hand up through the snow. I knew my hand was out of the snow and that I had an excellent chance. I quickly blacked out; the experience seemed painless, except for a firm pressure on my chest making it difficult to breathe. Returning to consciousness was a gradual process. At first it seemed I was able to breathe through the snow, then I saw figures standing above me. Finally, it became clear that the rescuers had found me and had opened an air space around my face."

Perla was a snow ranger at the time, and over the next 10 years, he became one of the foremost avalanche experts in the United States. In 1976, he and Pete Martinelli authored the *Avalanche Handbook* for the U.S. Forest Service.

There is one final story we must tell about cornice control. This one happened in the early 1970s at a western ski area, which we will mercifully let remain anonymous. In preparation for the blasting operation, the patrol had taken a roll of detonating cord from the powder cache and placed it on a table in the patrol room. (It must be mentioned that detonating cord looks for all the world like a spool of orange rope.) Minutes later, after booting up, the patrollers returned to the room to find the spool of explosive gone. They burst outside looking for any sort of suspicious character who had stolen it for God knows what nefarious purpose. They found nothing, but had to keep searching. A few minutes later a lift operator returned the empty spool and thanked the patrol for the rope. He had strung the entire lift maze with detonating cord!

Artillery

There are many instances at ski areas and along highways where it is impractical, or impossible, to control an area with hand-thrown charges. Artillery weapons are needed in these cases. These may be military weapons of World War I and II vintage, such as 75mm and 105mm howitzers and recoilless rifles. The larger caliber delivers a larger payload and is more accurate at greater distances. These weapons are obtained from military depots and are to be used only by Forest Service, highway, and ski-area employees trained at gunnery schools. Or they may be non-military weapons, like the avalauncher, that can be bought and operated by civilians.

The military weapons, both the howitzers and recoilless rifles, fire on a fairly flat trajectory and can deliver a charge with great accuracy up to several miles away. There is one major difference in these weapons. The howitzer recoils violently, so that its firing position must leave room or otherwise be designed for this reaction. The recoilless rifle, as its name implies, does not recoil; instead the weapon is designed so that a massive backblast, equal in force to what comes out the front, explodes out the rear. This means it can be fired from a pedestal mounted on a tower or flat-bed truck. The backblast is the main danger of these weapons; it can shake buildings and can break windows for great distances. And it can kill. The only person ever to die while firing such a weapon in the United States was a snow ranger at Crystal Mountain, Washington. In the 1960s that the man pulled the lanyard while standing behind the rifle. He was killed instantly.

Control by artillery has certainly carved an indispensible niche in the realm of control programs. It is difficult to see how certain highways could be kept open, or kept safe, without artillery control. In the United States, places like Red Mountain Pass, Colorado; Little Cottonwood Canyon, Utah; Carson Pass, California; and Stevens Pass, Washington, require weapons control. The most intense avalanche problem in North America, though, is along the Trans-Canada Highway in the vicinity of Rogers Pass, B.C. A full-time staff is responsible for forecasting and control, with the control being both passive (closures and a variety of structures) and active (artillery). There is even one gun placement which can be overrun by avalanches; an underground bunker was built for the gun crew to hide in after pulling the lanyard.

Many ski areas, too, find artillery control indispensible. Resorts like Alyeska, Alaska; Alpine Meadows, California; Jackson

Hole, Wyoming; and Alta and Snowbird, Utah, have avalanche-prone areas that are too difficult or dangerous to be controlled by patrollers on skis throwing bombs. Artillery has been a safe and reliable solution. Each year several thousand rounds are fired in the United States, and like hand charges, they get the job done about 99.9 percent of the time.

When problems do occur, it is most often because of an overshoot; that is, firing too high and putting a shell where it doesn't belong. This mistake has probably been made only 15 to 20 times in more than 30 years of artillery control. Once, a gunner at Alpine Meadows hit Lake Tahoe. At Mammoth Mountain, California, a shot once struck the snow at a low angle and skipped like a flat rock on a pond; it flew over the ridge and blew up somewhere in the backcountry. Then there was the time Snowbird shot Alta. The round went over Peruvian Ridge that separates the two areas, went through two corrugated metal walls of a lift house, and exploded on the snow several hundred yards farther on. There was also the time when the Forest Service invited the press to attend a demonstration shoot of an avalanche area outside of Ogden, Utah. The shot missed the ridge and flew into North Ogden, where it blew up a house under construction. You can imagine the press that came out of this!

Finally, there was the incident at Jackson Hole, Wyoming, in 1978. A gun crew was still controlling a closed part of the mountain when they fired over the ridge into an area that had been opened to skiing. The shell landed in a tree well and blew the tree to smithereens — all about a hundred yards from a chairlift loaded with skiers. Knowing that shrapnel is a problem with artillery shells, a patroller stationed himself at the upper lift terminal to check unloading skiers for possible injuries. Before he could question one woman, she excitedly asked him if it was safe to ski here. "Yes ma'am," he answered, "but why do you ask?" "Young man," she replied, "don't you know you have exploding trees at this ski area?"

We wish all incidents could have such endings, but there have been accidents where spectators have become victims. In one famous incident, a movie photographer died when a monstrous avalanche overran him and his camera. It was April 8, 1957, on Berthoud Pass, Colorado. Professional photographer John Hermann, 26, was under contract to Walt Disney to shoot footage of spectacular avalanches, and on this day he set up three cameras in anticipation of a large release. Seven days of storm (which dropped 79 inches of snow) had just ended, and the Colorado Department of Highways was going to shoot the Dam Slide, a path capable of large avalanches but which had not hit the highway since 1933. Hermann was warned not to stand by his camera on the highway, but that's where he was when the shooting began. The third round from the 75mm howitzer released the entire 50-acre starting zone to a depth of 12 feet. The avalanche swooped down on the highway at 100 miles per hour, throwing up a powder cloud hundreds of feet high and flicking 80-foot trees into the air like matchsticks. Hermann ran, but there was no escape; it buried him 16 feet deep. He died, as did a 21-year-old highway employee who was supposed to be stopping traffic well away from the avalanche path but had wound up standing next to Hermann, perhaps for a better view. Two of the three cameras were recovered, and they yielded the most spectacular avalanche scenes ever filmed. Hermann at least accomplished that goal.

We'll relate another story of burial involving people who were where they ought not have been, but this story has a twist. The date was December 30, 1973, and for days Alta and Snowbird, Utah had been under seige from a major storm and avalanches that came roaring off the steep canyon walls. Already, slides at Alta had smashed into buildings and parking lots, causing considerable damage. On the 30th, the Snowbird patrol prepared to shoot an unnamed path, one which had not run in the years that Snowbird had been controlling avalanches. They evacuated the area of possible runout, which included two house trailers serving as employee housing. Then they fired on the avalanche, which came out big — so big in fact that the gun crew and about a hundred spectators fled, fearing that their position would be overrun. That did not happen, but the avalanche did smash into the housing trailers and partly filled them with snow. As patrollers went to inspect the damage, they heard voices coming from inside. A few minutes later, they found themselves speechless when they dug out a young man and woman, both employees. Neither was injured, but also neither wore a stitch of clothing! It seems that privacy had been hard to come by in the cramped quarters, and the evacuation of the trailers had presented a unique opportunity for two lovers to be alone. But what a way to get caught! The path has been christened V's Climax Slide.

Avalauncher

Ever since military weapons were first used for avalanche control, their availability has been tightly restricted — for obvious reasons. At first only military or Forest Service personnel could fire them, but the regulations have been relaxed to include competently trained highway and ski-area personnel. Other problems have slowly become worse: these are, after all, surplus items from World War II, so that the weapons themselves, replacement parts, and ammunition (which are no longer manufactured) are steadily being depleted. All these factors created the need for a commercially available weapon that could be used by personnel at ski areas, highways, and mining operations.

7.5 Avalancher. Compressed air in the cylinder launches the projectile out of the barrel (D. Bachman photo).

The avalauncher, the first weapon designed specifically to throw explosives at avalanches, was invented to fill this need. Essentially a compressed-air mortar, the avalauncher consists of a long barrel attached to a thick cylinder which can be pressurized to lob a two-pound charge to more than a mile away. Manufactured in California, the avalauncher has found wide use in the United States at ski areas, highways, and mines. While it has neither the range nor accuracy of military guns, it is at least available and easy to operate. The design has gone through several revisions, and each new model is an improvement in reliability, accuracy, range, and safety.

The first avalaunchers, developed in the early 1960s, were, to be quite frank, unsafe. Thirteen were in use in the winter of 1962-63, and all performed commendably. But over the next few years, several accidents marred the reputation of the avalauncher. The worst incident happened in Chile, where several soldiers died when their avalauncher blew up. Surely some of the early problems came from poor procedures by the gunners, but there was a design problem. The projectile of the avalauncher would become armed when the compressed gas forced it up the barrel, causing a wire joining the bottom of the barrel to the projectile to separate, which in turn caused the fuse to be activated. (The projectiles of military weapons, by contrast, arm themselves by spinning during their flight, with centrifugal force causing the fuse to become activated.) What can happen, is that a slight gas leak from the cylinder can push a projectile partway up the barrel and activate the fuse. The gunner would have no idea that he had an armed projectile ticking away inside the barrel.

Word of this potential problem quickly made its way to all avalauncher operators. There was one case at Snowmass, Colorado, in the late 1960s when two patrollers were firing a series of rounds at a group of avalanche chutes. There came a point in the operation when one of the men thought he detected the hissing of a gas leak — just after he had loaded a fresh projectile in the chamber. Frantic, he yelled for his partner to help while he struggled to remove the barrel to get at the projectile. After a few seconds he realized he was struggling alone. He looked up to see his partner running for his life across the snow. The first man dove off the platform himself and rolled down an embankment. It all turned out to be a false alarm; there was no problem. But surely a new record was set in the 100-yard dash for running in snow while wearing ski boots.

A recent accident has unfortunately marred an otherwise good safety record over the last 10 to 15 years. On December 22, 1982, four men were killed and six others injured in a devastating explosion at a hydroelectric project in the Sierra of California. A projectile exploded inside the barrel of an avalauncher mounted on a truck, and this detonated an entire box of explosives on the bed of the truck. Total destruction over a large area was the grisly result. The cause? We don't really know, but we do know that the gun crew had modified the projectiles to permit more rapid loading and firing.

POST-CONTROL RELEASE

Explosives (hand charges, artillery, and avalauncher) do the job as intended more than 99.9 percent of the time; that is, the explosive either sets off an avalanche, or it blows a crater in the snow and gives a good indication of stable snow. Still, 99.9 percent is not 100 percent.This means there are those few times when explosives do not get the job done. The result is a *post-control avalanche*, which we will define as an avalanche that releases minutes to hours following explosive control. Data snow that there are bout 20 to 25 post-control avalanches per winter. Some of these have been killers.

The prospect of a post-control release poses an ever-present problem. Suppose you are in charge of the snow safety program at a ski area; you have sent out your control teams in the morning and they have come back with typical results — a few slides released, but most of the bombs went off in the snow without shaking anything loose. You give the all-clear, the lifts start running, and soon skiers are all over the mountain. An hour or so later, a skier enters a steep slope, skis past a bomb crater, and releases an avalanche that tumbles him down the hill. He — and you — have just been victimized by a post-control avalanche.

The causes of these unkind events are not fully understood, but we do have some strong speculations. First, they are more likely to happen on slopes that have not had the benefit of compaction by skier traffic, or slopes with significant depth hoar at the bottom of the snowpack. A program of continued explosive control, followed by as much ski compaction as possible, has been a good solution at many areas. Second, we know that snow in a starting zone can be quite variable, so that a charge placed in a strong area will not release an avalanche, whereas one placed in a weak area will. The solutions to this problem are to know your avalanche paths well so that charges are properly placed, to throw more explosives so that more area is covered, to throw larger explosives, or to suspend charges over the snow to maximize the blase. Third, snow stability can worsen over the course of a day, if snowfall, wind or temperature are acting to increase stress. This problem can be handled by closures for additional control during the day. Fourth, and most troublesome, we suspect that bombs can occasionally make the snow weaker without releasing an avalanche. This could happen when a blast jolts the snow and causes partial cracking, partial slippage on a weak layer, or partial collapse of a depth-hoar layer. (In the vast majority of cases, the cracking is complete enough to cause failure, or it is absorbed by the snowpack without worsening stability.) In these cases, the blast may cause what has been termed a *hangfire avalanche*, one which can release on its own as stress slowly increases to the breaking point, or which releases with the next pass of a skier.

Such is the nature of post-control avalanches. Explosives must not be indicated as the cause, even though we suspect a cause and effect relationship in a very small number of cases. We certainly cannot abandon explosive control, for then we would lose our ability to attack avalanches. We just have to remember that if our attack is not thorough, the avalanche has a way to counterattack — through a post-control release.

The worst post-control avalanches have occurred in ski areas, even though they have also plagued highways, mining operations, and helicopter skiing ventures. The disaster at Alpine Meadows in 1982, which we refer to several times in this book, was a post-control avalanche; the killing slope was fired on with at least a dozen rounds of the 75mm howitzer and recoiless rifle. Bad weather obscured any small slides that may have released. Six hours later the lethal one came down.

In January 1973 near Sun Valley, Idaho, a control team flew by helicopter to a backcountry area to test stability before flying clients to the site for a day of skiing. They threw 14 hand charges and did protective skiing, without releasing a single slide or noting any signs of unstable snow, such as settling or fracturing. Two hours later the slope broke and caught five skiers; one died.

The winter of 1983-84 was a bad one for ski patrollers in Colorado; four of them died in post-control avalanches. On December 18 at Copper Mountain, a control team went to a known avalanche area outside the ski-area boundary that is periodically checked and controlled. Several hand charges produced only potholes. Ski cutting indicated stability, so the patrollers skied down one at a time. The third man triggered a massive slide that swallowed him up. Although his rescuers located him with a rescue beacon in two minutes, he died of internal injuries from the fall.

The second incident was even worse. On March 31 three men of the Aspen Highlands patrol headed off to run a control route in Highlands Bowl, an out-of-bounds area in which they lead guided powder tours. (The tours avoid the open part of the bowl in favor of the relative safety of gladed runs along the edge.) A winter-long program of control and snow pits gave confidence that there was no great danger on this day. The men threw charges from the ridge into the bowl; nothing moved. They then skied past their shot holes and stopped on a small bench. Normally at this point they would throw several bombs with extra-long fuses and retreat to the safety of the trees. Today, though, they felt confident that the snow was stable; they threw two bombs below the bench and waited. The second bomb released a huge avalanche. The fracture broke first below the bench, but seconds later propagated above the men and pulled out the snow that they had bombed and skied 10 minutes earlier. The men were in a hopeless position, caught in the center of an enormous avalanche. None of the three survived.

Avalanche control is hazardous duty. It is a tough, dangerous job that becomes stripped of glory with stories such as these. There is little room for error and no room for overconfidence. We could eliminate post-control releases altogether — if we had enough manpower, weaponry, and money to saturate slopes with explosives or to cover them with supporting structures. But the price paid — monetarily, aesthetically, and environmentally — would be horrendous. No, that is not the answer. We will have to live, and sadly a few of us die, with 99.9 percent success.

7.6 This avalanche killed three ski patrollers at Highlands Bowl, Colorado, on March 31, 1984. The fracture is visible across the middle of the left half of the bowl (D. Driskell photo)

Ketchum, Idaho, real estate sign noting that the property is in an avalanche zone. Note the construction of the house on the right; the uphill side is designed to allow avalanche debris to flow up and over the home (Douglas N. Greene photo)

8 AVALANCHES AND THE LAW

RECOGNITION AND ACTION

FOR CENTURIES IN THE SWISS ALPS, farmers and villagers cleared or overcut the forests on the steep slopes above the valley floors. They used the trees for building materials, the cleared areas for grazing and farming. What resulted was a sharp decrease in the forest cover and a drop in the elevation of the treeline in the mountain regions. A concurrent result was an increase in mud slides, landslides, and snow avalanches. As time went on, avalanches more and more frequently devastated what was left of the forests, and endangered houses, barns, and occasionally entire communities. This deforestation is well-documented in the historical record, as is the response: the beginnings of recognition and action to control destructive avalanches. Hans Frutiger, engineer and avalanche authority with the Swiss Federal Institute for Snow and Avalanche Research in Davos, Switzerland, is well-known for his work in avalanche protection, both in designing protective structures and developing avalanche-hazard mapping and zoning techniques. His writings on Switzerland's land-use history and policies form the basis for this chapter. Frutiger found several references in the historical record which noted an increase in deforestation in Switzerland from the 17th to the 19th centuries, accompanied by increased numbers of avalanche accidents. In the Valais region of Switzerland, where the Valasians were rapidly removing the trees from the slopes, the local officials responded legally by issuing interdicts which prohibited tree cutting above inhabited areas. The Valaisans who settled this area were responsible for major decimation of the forests; as Frutiger notes, "it is not an accident that valleys settled by Valaisans

The welfare of the people is the chief law.
—CICERO

frequently have the reputation of being avalanche valleys."

Switzerland adopted its first federal constitution in 1848 but not until 1872, when Johann Coaz, a pioneer in the field of avalanche protection, drew up the first maps of avalanche areas, did the federal government begin its efforts to protect the public from natural disaster. This was at the request of the forestry inspectorate of the Canton of Graubuenden, which commissioned its chief foresters to collect avalanche statistics from the cantons. These statistics became Europe's first avalanche cadastre, or written record, of where and how often avalanches occurred. The office of the Swiss Federal Forest Inspectorate was created in 1874, with Coaz as chief forest inspector. Two years later, the Swiss government enacted its first forest protection legislation designed to preserve forests which protected inhabited areas and to reforest those areas which had been thinned by humans, grazing animals, and avalanches.

In 1910 Chief Forest Inspector Coaz published *Statistics and Structural Control of Avalanches in the Swiss Alps*, a document which contained maps of forest cover and avalanche paths in Switzerland on a scale of 1:100,000. Unfortunately, the systematic collection of avalanche statistics was not continued after that and no copy of the original publication containing the maps exists. Not until after the disastrous avalanche winter of 1950-51, was the idea of creating a comprehensive survey of avalanche occurrence reborn. During January 1951, avalanches in the Swiss Alps injured 234 people, killed 98 people and 884 animals, and destroyed 187 houses, 1,302 outbuildings, and thousands of acres of forest. By this time, the European Alpine countries were seeing major population increases in avalanche-prone valleys, due to tourism and the increasing popularity of winter recreation.

In the United States, mountain dwellers of the western states were also forced to recognize the avalanche hazard and to consider legal measures to protect themselves and their property. In Colorado's high country, mining was reaching its peak in the late 19th century, as was the population in the towns and the surrounding high-elevation mines and mills. In the 1880s, avalanches were taking their toll, and a few far-sighted individuals thought something should be done.

The mayor of Animas Forks up the Animas River drainage from Silverton, Colorado was quoted in the Lake City *Mining Register* in 1881, saying he "deplored the fact that the timber south of us is being so rapidly destroyed as to endanger our town

8.1 This example of massive deforestation, in Colorado's Red Mountain mining district in the 1880s (San Juan Mountains) is most probably the result of human cutting for mining and building purposes. The bare slopes did allow avalanches from the slopes above treeline to travel long distances and damage the mine buildings in the valley (Colorado State Historical Society photo)

from sliding snows." The mayor was right: the deforestation of the steep slopes above the little settlement allowed avalanches to come right into town. In March of 1884, "one slide came down Wood Mountain, 200 yards from town, filled the Animas Canyon with snow and continued running until it struck the shaft-house of the Columbus Mine" (from the Animas Forks *Pioneer* of March 8, 1884). That same winter an even larger avalanche ripped off Cinnamon Mountain above Animas Forks, and "after crossing the Animas River near the Eclipse smelter, ran up the other mountain and then folded over and fell back like an immense wave" (the *Pioneer*, March 15, 1884). Also that March, an avalanche struck the Sampson Mine buildings. Two men were inside; only one survived. The *LaPlata Miner* (March 15) in Silverton reported:

. . . a terrible snowslide . . . started near the top of Bonita Mountain and, in its downward course, struck the buildings belonging to the Sampson, completely demolishing them, as well as the extensive plant of machinery recently put up by the company to treat the product of the mine. The works consisted of smelters, mill concentrator, tramway and boarding house and stable. These works were entirely new, having been

completed last December, at a total cost of over $70,000.

It appears . . . that the works could have hardly been established in a more dangerous locality, to the destruction of property and life, and presents a phase of ignorance on the part of those locating the buildings, which charity alone prevents us from characterizing as criminal. The location of these works in the path of snowslides against the advice of experienced men conversant with the country was at the time regarded as an act of folly.

The mine was equipped with the most costly and complete plant of machinery ever placed on property in San Juan, and the destruction of life and property thro' careless location, should be obviated hereafter by the employment of men familiar with the country, and whose experience should point the way to proper location.

This is a long-winded way of saying that expert advice should be sought when locating structures in potential avalanche terrain — an idea which was revolutionary in the rough-and-tough mining days of the American west and which is still being fought by modern-day pioneers, as we shall soon see.

More avalanche destruction in the 1886-87 winter prompted more editorials. When avalanches struck the Highland Mary Mine in January, crushing all the buildings and "sweeping them in the form of kindling far from their original site," many were surprised. The buildings had been standing for at least 13 years and were considered to be in an absolutely safe location. "This goes to show that nowhere in the deep gulches of the San Juan can safety be relied on. The fact that a snowslide has never been known to occur in a particular locality is no guarantee of safety whatever," wrote the Silverton *Democrat* on January 29, 1887. The accident at the Highland Mary probably prompted this January 27th editorial in Silverton's second newspaper, the *San Juan* :

Again, buildings should not be put up where there is . . . danger of slides, and we believe that the Colorado Legislature should pass a law making it a penal offense for mining superintendents who have buildings put up in dangerous places or where there is the possibility of a slide sweeping them away. Until such a law is passed, there will be lots of chances taken in the erection of buildings.

This was one of the earliest public calls for a government body to enact some form of avalanche hazard legislation.

In Telluride, over the ridge from Silverton, the *Journal* editor observed on January 27, 1904, that the situation was ripe for a disaster. Referring to the 1886 Sheridan Mine disaster, when avalanches caught 21 people, killing four and destroying buildings:

At present there isn't enough snow in that locality to cover the ground and in recent years all kinds of traffic into and out of the basin goes forward daily throughout the winter the same as in the summer. Today thousands of men are employed in the hills where then there was a hundred. Were we to have the great snow falls characteristic of the early years, with the heavy winds, timber removed and men and animals going back and forth constantly over the roads and trails, the death list from snow slides would be appalling.

After a disastrous 1905-1906 winter in the San Juans, with dozens of fatalities and thousands of dollars' worth of property demolished by avalanches, the editor of the Silverton *Standard*, the conscience of the high country, proposed a full scale zoning plan for the area. The editorial, entitled "Snowslide Commission," appeared in the April 7, 1906 edition and proposed the enactment of a state law which would establish a commission with the power to protect lives and property from avalanches.

Upon such a commission should the power be bestowed to decide whether sites for such buildings are safe or unsafe, and their licenses issued accordingly . . . Had a commission composed of practical mining men been consulted the Green Mountain mill would not have been built where it now is and one life and much financially been saved. Had there been inspectors to watch the safety of the working miners perhaps the men would have been called away from the Shenandoah mine before the avalanche swept them to their death. Invested with police powers a commission like this would be a force for good, when great snowfalls load the mountainsides with their freightage of death and devastation.

But these duties would be but incidental to the true object of the commission . . . There are certain defined places where snowslides run. Statistics, old and new, should be gathered in order that the danger may be known and avoided . . . It is said conditions change and that slides came down last month where never before. The more reason that an official record should be kept of them, for memory is treacherous.

The Green Mountain Mill mentioned above had just been completed a few weeks before a large avalanche destroyed the assay office, engine room, and a major portion of the aerial tramway. The next day, another avalanche finished the job, destroying the boarding house, with damages totaling between $50,000 and $75,000. The Shenandoah Mine disaster, described in Chapter 2, claimed twelve lives when an avalanche destroyed their boarding house.

This editorial was quite revolutionary for the times since it proposed three different types of protective controls: the power to issue or withhold building permits or licenses based on the location of the building, the gathering of statistics on avalanche location and frequency, and the actual forecasting of avalanche events so that buildings could be evacuated. Eventually, all of these goals would be met — but not for more than half a century.

We wonder if some of these ideas might have been acted upon had Colorado's mining boom continued. But, as we discussed in Chapter 2, it did not, and the mines gradually closed, as miners and their families left the area, leaving only small settlements and scattered mining operations. The populations throughout Colorado's mining areas were drastically reduced, and avalanche threat to life and property concurrently decreased. The issue of avalanche protection slipped into temporary oblivion as economic survival became the dominant concern.

CHANGE AND TRANSITION

Not until the 1950s, both in North America and, as we've seen, in Europe as well, was there a resurgence of concern for avalanche dangers. The post-World War II period was one of change and transition. In the European Alps, land prices began a rapid spiral of increasing value as farming activity decreased and tourism increased. Land speculation caused Alpine land values to rise 20 to 50 times faster than pre-war prices as the unoccupied farm land became potential building sites for the expanding tourist resorts. Before long, however, the factors of increasing mountain development and the changing makeup of the population brought serious consequences. In the Alpine countries, the loss of the long-time farmers and villagers often meant an end to the passing down of knowledge and local lore. For centuries, villagers had been forced to cope with the natural hazards of their environment. Knowledge of where the avalanche runs were, how often and how far the moving snow traveled out on the valley floor, and what kind of a storm produced destructive avalanches — this kind of oral history was passed on from generation to generation. Houses and barns were squeezed together in the safe areas between avalanche paths. In some avalanche-prone valleys, such as the Lötchenthal in Switzerland, houses were built over the barns to consolidate space in the safe areas. This collective knowledge preserved a majority of the villagers for centuries. But the new residents, or part-time residents, knew little, sometimes nothing, about their new surroundings. They didn't know, for example, that their vacation chalet might be situated in an area that the former owner, the farmer, had left undeveloped because avalanches occasionally swept across the valley to that point.

Conflicts were inevitable between the property owners, who wanted to build, and the public officials, whose responsibility it was to provide for public welfare and for the safety of the inhabitants of the "commune" or community. The winter of 1950-51 brought these conflicts to a head, when the European Alps experienced two periods of catastrophic avalanches, the worst in more than a century. We listed the Swiss accident tolls from the January avalanche cycle on page 169 of this chapter. In the entire Alpine region, this winter killed 279 people, injuring 285; avalanches also killed 1,400 head of domestic livestock, destroyed or damaged 2,500 buildings and ripped out 15,000 acres of trees, according to Colin Fraser.

With public attention stirred, the time was ripe for the Swiss government to resume collecting avalanche statistics and consider legal methods to decrease avalanche danger. In 1952 the federal government enacted guidelines which called for setting up avalanche surveys and avalanche zone plans, and giving to the cantons and communes the responsibility for establishing them. (A canton is the Swiss equivalent to a state in the United States.) The purpose was first to identify dangerous areas (the avalanche survey or cadestre) and then to provide maps of the danger zones. These maps would be incorporated into a regional plan to prevent further development and construction in those areas. But Hans Frutiger, who has chronicled the history of Swiss avalanche mapping and zoning, reports that many of the cantons ignored the guidelines, arguing that avalanche zoning was the responsibility of the federal government. A second appeal to the cantons from the federal government in 1959 repeated the fact that "the production of avalanche zoning plans and cadastral surveys is essential if in the future the loss of life and property is to be prevented." The federal government stated that it could not subsidize resettlement or expensive avalanche protection structures when "the choice of the construction site was made without consideration of the avalanche zoning plan, or, where none exists, the warnings of those familiar with the area were disregarded." The avalanche disasters in 1951 and again in 1954 (when 33 people were killed and 63 houses destroyed) had been quickly forgotten, and construction again resumed "with irresponsible negligence" in areas threatened by avalanches. It took the avalanche catastrophe of 1968 to stir public opinion and provoke action both on the federal and the cantonal level.

Avalanches in January — more than 400 of them — injured 106 people; killed 37 people and 23 animals; destroyed 23 houses and 307 buildings.

Decisions by the Swiss Supreme Court gave the cantons ultimate responsibility for restricting the rights of private property owners, as provided for by cantonal law. What if the land had been zoned in an avalanche area and now the canton denied permission to build? Would the property owner be compensated? The highest court ruled that compensation would be awarded to property owners only when their land had been classified in the past as a building site. From now on, if the site was one visited by avalanches on a regular basis, the land would generally not be classified a building site. This clarified the responsibilities of both the Confederation, or federal government, and the cantonal governments. The cantons had the prime responsibility for enacting and enforcing avalanche zoning laws.

Frutiger describes two different Swiss Supreme Court decisions on similar cases — good examples of how the individual cantons must enact their own laws and define their zoning explicitly. Two communes were trying to halt construction in skiing terrain. The commune in Berne received a favorable decision from the court and was able to keep the terrain free of construction. The commune won its case because the cantonal building code was strongly written to allow zoning in skiing terrain. The commune from the canton of Vaud lost its case because the canton's building code was not strong enough to support the right to keep land free for the purpose of skiing, since skiing terrain was not expressly mentioned in the code.

Although the cantons had the authority to enact zoning laws which included avalanche zoning, few actually did so. In 1969, the Swiss Institute for Local, Regional and National Land-Use Planning surveyed the cantons to inventory building and zoning codes. Of twelve Alpine cantons, only 25 percent had enacted zoning codes. Another federal act passed in 1969 redefined the constitutional basis for land-use planning. and in the early 1970s, several additional Alpine cantons enacted new building and zoning laws. These Swiss avalanche zoning laws, and the court and administrative decisions which refine the laws whenever specific regulations do not exist, have set the legal standard for avalanche zoning. The most significant fact to be noted from this bit of legal history is that the Swiss government has established that the communes do have the authority, and responsibility, to prevent construction in avalanche areas. In areas where specific avalanche zoning does not exist, where a detailed avalanche map was not adopted by the canton, the general police powers are sufficient enough to deny construction permits.

The Swiss define an avalanche hazard map as a large-scale topographic map which shows avalanche areas. Three levels of hazard are usually noted: white for no hazard, blue for moderate hazard, and red for high hazard. The map is used by the communal authority as an advisory tool for planning. When the commune enacts a land-use plan which addresses avalanche hazard specifically, then the map becomes part of the avalanche zone plan. The map is used to determine which areas are endangered by avalanches, and the commune has the authority to limit property rights in these areas. Thus, avalanche zoning, as defined in Switzerland, means "preventing an improper use of land" which prevents building in avalanche-prone terrain. Another significant point is that building permits can be denied if the building site itself is safe from avalanches but the only access is through avalanche terrain. Thus, safe access is required.

A final point regarding Swiss avalanche zoning: the unsuspecting land buyer is protected from the unscrupulous land developer. In the 1970s, Swiss courts decided three separate cases in favor of the land purchaser in circumstances when the buyer had purchased property situated in avalanche terrain without knowing about the avalanche hazard and without knowing that he would not obtain a building permit because of the hazard. In all three cases, the buyers contested the contract and the sellers were required to pay back the full purchase price and take back the land. Swiss law states that the seller can be charged with committing intentional fraud if he knows about a hazard but does not inform the buyer.

Planning is not always as effective or as thorough as is expected, as we shall see from this next example from Hans Frutiger. A new ski area was in the planning stages in the early 1970s, and an authorized planning commission provided expert opinions on skiing and the required protective measures against avalanches on the ski runs. Operations began in the winter of 1974-75, with the opening of the access road, the access chair, lift and three ski-area lifts. The first seasonal residents were already occupying their newly built vacation homes when the heavy snowfall of April 1975 caused a major avalanche. The avalanche destroyed three unoccupied vacation homes, tore out a chairlift, and destroyed a barn which had been remodeled into a vacation home and was occupied by seven vacationers. Five were killed and the two survivors were injured.

The avalanche traveled into terrain which had been planned for use as residential space and as the central shopping area for the ski area. Public officials responded to this disaster in a strange fashion, stating, "In fact no one could have foretold that an avalanche could penetrate into this area where the house stood and where at no time in human memory had such an event been noted." A local newspaper stated, "Farmers often speak of 'Fate.' This avalanche should simply never have occurred, at least not with such magnitude."

However, the public officials and the newspapers had not done their homework. Avalanche experts found it quite simple to reconstruct the history of avalanche activity in this area. They learned that this particular avalanche had run in December 1961, just 14 years earlier, and had run even farther in 1961 than it had in 1975! The experts also found a reference from the year 1925 that this same avalanche had reached an area where one of the resort buildings was to be constructed. In this situation, the planners had not recognized, whether out of ignorance or haste, the enormity of the avalanche hazard — a tragic oversight which ultimately cost lives and property damage.

A 1979 meeting of the International Glaciological Society, featuring the theme "Snow in Motion," brought together snow scientists from around the world, who presented their research findings. Results were published in the *Journal of Glaciology* and are excerpted here to describe how other countries are contending with avalanches as a land-use issue. L. DeCrècy of the Snow Division of Grenoble's Center for Technology described the French approach. Zoning is the obligation of the state, and zoning plans define the hazard areas before building permits are issued. Like the Swiss, the French plans differentiate between three hazard zones, with white zones denoting areas of no danger, red zones denoting dangerous areas with no construction allowed, and blue zones signaling that avalanches are "doubtful." Blue zones are the most difficult to define and expert opinion must be sought to determine just how far an avalanche will travel. The blue zone includes infrequent avalanches which have a return period of 300 years or more, and also more frequent avalanches, with return periods of 30 to 50 years but which involve less snow and travel a shorter distance. The French zoning plans call for additional safety measures in blue zones when construction has been permitted: architectural means to reinforce the structure; construction and maintenance of protective structures on the steep slopes above the buildings, and an evacuation plan.

E. Hestnes and K. Lied report that in Norway, narrow valleys and steep mountainsides and cliffs are common terrain, and avalanches are also common. Almost 1,500 people have died in natural hazards accidents in Norway from 1871 to 1970, with 55 percent of the fatalities from the snow avalanche, slush avalanche, and the blasts of air which precede and are generated by snow avalanches. Avalanche zoning is a necessity, and avalanche hazard mapping has been ongoing since the early 1980s.

In the picturesque province of British Columbia in western Canada, 80 percent of the terrain is mountainous. The climate produces average annual snowfalls of 275 to almost 800 inches, and the population is growing, the developers are active — and the avalanche threat is a constant.

The present legal basis for avalanche zoning in British Columbia is an avalanche management program within the Snow Avalanche Section of the British Columbia Ministry of Transportation, Communications, and Highways. The Snow Avalanche Section conducts hazard studies for zoning purposes on behalf of the other provincial agencies involved in land-use zoning. Ninety percent of British Columbia land is publicly owned. Control and prohibition of development is relatively simple in cases involving public land. In more complicated situations involving private land development, a section of the Land Registry Act of 1961 allows the approving officer, who reviews a development plan, to refuse approval of the plan if it is subject to flooding, erosion, or land slips, or is against the public interest. The British Columbia Supreme Court has upheld this section in a natural hazards case involving rockslides. In 1979 the Land Titles Act was enacted, which included avalanches in the list of natural hazards, thus making clear the province's role in avalanche hazard zoning.

The British Columbia plan involves developing an avalanche cadastral survey similar to the Swiss plan, to identify the sites of avalanche potential. Because of the magnitude of the avalanche problem in the province, the Avalanche Section undertakes detailed studies only after the Provincial Government, Regional District, municipality, or another agency refers to them an application for development. For detailed studies, the Avalanche

Section uses the concept of the avalanche hazard line to define the boundary of large infrequent avalanches. The line corresponds to the Swiss avalanche zoning system's boundary between the white zone and the blue zone. The avalanche hazard line represents the maximum distance, and then some, that a big avalanche can "reasonably" be expected to travel.

Most modern zoning plans, European or North American, generally follow similar formats. Information on avalanche path location, how often it has been observed to run (frequency), how far it has run (the maximum run-out distance) is collected in an ongoing data survey. Avalanche areas are marked on small-scale maps, anywhere from 1:24,000 scale up to 1:250, 000 scale for the larger areas. When a developer or property owner decides to build, the local licensing organization will review the application based on existing information — maps, data and regulations. If an actual avalanche zoning law is in effect, the local government has usually adopted avalanche maps. These are either small scale for consultation purposes, or large scale — usually 1:5,000 or 1:10,000 scale — for pinpointing exact locations. On the large-scale maps, avalanche areas are often divided into the three hazard zones which originated with the Swiss: white, blue, and red. In the red, or high-hazard zone, construction is usually not permitted. In the blue zone of moderate hazard, building is permitted according to specific criteria designed to make the building withstand the impact forces of an avalanche. The white zone is considered generally safe. Depending on the scale of the maps available to the governing body and on the proposed location of the building site, the agency in charge of issuing permits decides can deny the building permit request, require additional studies, or grant the request, occasionally with detailed stipulations.

AVALANCHE HAZARD ZONING POLICIES IN THE UNITED STATES

The ski resort of Vail, a community built from scratch in 1962 from pasture land in Colorado's high country, presents a good example of municipal control and planning. Ranching was the only industry of the sparsely settled area until the skiers came. Although avalanche paths are obvious along the slopes of the Gore Creek Valleys, no historical record of avalanche activity or frequency existed when the town was developed. When the town expanded eastward in 1975, the city fathers found themselves confronting several major and many minor avalanche paths whose run-out zones extended into privately owned property. Not unprepared, the Eagle County government and the town of

Vail had, in the early 1970s, authorized several avalanche studies. These studies formed the basis for establishing avalanche-hazard zones as part of Vail's comprehensive land-use plan. Avalanche experts, utilizing their recent work plus the earlier studies, identified zones of avalanche influence — areas where avalanches may present a hazard — and mapped these zones on large-scale maps.

Vail's avalanche zoning plan works this way. The property owner applies for a building permit. The local government checks to see if the property lies within a zone of avalanche influence. If it does, then it is the responsibility of the property owner to produce, at his own expense, a detailed study which specifies zones of high hazard (red) and moderate hazard (blue), based on quantitative techniques for determining both avalanche impact forces and avalanche return periods. Thus, the responsibility for proving that a safe building can be erected in the zone of avalanche influence apparently belongs to the property owner or his consultant rather than to the town of Vail. To date, this burden of responsibility has not been tested in the courts.

A second example of U.S. avalanche zoning policies takes us north to Alaska, to the capital city of Juneau. Juneau sits on a narrow sliver of flat land, facing the Gastineau Channel on one side, and butting up against huge Mount Juneau on the other. Several large avalanche paths from Mount Juneau have a history of sending avalanches into the city. In November 1936, an avalanche of snow and rocks slammed into the southern end of downtown Juneau, killing 14 people and injuring nine, and burying a boarding house and two homes in the subdivision of Gastineau Heights. The Behrends Avenue avalanche was named for its habit of releasing from Mount Juneau and running right down Behrends Avenue, occasionally reaching tidewater. Since 1890, hundreds of avalanches have traveled down this path; six were large enough to reach that portion of Juneau which is presently developed with 40 homes, a motel, a highway, and hundreds of boats moored at the Aurora Basin harbor.

Detailed studies of Juneau's avalanche potential began in 1967, when Keith Hart, then Juneau's planner, wrote a report on the Behrends Avenue avalanche path. In 1972 a comprehensive geophysical hazards investigation, incorporating Hart's report, was given to the city. The city's avalanche zones were divided into areas of high, potential, and no hazard, similar to the Swiss system. Several additional studies in the 1970s pointed out that dozens of homes were currently in dangerous locations. The study further recommended that no new development be permitted in known avalanche areas, and that high hazard zones be cleared of structures, and the people relocated elsewhere. The recommendations remain only that — recommendations — since the elected officials have yet to act on a comprehensive avalanche zoning ordinance. In 1973 the city did adopt regulations which allow the planning commission to turn down the development of entire new subdivisions in known avalanche areas. However, no restrictions exist to prevent residents from building new individual homes in hazardous locations. In the late 1970s Juneau's municipal assembly overruled a move by the city building director to prevent new home construction in the already existing White subdivision — an avalanche hazard area near the Behrends Avenue avalanche area — and construction continued.

At 5 a.m., March 22, 1962, a huge avalanche tundered down the Behrends Avenue avalanche path, finally losing steam by the time it reached the Gastineau Channel — but not before it had blown chimneys more than 135 feet through the air, snapped utility poles, removed roofs, collapsed walls, broken windows, and physically relocated two dozen homes. Another avalanche followed the same course in February 1985, bringing hundreds of tons of heavy, wet snow into the city. After snapping trees and a power pole, the avalanche came to rest just above the neighborhood of single-family homes. Jim and Leslie Dumont had lived in the Behrends Avenue neighborhood for nine years and had put an addition on their house. Their two young children walk to school, which is close. The February 1985 avalanche stopped in their back yard. Interviewed in the Anchorage *Daily News* of March 4, 1985, Jim Dumont said, "I'm just glad it stopped. This really was the one house that was in the direct path."

A friend of the Dumonts had been interested in purchasing the lot directly above theirs, but changed his mind after the February avalanche. The Dumonts were concerned and they knew they were lucky, but they have stayed put. And they have no plans to take out avalanche insurance. In 1982 Jim summed up their philosophy to a National Geographic writer this *way:* "If it comes down and does a little bit of damage, we could eventually replace that. If it comes down and wipes us out, then it will be too late to worry." In the 1985 Anchorage *Daily News* interview, he said he has not changed his mind today, noting that he "weighs the positive aspects of this location and the hazards, and

8.2 Mrs. Dorothy Tow's home in the White Subdivision in Anchorage, Alaska. Avalanche debris from the Behrends Avenue avalanche surrounded and partially buried her house in 1985 (D. Fesler photo)

the location wins every time." Winter must bring many nervous moments to the Dumonts.

A second February 1985 avalanche from Mount Juneau came crashing into the White subdivision, and surrounded Dorothy Tow's home on Wickersham Avenue with very heavy, wet snow (Figure 8.2). Although there was no damage, the family was trapped in the house for several hours. Mrs. Tow had built the house in 1984 and when she applied to the municipality of Juneau for a building permit, she was not told that her building site was within the runout zone of the avalanche. Nor was she informed of the danger by the former landowner or by the builder. At 5:30 a.m. on March 18, just four weeks later, another avalanche came down Mount Juneau, trapping Mrs. Tow inside her house with a 16-foot wall of snow. Mrs. Tow reported to the Juneau *Empire*, "The snow was so deep I couldn't see out the first story windows. The door burst open and snowballs started rolling in." A third avalanche the same winter came within 30 feet of her house.

We'll conclude our discussion of the Juneau avalanche hazard issue with a comment from the city land manager, Steve Gilbertson. Commenting in the Anchorage *Daily News*, in response to the assembly's refusal to prevent construction in avalanche hazard areas, Gilbertson said, "I think the feeling on the assembly was that people should have control over their destiny, and if they wanted to live there they could."

It seems that the city of Anchorage, Alaska, shares similar

sentiments. The Anchorage Assembly in May 1985, voted down a proposal to establish avalanche hazard zones in the municipality — which would have affected potential development in the Eagle River Valley and Girdwood areas. The law would have identified potentially dangerous avalanche areas (based on maps assembled by avalanche experts) required landowners to notify prospective buyers or lessors of the hazard; restricted development in the zones; and imposed strict building standards for structures in the areas. A final vote of seven to two killed the matter.

An editorial in the Anchorage *Daily News* (March 4, 1985) suggested that the assembly's vote against avalanche zoning showed too much concern with property values to prohibit development in high risk areas, and not enough concern for public safety to purchase the rights of development.

But you'd think local officials charged with protecting public safety would be willing to at least require disclosure of the hazards as a truth-in-marketing measure . . . to at least mitigate the risks at new subdivisions. But no, the assembly wouldn't even do that . . . Maybe they think protecting real estate values is more important than protecting lives and property. Maybe they don't think government should get involved . . . But it will, someday, under far more pressing circumstances. Some day one of those high-risk areas on the experts' avalanche risk maps will prove why it earned the designation. Then government will send rescuers and public safety officials to render aid. And once lives or property have been lost, people will want to know why on earth the biggest city in Alaska has no serious, established controls to mitigate avalanche dangers in a place where snow, mountains and avalanches are as common as the change of the seasons.

Exactly one year before, in May 1984, a good-sized avalanche released in one of the three starting zones of what is called the Three Bowl Slide, north of Anchorage, so named for the multiple areas where avalanches can start. This particular avalanche traveled down the main gully, knocking over trees as it went, and stopped just short of Hiland Road in the Eagle River area. The moving snow also stopped just 150 feet short of a new home currently under construction. Local avalanche expert Jill Fredston, snow specialist and avalanche forecaster with the University of Alaska's Avalanche Forecast Center, noted that this particular avalanche path runs fairly frequently. The last recorded event was in 1974, when an avalanche did cross the road. Fredston noted that another new home under construction below the Hiland Road also "has a definite chance of being wiped out. It could have been reduced to splinters." On the already existing maps, these houses are situated just outside the high-hazard "red" zone, and within the moderate hazard "blue" zone.

Current avalanche hazard zoning in Europe and North America can claim many successes and some failures. Dozens of municipalities have incorporated avalanche hazard into their land-use planning codes. Much of the early impetus came in the decade of the 1970s. In Colorado in 1974 the state legislature spurred the individual counties to action by passing House Bill 1041. This bill required the counties to consider assessment of natural hazards as a factor in land-use decision-making. As a result of this legislation and financial support from the state, most mountainous counties in Colorado presently have some type of natural hazards plan, and a specific avalanche hazard section, in their land-use plans.

To date, very few of the enacted laws and ordinances have been tested in court. The rest of this chapter will discuss the few cases of avalanche litigation which have made it through the legal system, and their implications.

RESPONSIBILITY AND LIABILITY

What happens when an avalanche destroys property or takes a human life? Who is responsible? An avalanche caused by a snowmobiler or cross-country skier in the backcountry, far away from developed ski areas or towns, is almost always considered an accident, and is most often blamed on errors in judgment on the part of the recreationist, or just bad luck. But what about the structure which is destroyed, or the alpine skier in or near a developed ski area who is caught, injured or killed by avalanche? Whose responsibility is it to restrict mountain construction in potential avalanche danger areas? Philosophies differ, obviously, as we have seen from the contrasting examples of Vail, which is pro-planning and zoning, and Juneau, which is not. One philosophy allows the individual to make the decisions which might endanger his property or his life, the other removes the individual responsibility, assigning responsibility to a larger body such as a municipal law or government restrictions. In Chapter 5 we discussed the concept of individual risk: what is an acceptable risk for one individual might be unacceptable to another. One daring or fearless individual might ski down avalanche paths or choose to build in avalanche runout zones, but in terms of responsibility, it is the concept of public safety which justifies many of the restrictions and ordinances currently in effect.

Say, for example, that the Snowflake family wants to build their dream vacation home in Avalanche Valley. Their building site is located on a grassy, gentle slope which also happens to be the runout area of a large but infrequently running avalanche. The family plans to occupy their home only during the summer months. When the local government informs the family that their building site is potentially dangerous, the Snowflakes counter with the argument that they could rebuild the house in the unlikely chance that an avalanche would damage it, but they wouldn't be hurt since they would never be there in avalanche season. All sorts of different scenarios arise from this situation. If the local government had previously enacted an avalanche zone plan, it would have the power to deny the Snowflake family a building permit, or to at least require more detailed studies of the site before they decided to issue a permit. But if no avalanche zoning plan was in effect, the family could go ahead and build their vacation home. Let's say they do. After a few years, the Snowflakes decide that mountain living is not for them and instead buy a condominium in the Bahamas. They then sell their summer house to Mr. and Mrs. Unsuspecting from Iowa, who have always wanted to live year-round in the mountains. The disaster scenario begins to unfold . . .

A major storm is under way, with howling winds and unabated heavy snowfall. Mr. Unsuspecting gets a pain in his stomach and calls the town's emergency service telephone, requesting an ambulance. The local emergency medical technicians, who are familiar with the Unsuspecting's location, refuse to respond to the call, saying that it is too dangerous: the access road and the house itself could all be hit by avalanches. But should they go? A variation on this scenario: the inevitable occurs, and a major avalanche crushes a portion of the house. The Unsuspectings are able to use the telephone and call for help. The rescue group ponders their responsibility: should they risk their lives by venturing out in the storm to aid these people while the house is still threatened by additional avalanching, and while the access road is also dangerous?

Who is responsible for informing the property owners of the risk they undertake, knowingly or unknowingly, when they build or move into a house in a potentially dangerous location? Is it the municipality, the original property owner, the builder? And who is ultimately responsible for any ensuing injury, death, or property damage? Because few cases of avalanche litigation have been tried and appealed through the courts, most of these questions cannot be answered. But as more and more people venture into the mountains for recreation or to live or vacation, and as avalanche litigation develops its own data base, responsibility will eventually be determined.

Most cases involving avalanches have been settled out of court. Of the few that actually go to trial, only the cases that are appealed can be used as precedent in other cases. The appellate court decision is, then, one which becomes a binding precedent in cases appearing within the same state, while in other states, the decision can be used as "persuasive argument" but is not necessarily binding. We thank Dr. Sue Ferguson, publisher of the monthly journal *The Avalanche Review*, and head of the Utah Avalanche Forecast Center, and Mr. James L. Kennedy, Jr., attorney-at-law in Ketchum, Idaho, and an expert in avalanche zoning and natural hazards analysis, for compiling much of the following information on one of the two avalanche cases within the United States which has reached the appellate court level of our judicial system. This is the Yodelin, Washington, case. (The other case involved a skier near a developed ski area, and has no bearing on zoning or planning.)

In 1966 Skip Vorheese, of Resort Counseling Associates, hired Ed LaChapelle, avalanche expert and then associate professor of geophysics at the University of Washington and director of the U.S. Forest Service Avalanche Study Center at Alta, Utah, to conduct a feasibility study for developing property owned by Robinson Plywood and Timber Company in the Stevens Pass area of Washington's Cascade Mountains. LaChapelle's report warned against any construction in what was called the Yodelin area because of avalanche danger.

Robinson Plywood and Timber Company sold the property to Wendell Carlson of Nason Properties. Mr. Robinson claimed he sold the Voorhees-LaChapelle study separately to the new owner. (A former partner of the new owner said later that he had never heard of the study). Construction began, with a ski area built on one side of the east-west highway and vacation homes on the other side.

During the summer of 1968, LaChapelle drove past the area and noticed that houses stood within the avalanche areas he had identified two years earlier. Taking the initiative, he called the State Real Estate Division (of the Washington State Department of Motor Vehicles) to express his concern that houses had been built in potentially hazardous terrain. Because LaChapelle did not own the report he had previously put together, he compiled a new report based on observations of actual avalanche events on the slopes above the development — avalanche hazard maps and eyewitness reports from snow rangers and others familiar with the area. LaChapelle sent this new report to the Real Estate Division in the state capitol in Olympia.

The State Real Estate Division felt compelled to send a letter to MacPherson's Inc., the real estate agency for Nason Properties, warning them that an avalanche problem existed and that they should do something about it. The letter from the state prompted owner Carlson to threaten legal action against the state, claiming damages against Nason Properties. The State Attorney General's office advised Carlson to drop the matter, since he would have to defend himself personally, paying all court costs. The matter was dropped. The real estate agency cautioned its agents to "make no claim about avalanche safety and in fact to state that a thorough study of the situation was being conducted."

In spring of 1970 a small avalanche pushed its way into the kitchen of one of the cabins owned by Barton Edgers. Early the next winter, another small avalanche struck the cabin. Edgers ran a cable from the main floor and attached it to a large rock behind the cabin, hoping this would keep the cabin on its foundation. He also boarded up the back windows and door during the winter months. (In his 1975 book, *The Snowy Torrents*, Knox Williams described this response as a "classic underestimation of the destructive forces involved.")

On January 24, 1971, 16 people were vacationing in two cabins in the Yodelin area — one was Barton Edgers' cabin, the other was owned by Milo Stoen. Both cabins sat at the foot of the steep mountainside. A major storm, accompanied by howling winds, caused the slope above the cabins to avalanche just after midnight, killing four, injuring four others, burying 13, with three others caught but not buried. Seven cabins were damaged, but, fortunately, only these two cabins were occupied. More than half a dozen law suits ensued in the legal battle which followed. Sue Ferguson, with the help of attorney Jim Kennedy, presented the story in the February 1985 issue of *The Avalanche Review*. It is her description we use here. In 1975 the residents of the Yodelin development sued the State of Washington (specifically, the Department of Motor Vehicles, Real Estate Division), MacPherson's Realty, and Nason Properties to recover for the loss of life and property caused by the avalanche; the case is known as Brown v. MacPherson's Inc. Before Brown v. MacPherson's Inc. went to trial, the State of Washington requested that the court dismiss the case against its Department of Motor Vehicles Real Estate Division. The court decided, in a five to four vote, that the State of Washington "did not have the power or authority to warn the general public and owners and occupants of the property development that there was an extreme avalanche hazard. Therefore they cannot be held liable for failure to do so." The case against the state was dismissed in 1975. (The outcome of the original case of Brown v. MacPherson's Inc., is not known but the assumption is that it was settled out of court.)

This dismissal was appealed in 1975. Remember: it is the appellate court decision that becomes precedent for other cases. The higher court found that the State of Washington could be tried for negligence. The decision was based on four facts: 1) an avalanche expert (LaChapelle) told a state employee that cabins located in the development were in a high-risk avalanche area (the state became aware of the hazard); 2) the state employee led the expert to believe that the state would deal with the matter, and warn residents in the area (the state assumed the responsibility for warning of the hazard); 3) the expert refrained from relaying any additional information because of the state's response; and 4) the state terminated its involvement in the issue without informing the property owners of the avalanche danger.

The decision of the appellate court acknowledged that the state could be tried for negligence if it could be proved that they had undertaken to do something and had either done it improperly, or had not done it at all. It was LaChapelle's reasonable reliance on the state, and the state's initial response from its real estate division, which created the state's "duty to warn." The state did not comply, and therefore the state could be held liable.

In 1973 the State of Washington enacted the Land Development Act, in response to the Yodelin accident. The law requires the disclosure of "any hazard on or around the development." However, the law only applies to developments of 10 lots or more, with single lots exempt from the requirement.

Spurred on by Washington State's appellate court decision, which recognizes a "duty to warn" of known hazards, officials in Ketchum, Idaho, took action. The municipal government was already aware of their own avalanche problems, and they were

8.3 In Ketchum, Idaho, a sign warns of the avalanche slope which threatens the home at its base (Douglas N. Greene photo)

determined to spell out detailed requirements in their zoning ordinance, which provides that the public be notified of avalanche potential within all designated avalanche areas, as determined by detailed studies. A few features from the zoning ordinance illustrate the "duty to warn" concern. All subdivision plats which are located in an avalanche zone will be stamped or so marked. Applications for building permits for construction within an avalanche zone will be stamped "Avalanche Zone." Before a building permit is issued for construction within an avalanche zone, the applicant must appear before the city council to receive personal notice of the fact that the proposed building is within an avalanche zone.

Further, the city must post signs in public right-of-ways identifying boundaries of avalanche zones Figure 8.3). Those who rent, lease, or sublet structures within an avalanche zone are required to provide the future occupant with written notice that the structure is within an avalanche zone before occupancy. Real estate agents who show property within an avalanche zone are required to give written notice "prior to viewing" that the property or structure is within an avalanche zone. And finally, all brochures and advertisements which solicit sale or reservations of "living units" within an avalanche zone must note that fact. These requirements unequivocally fulfill the obligation of a "duty to warn," and they answer many of the questions raised above as to who is responsible. The Ketchum government assumes that it is its responsibility to warn; after that, it's up to the individual to decide if he/she wants to assume the risk.

We have examined the history of avalanche hazard recognition, historic and contemporary efforts at managing the hazard, and legal definitions of responsibility. Recall for a moment the account in Chapter 2 of the calamitous 1910 avalanche in Wellington, Washington, which killed nearly 100 people. Read the following description from the Cordova Daily Alaskan (April 4, 1910) [laboriously uncovered by Alaska avalanche expert and history buff Doug Fesler], of the inquiry outcome into the accident.

A jury of men with "sound judgment and good understanding" went to the scene of the disaster to hear the testimony. "Evidence was received from men who were acquainted with conditions before the avalanche as well as from those who survived it." The questions were whether any human responsibility existed and whether the Great Northern Railroad could have done something to prevent the disaster. The verdict: " . . . the jury relieves man of all responsibility: and attributes the death of 100 persons

8.4 In Ketchum, Idaho, this home, built into the avalanche slope, is designed to allow the avalanche to past over it without damaging the structure (Douglas N. Greene photo)

to the decree of God alone." The "act of God" response is a far cry from the "duty to warn." As our legal system finds itself faced with more and more decisions which must define responsibility of the individual vs. responsibility of the governing agency, we will see more precedents set. It will be interesting to see which way the pendulum swings.

Jumping from 1910 to 1985 brings us to the most recent avalanche litigation case, the lawsuit filed by the families of three people killed in the Alpine Meadows, California, avalanche of March 1982, described in Chapter 1. Dick Penniman, mountain environment specialist and avalanche consultant to the Forest Service, reported the results of the trial, which lasted nearly three and a half months. On December 20, 1985, a Placer County jury found that the Alpine Meadows ski area was not negligent in the deaths of three people who were killed by a massive avalanche as they walked through the ski area's parking lot on March 31, 1982. The jury decision was nine to three, the least needed in a California civil suit, to award no damages to the heirs of the victims. The plaintiff's attorneys contended that Alpine Meadows was negligent for not having warned visitors of the danger in the parking lot, and for not taking proper precautions to prevent the disaster. Attorneys for the defense argued that Alpine Meadows had followed proper avalanche control procedures and that the avalanche was an act of God. Expert witnesses testified for both sides, with experts on behalf of the plaintiffs claiming that the avalanche was foreseeable and that the ski area failed to use adequate avalanche control measures for those conditions. Experts for the defense argued that, given the historical weather data from previous storms, the performance record of the avalanche paths, and the current state-of-the-art of stability evaluation, the avalanche forecast on March 31 was correct, the avalanche could not have been predicted, and Alpine Meadows took every precaution that could have been expected from them.

Penniman reported that when the jury reached an impasse in its deliberations, presiding Superior Court Judge James Garbolino instructed them that, in order to find Alpine Meadows negligent, they (the jury) would have to rule that the ski area had failed to exercise "ordinary care," or the caution expected of ordinary prudence. The jury was not instructed to consider "extraordinary care," or the conduct required in places of extreme danger. As of this writing, the decision is being appealed. The plaintiffs have also filed a wrongful death suit against the U.S. Forest Service, which issues the permit under which Alpine Meadows operates. That case was scheduled to be tried in 1986. Two additional negligence suits which resulted from the Alpine Meadows avalanche, filed by a survivor and by the heirs of another person who was killed, were settled out of court for undisclosed damages.

A final, thought-provoking case study comes from Jim Kennedy in Ketchum. A private land owner tried to stop the Sun Valley ski area from cutting down trees on the slope above his property. The ski area (owners of the land) planned a new ski run down the slope. However, the property owner complained that removing the forest cover would increase the likelihood of destructive avalanches reaching his home. When the case was brought to trial, the presiding judge decided that the ski area's avalanche control program was sufficient to prevent major avalanches from destroying the private land owner's property, and the ski area was allowed to cut the run. When the judge was asked the hypothetical question, "What if Sun Valley ceased to exist, and stopped their avalanche control?" he said he did not believe that was possible.

We will ponder that one a while . . .

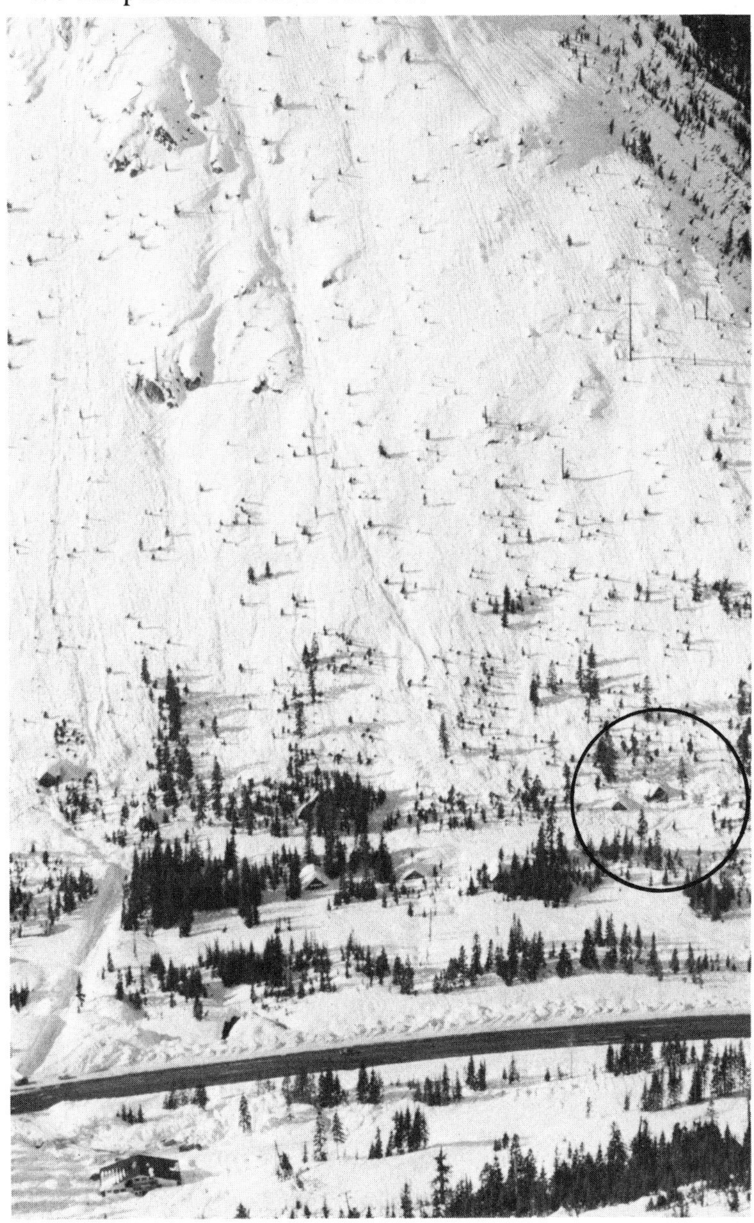

8.5 Yodelin, Stevens Pass, Washington. The photo is an aerial view of the Yodelin development, four days after the accident of January 24, 1971. Within the circled area is where the cabin, and many trees, were destroyed by the avalanche (A. Judson photo).

In Telluride, Colorado, spectators observe this large powder avalanche which was triggered by explosives (©1985, Bill Ellzey)

9 AVALANCHE STUDIES

WITHIN THE SCIENTIFIC COMMUNITY, the field of snow and avalanche research is a relatively young discipline. Not until the 20th century did scientists attempt any systematic studies of the physical aspects of the mountain snowpack and the mechanical forces that caused avalanches. Interest in avalanche studies developed hand in hand with the growing desire to not just climb mountains but also to ski across them. And this was what was happening in the European Alps around the turn of the century, and half a century later in the United States. This final chapter examines the field of snow avalanches from both an historical and a contemporary perspective. The purpose of much research is to find solutions to practical problems, and snow and avalanche research is no exception. Many aspects of this research can have dramatic applications . . . from new equations for calculating the distances avalanches will travel — which can save millions of dollars in damage by encouraging safe placement of structures — to developing more refined theories on the complex interactions between snow and climate — which can improve avalanche forecasts.

AVALANCHE RESEARCH: A BRIEF HISTORY

Every question we answer leads on to another question.
DESMOND MORRIS

Europe

During the Middle Ages mountain inhabitants viewed avalanches as punishment sent down from the lofty peaks by the resident demons and spirits, or as an "act of God" which could not be avoided or prevented. Possibly the capricious nature of avalanches themselves contributed to these beliefs. Such superstitions accounted for the notable lack of curiosity in exploring the surrounding mountains; this was a good way to avoid both the demons and the avalanches. Colin Fraser describes a "witch trial" in the Hinterrhein Valley of Switzerland in 1652: the verdict was not only that the defendant was a witch but it was stated that "witches are the causes of avalanches."

And in the Canton of Uri, a legend is told of a woman dressed in black who occasionally wandered into the village of Erstfeld. No one knew where she lived or who she was, but villagers began to notice that whenever something was awry — illness or missing animals, for example — the mysterious woman had been spotted nearby. One day a big avalanche came crashing into the valley, and who was sitting on the snow "quietly turning her spinning wheel" but the woman dressed in black. "Just as she was thanking Providence for having spared her life, four men grabbed her up out of the snow and carted her up into a clearing . . . flung her on a heap of firewood and summarily burnt her alive." These superstitions and beliefs provided one way to cope with the constant threat of avalanche disaster. Because the villagers thought they had no control over their fate, it was easy to concede that the dreaded avalanche was an act of God or the act of evil forces from above. By burning an occasional witch, the villagers were able to vent some of their frustrations, but this appeared to be their only method of fighting back.

Not until around the 18th century did mountain inhabitants begin to defend themselves. From Johann Scheuchzer's *Description of the Natural History of Switzerland*, published in Zurich in 1706, come some interesting observations from that time. Describing means of protection, he notes that high mountain dwellers "practically never erect buildings at the foot of a steep mountain unless there is a hill or a wood appropriately located on the slope which would divert the rolling avalanche to the sides, or force it temporarily to lose its power upon arrival in the valley." Triangular-shaped "patches of pine woods" above villages were protected by law, and "severe punishment is meted out to anyone damaging the woods, even though a great shortage of lumber exists." Scheuchzer noted that everywhere in Switzerland, "triangular walls are found at the foot of mountains, their apexes pointed in the direction of the most dangerous walls, so as to break up the avalanche and keep them from doing damage to buildings."

Beginning in the 18th century, curiosity began to grow among both mountain dwellers and the burgeoning group of climbers as to the "nature of the beast," and systematic studies of the avalanche phenomenon began. Johann Scheuchzer summarized the 17th-century concept of avalanches:

An avalanche can be created by anything that can put the snow lying on the mountains in motion, the newly fallen snow itself, which is more easily movable than the old snow lying on the ground; the snowflakes falling from trees or cliffs, or snow blown from the top of snowdrifts;. . . the sound of bells, pistols, or other firearms; shouting, or even the voices of travelers talking to one another; rain; warm spring weather; mountain goats; snow fowls and all other birds. Each of these causes is capable of loosening the snow a little . . . The snow subsequently increases in size and power as it rolls downward, until it eventually assumes the form of a huge snowball the size of a house or mountain, which snowball carries everything in its path down with it: trees, rocks, mountain goats and other animals, men, houses, etc.

Much of this early definition is correct; any sudden force on an unstable snowpack, including "snow fowls and all other birds," could be enough of a trigger to cause the snowpack to fail. The concept of an avalanche as a huge snowball, although inaccurate, was the prevailing theory for centuries. Old engravings and woodcuts show the snowball, studded with cows and trees and houses descending to the unsuspecting village below. Not until the 18th century was this myth — plus no doubt many others — dispelled.

The first avalanche researchers were the climbers and the early skiers, who learned, often the hard way, of the volatile and often unpredictable nature of the avalanche. Most of their knowledge was intuitive, gained from years of observation and experience. Mountaineers learn today much the same way; however, today's mountaineers can also draw from almost a century of scientific work to test their intuitive feelings. We know from Chapter 8 that it was Johann Coaz, the Swiss forester, who published the first study on avalanches. Beginning in the 1880s, he investigated the phenomemon for a dual purpose: to learn about avalanche forces so that avalanche defense structures could be designed, and also to learn where and how often avalanches occurred, so that a long-term record would exist for planning purposes, for locating protection structures and for reforestation projects. His book, *Avalanches of the Swiss Alps*, published in 1881, was followed by a 1910 compilation of Swiss avalanche statistics and information on avalanche protection structures.

Early in the 20th century, avalanche lore and knowledge began appearing in print as mountaineers and scientists wrote down their observations and theories. Much of the early work was closely tied to "ski-ing," a sport still in its infancy in Europe and barely born in North America. The first edition of *The Ski-Runner*, published in 1903 and edited by E. C. Richardson, contained a section on avalanches written by Dr. W. R. Rickmers. It was Dr. Rickmers' purpose to bring to the skiing public's attention the avalanche threat to winter mountaineering. Richardson's 1909 revision of *The Ski-Runner* also contained a chapter on avalanches. Richardson was probably the first to classify avalanches according to their prime causes — wind, snowfall, rain, etc. Another famous British name in avalanche research history is Arnold Lunn, whose detailed analyses of the avalanche phenomenon formed an important section of G. W. Young's book, *Mountain Craft*, which appeared in 1920.

Swiss forester E. Eugster published his observations on avalanches in 1927, and German researcher Dr. W. Paulcke, who began his "snowcraft" investigations in the late 1800s, published his descriptions in the 1920s. Dr. H. Hoek's *The Ski*, both the 1908 and 1925 editions, treated in detail the new field of avalanche studies. M. Zdarsky, the Austrian ski pioneer, published his work in the 1920s. And the Austrian colonel, G. Bilgeri, more practitioner than researcher, published a ski-mountaineering handbook, also in the 1920s, which described how to avoid avalanche danger. This very brief chronology of avalanche research would not be complete without mention of G. Seligman's classic 1936 work, *Snow Structure and Ski Fields: being an account of snow and ice forms met with in nature and a study on avalanches and snowcraft*. This work, based on Dr. Seligman's snow studies, which he undertook in the Swiss Bernese Oberland, drew together everything hitherto known about snow and avalanches.

The Swiss, long the pioneers in avalanche awareness and application, became increasingly convinced that they had to take preventative measures to protect both the endangered villages and the tourists partaking in winter sports. The Snow and Avalanche Research Commission of Switzerland was founded in 1931, and in the winter of 1934-35, the first research began at the Swiss Federal Institute for Snow and Avalanche Research, located atop the Weissflujoch above the village of Davos. Names like Henri Bader, Robert Haefli, and E. Bucher represent the Swiss innovators of snow science, and their book *Snow and Its Metamorphism*, published in 1939, was the first to describe their systematic research into the alpine winter snow cover. These early snow scientists tackled the problems of changes in the snowpack caused by variations in temperature, weight of the overlying snowpack, and pressures due to creep and deformation. Winterlong studies monitored the developing mountain snow cover, measuring the different layers within the snowpack, and the effects of the immediate environment: slope angle, slope aspect, and elevation.

In the 1940s and early 1950s, scientists concentrated on the mechanical aspects — snow mechanics and avalanche formation — as well as the physical properties of snow — snowpack structure and metamorphism. Field sites in the Swiss mountains, especially from the Weissflujoch station, provided the researchers with much-needed information on how a mountain snowpack behaves, and brought an overwhelming amount of "real" data to the scientists who before had only theories and intuition on which to base their conclusions. The research accomplished by Weissflujoch scientists through these years laid the foundation of snow and avalanche knowledge which is still studied today. Although contemporary researchers have made considerable progress, it is the basic concepts, defined in the 1930s, 1940s, and 1950s, which have stood the test of time. The state-of-the-art snow science presented in Chapter 3 traces its history to these early research efforts.

Investigations into the mechanical properties of the snowpack requires instruments for measuring the hardness, or strength, of snow. One instrument, a cone-shaped, incremented rod with differently weighted hammers, was called a rammsonde or a ram penetrometer. The snow worker places the tip of the cone on the snow surface and allows the rod to fall into the snow. The distance the cone has moved into the snow is recorded, and then another rod with a weighted hammer is attached. The hammer is dropped from known heights, such as 10 cm, or 20 cm, for a counted number of drops, and the penetration depth of the rod is recorded, until the rod reaches the ground. The stronger or tougher layers, like ice layers or wind-blown snow, require more drops, often from a greater height, than do the soft layers of snow. The end result is a profile of the snowpack obtained without having to dig a snowpit. This is a relatively subjective test, since a heavy-handed snow tester could miss the thin snow layers that a more delicate tester could detect. However, if the results are used as index values, this test was and still is a valuable tool for monitoring the snowpack changes.

The Swiss devised another technique for testing snow hardness which has become an internationally accepted method. This is a very inexpensive technique, requiring no sophisticated instrumentation, only the use of the hand. The hand hardness test is part of the International Snow Classification system, and is widely used by ski patrollers and snow workers. The technique is simple: use your hand to investigate the individual snow layers that make up the snowpit wall, and judge the hardness of the individual layers. If you can push your entire fist into the snow, it is very soft. Just four fingers of penetration indicates the snow layer is soft. If you can push only one finger into the snow, that layer would be considered medium hard. If only a pencil will penetrate, the snow is hard; if a knife is required, consider that particular snow layer very hard. (Henri Bader, the famous Swiss scientist, came up with an idea for testing snow hardness that sounded better on paper than in the field. His idea was to fire a pistol at a snowpit wall to see how resistant the snow was to the bullet. He had to abandon this idea due to problems of determining not only how to calculate the results but of even finding the bullet in the soft snow.)

While snow scientists conducted their investigations in laboratories and snow study sites, the fledgling ski-area workers were also learning about the nature of snow and avalanches. This learning process was by necessity, since it was their role to protect the flocks of alpine tourists who were testing out the new sport of skiing. In Switzerland, the ski patrol of Davos, called the Parsenndienst, worked hand-in-hand with the researchers of the Federal Snow and Avalanche Institute.

The United States

In the United States, as in Europe, it was the rise of alpine skiing that prompted the first research efforts into the nature of snow avalanches. The U.S. Forest Service started its first avalanche research program in Utah during the winter of 1937-38. Even before the lifts were built at the Alta ski area, the Forest Service assigned C. D. Wadsworth as the first full-time snow and avalanche observer, a position later called "snow ranger." The National Weather Service, then called the U.S. Weather Bureau, cooperated with the Forest Service by installing instruments at Alta to monitor the weather. Why Alta for the site of the nation's first avalanche research center? Although other ski areas around the country were being developed concurrently, it is

Alta's physical setting that provided a generation of snow rangers with a perfect laboratory for their investigations. Alta is located just east of Salt Lake City, in Little Cottonwood Canyon, a narrow, incised mountain valley surrounded by steep-sided slopes with much of its terrain above treeline.

During the first few years, the Alta snow rangers recorded their observations of weather, snow, and avalanches, placing more emphasis on passive control than active research. Areas that they considered dangerous were closed to the public until they felt the hazard had diminished, and they were empowered to close Little Cottonwood Canyon to traffic when they anticipated high avalanche hazard. This procedure continued until after World War II, when stage two of avalanche research began. Its origins lie with the Tenth Mountain Division, the group of ski-mountaineers who trained in Colorado's high country for mountain warfare in Europe. Who would be better qualified to get the research effort on its feet than a veteran Tenth Mountaineer, one with skiing ability who knew a little something about snow and avalanches?

Montgomery "Monty" Atwater arrived in Alta in the fall of 1945, a recent graduate of the Tenth and an aspiring writer. He definitely qualifies as the premier pioneer of American avalanche research. When Atwater arrived in Alta, he had little available to him beyond his own abilities and imagination. Working with the encouragement of Felix Koziol, the supervisor of the Wasatch National Forest, Atwater delved into the technology of avalanche control, using just about any cannon he could get his hands on to see its effect on the avalanche slopes surrounding Alta. He wrote down his ideas on forecasting avalanche hazard and controlling avalanche slopes in 1949, in a publication called *Alta Avalanche Studies*, the first of a long series of technical and applied works which continued until the center closed in 1971. Also in 1949 he organized the first "avalanche school" at Alta for the small but growing group of snow workers, mostly Forest Service snow rangers. This school was the predecessor of the many schools, training sessions, and university courses which are available today to anyone interested in the subject.

Another event of 1949 was the visit of famous Swiss avalanche expert Andre Roch. He toured the western United States, to observe avalanche areas and make recommendations. His report, *Avalanches in the U.S.A. 1949*, introduced many of the Swiss methods of avalanche control to American snow workers.

9.1 Powder avalanche in Alta, Utah, triggered artificially. The powder cloud is engulfing the U.S. Forest Service Guard Station (E. LaChapelle photo)

Roch also introduced his classification of North American climatic zones and his description of the corresponding different snow and avalanche conditions, which are still used today. One of the effects of Roch's report on avalanches, spurred on by the mushrooming ski development on Forest Service lands, was the establishiment of study areas in the other climatic snow and avalanche zones — in the coastal zone, at Stevens Pass in the Cascade Mountains, and in the continental zone at Berthoud Pass in Colorado.

By the early 1950s snow rangers in the three climatic zones were recording avalanches, weather conditions, and snowpack changes, all in an effort to decipher the "dreaded avalanche." In 1952 Atwater and Koziol collaborated on the first *Avalanche Handbook*, a comprehensive compilation of the growing knowledge of snow and avalanches, and the methodology to study and control them. In this first handbook, the authors introduced many of the principles that contemporary snow workers still rely on: concepts such as contributory factor analysis, described in Chapter 4, methods for observing snow and avalanches, and basic policies for preserving snow safety on National Forest Lands.

Ed LaChapelle arrived in Alta late in 1952 to assume the duties of assistant snow ranger, after spending a year working at the Swiss Federal Institute for Snow and Avalanche Research. After a few years at Alta, LaChapelle was assigned to full-time research, publications, and training, and snow ranger work was assigned to others. Ed describes the result of this reorganization: "The hitherto *ad hoc* nature of the studies was now formalized as the Alta Avalanche Study Center," its earlier name — the Alta Study Station — dropped due to an unsuitable acronym.

A brief aside gives a glimpse into the free-form "research and development" techniques the Alta snow scientists often used. When LaChapelle returned to Alta after a year's study at the Swiss Federal Institute for Avalanche Research, he described to Monty Atwater and his friend Lowell Thomas, the famous journalist, how the Europeans use dogs to search out buried avalanche victims. Lowell Thomas decided that the Alta Center needed an avalanche dog and presented the Forest Service with a German Shepherd puppy. Thomas and Atwater pondered a name, finally arriving upon PIF, an acronym for Precipitation Intensity Factor, and training began. Unfortunately, PIF never developed into much of a search dog. Her problems were a nervous temperament and a constantly changing home. She lived her first few months at Alta with the LaChapelle family. But when it was time for them to return to Seattle, PIF had to stay in Alta. Why?

9.2 PIF, possibly the first American avalanche dog, flanked (from left to right) by Lowell Thomas (reclining), Monty Atwater and Ed LaChapelle, in the early 1950s (Utah State Historical Society photo)

Because she was government property! Her constantly changing masters and homes only exacerbated her overstrung nature and she met an untimely death when she drank antifreeze while spending some time in a Forest Service garage.

The publications of the Alta Study Center covered a broad range of topics. Several were translations of Russian, Austrian, and Swiss work on zoning, avalanche-dog training, physical and mechanical changes in the snowpack, and avalanche dynamics. Others, written by American snow workers, covered similar aspects of the snow and avalanche field. Snow workers throughout the west published their studies through the Alta Center, with reports such as snow avalanche fatalities in Colorado, snow and avalanche conditions at Mount Baldy, California, and the nature and control of snow cornices in the Bridger Range of southwestern Montana.

Occasionally, a publication resulted from a great idea that turned out to be less than great in practice. Ed LaChapelle tells the story of the Alta research tower, a 15-foot steel tower set up at the Alta snow study plot. The tower supported an assortment of gauges and experimental instruments to measure snow and weather. The instrumentation was sound but the tower's location was not. "In 1953 an avalanche swept away the tower and distributed the instruments all over the valley floor. Monty Atwater intercepted this pass and ran it back for a touchdown by mapping all the pieces as they melted out in the spring and publishing a paper on 'The Debris Distribution of a Major Avalanche'."

By the mid 1960s the Alta Center was the hub of research and operational avalanche management activities. Ron Perla joined the Alta group in 1966. A New Yorker, Ron was bitten by the ski bug and took a snow ranger position at Alta while working on his Ph.D. at the University of Utah. Research took another great leap forward with the addition of Perla to the team, and the publication output became prodigious. But productivity and success often draws attention to the producers, and in this case it proved to be the downfall of the Alta Center.

As LaChapelle describes its history, the Forest Service had originally created the Center under the auspices of "administrative studies," the justification being that Forest Service fiscal policy would support certain practical areas of research with National Forest Administration funds. By 1966 many were of the opinion that the activities of the Alta Center were more appropriate to the research branch of the Forest Service, and the decision was made to phase out the Center and transfer the operation to the Alpine Snow and Avalanche Project of the U.S. Forest Service's Rocky Mountain Forest and Range Experiment Station in Fort Collins, Colorado. By 1971 all research had ceased at Alta, and the Alta Avalanche Study Center was history.

Research continued at the Rocky Mountain Station throughout the 1970s, where project scientists investigated a broad range of snow and avalanche topics. Project Leader Pete Martinelli produced many publications describing identification of avalanche areas; Dick Sommerfeld delved into the intricacies of snow metamorphism; Art Judson quantified the northern Colorado mountain climate and developed a computer model for forecasting avalanches. Judson's foremost contribution to the avalanche world was the organization of the first avalanche warning system in the United States. We'll talk more about this later. R.A. Schmidt continues to work on the problems of blowing snow — how to measure it, how to model it, even how to stand up in it. His work is applied not only to avalanche problems but also to snow management problems. For example, ski area management needs to know how to keep the snow on the slope and not blown away to a nearby forest. Highway engineers need to know how to keep highways open in areas where winds and snow combine to reduce or totally obscure visability.

However, the work undertaken at the Rocky Mountain Station was a different type of research. No longer were operational people and researchers working and living together in a confined environment, with constant exchanges of ideas. Alta had been a living laboratory. The operations people tried out a new method, and the success or lack of it was immediately discussed with the researchers who were investigating it. Or vice versa — the researchers would ponder an idea, conduct a few experiments, and bounce it off the operational field workers. Transfer of information, and results, both positive or negative, was immediate. The field worker didn't have to wait for results to be published in a professional journal, to learn about new ideas or techniques. The researchers, on the other hand, knew immediately whether their ideas would "hold water" or were impractical when applied.

Since the demise of the Alta Avalanche Study Center, the gap between the researcher and the field person remains open. The most recent blow to American snow and avalanche research was the termination in 1985 of the U.S. Forest Service's snow and avalanche research group in Ft. Collins, Colorado.

THE PRESENT: ADVANCES IN INSTRUMENTATION

Even with the demise of the Forest Service snow and avalanche research project, avalanche work in the United States, and Canada too, is holding its own — not soaring but not drowning either. Let us explain by first looking at the state of snow and avalanche studies in North America, and then continue by showing how the results of these studies are disseminated to those who actually apply them for work or for recreation.

Many of the principles of snow physics and avalanche dynamics were established in the 1940s and 1950s. Significant advances in the last thirty years have concentrated on refining these principles. A revolution in instrumentation is responsible for many of these refinements, and for the progress we have made in observing and understanding avalanches. Even as recently as the early 1970s, some instruments which measured snow and weather data had to be read directly, like reading a glass bulb thermometer for air temperature. But some instruments could record data on charts — for example, the hygrothermograph, which records relative humidity and air temperature; or the anemometer, which records wind speed; or the precipitation gauge, which records rain or the water-equivalent of snowfall. After a week or a month, the charts had to be removed by hand from the instruments in the field, and replaced with a new chart. The data on the chart, so-called analog data, are simply continuous, inked lines or traces: for example, air temperature over a week's time. In contrast, digital data represents the actual values being measured expressed in numbers. (A good example is the analog watch, which has a dial face which shows the path of the hands' passage through time, compared to the digital watch, which gives a number representing the current time.)

After the data is recorded and the chart is retrieved, the next step is transforming the lines into numbers. This requires either a patient and careful human, or a patient and careful human with a computer who traces the line with a "digitizer." The digitizer is calibrated according to the scale of the chart so that each move of the digitizing pen on the chart, from one point to the next, transforms the lines into numbers. The human does the same thing. Both methods are adequate, but time-consuming and error-prone. The researcher uses the numbers to analyze the parameter. In the past, statistical analysis such as mean, standard deviation, regression, etc., was either done by hand, or, by the late 1960s, with calculators or large main-frame computers. If the analysis needed to be presented graphically, the researcher used pencils and graph paper. If the graphs needed to be published, the skills of a draftsperson were required, unless the researcher had a bit of the artist in him.

And, we must not forget how these analog charts got into the hands of the researcher. The researcher, or a field assistant, had to travel to the instrument, under whatever weather conditions, to remove the chart and replace it with a clean one. Skiing or snowshoeing through blizzard conditions to get to the snow-study plot could be miserable. But on the other hand, most snow-workers can recall many "bluebird" days, with sunny skies, fresh powder snow and calm winds, where the quest for the chart was a good excuse for a grand outing. We confess that, occasionally, even when it was not yet time to change charts, but snow conditions were excellent, we felt a strong need to go check the recording instrument to make sure it was working!

In the past, all information about the snowpack came from the close relationship between snow workers and their shovels. To learn about the layering in the snowpack — the strengths and weaknesses, changes in temperature and texture — the snow worker dug a hole in the snow called a snow pit. Once in the pit, hours could be spent examining each layer, using magnifying hand lenses, scales and thermometers. What has changed? Plenty and almost nothing. The snow worker still digs snow pits and the backcountry recreationist digs "hasty" pits for observing the prevailing snowpack conditions. The hand hardness test still is the easiest and fastest method for determing snow resistance. But the computer age has brought data collection and analysis great leaps forward.

The instrument sensors still record air temperature, wind speed and direction, precipitation, and relative humidity. But they can also record snow depth and snowpack water-equivalent; information that in the past required often slow and tedious on-site measurements. Measuring snow depth the cheap way requires an incremented rod, with a length greater than the maximum snow depth expected at a particular site, which is fixed vertically in the ground before the snow falls. The snow worker notes the height of the snow around the stake, and the increase or decrease (from snow settlement) since the last observation. Measuring snow depth the new way — and by the way, the expensive way — is with an ultrasonic snow-depth gauge. This device measures the time it takes an ultrasonic wave, which is emitted by a sonic transmitter located well above the snow surface, to be reflected from the snow surface and back to the receiver. The receiver then transmits this information to a data-collecting computer. The computer then sends the data via satellite to a central computer which the forecaster can access. The fast transmittal of data gives the operational forecaster almost instant knowledge of how fast the snowpack is deepening, and, consequently, of how fast the unstable slopes are being loaded with new snow.

Another advance in measurement is the technique for remotely measuring snow water-equivalent, or the amount of frozen water which composes the snowpack. One of the traditional methods required the digging of a snow pit to the ground. Individual samples of the snow from top to bottom were weighed and the water equivalent was calculated from these measurements. Although not a major undertaking in the continental snow climate of the Rocky Mountains, it could be a full day's work in the maritime snow climate, where snow pits of 10 feet or more are common. The contemporary method uses a "snow pillow," usually constructed of thin stainless steel and filled with a liquid. As the thickness of the snow cover resting on the "pillow" increases over the winter, the increase in pressure exerted downward by the snow is measured and converted to water equivalent. Hundreds of these snow pillows provide twice-daily information to the U.S. Soil Conservation Service, as part of that agency's snow and weather data collection system called Snotel. Aside from an elk taking a snooze on a snow pillow, the instruments are quite reliable for measuring the developing winter snowpack.

The amount of blowing snow during a storm is a very important parameter which could only be approximated, or guessed at, in the past. R. A. Schmidt, research hydrologist at the U.S. Forest Service's Rocky Mountain Station in Fort Collins, Colorado, has been instrumental in developing snow particle counters, which, when combined with wind-speed sensors, can measure from afar the amount of snow being transported from one place to another. These measurements help the avalanche forecaster estimate how much snow loading is taking place in avalanche release zones.

The dramatic changes in instrumentation have taken place not only with the instruments themselves, but also in how the data are received. We have alluded to this earlier, but here are a few more details. Analog charts are slowly being replaced with "dataloggers" or small computers which store the data on a computer chip. These dataloggers are capable of recording and storing thousands of data points per hour, and can operate for weeks and months at a time without attention. By the time the field worker retrieves the data it has already gone through a pre-programmed analysis on the microcomputer. The researcher can take the analyzed data, and enter it into a computer graphics program, which will perform statistical analysis and produce the desired graphical form: bar graph, line graph, pie graph, or scatter diagram. Thus, many steps can be omitted using the new technology, and the margin for error decreases accordingly.

The modern techniques are excellent for research, where the results are not needed on a real-time basis. However, for many researchers and operational workers, immediate data are required. And the technology now exists to provide it. Remote weather stations, often solar powered, can send data from their sensors to satellites circling the earth, sometimes as often as every 15 minutes. The U.S. Soil Conservation Service uses another method for transmitting instrument data; this is called meteorburst telemetry and works on the exotic principle of using the frequent meteor showers, which come into the earth's atmosphere several times each day, to relay the data to a central computer. Both these methods of data collection allow access to the data, via large main-frame computers, within minutes of transmission. Operational workers — not only avalanche forecasters but those forecasting floods, snow-melt runoff, and day-to-day weather — use these tools, both to compose their forecasts, and later, to verify their accuracy.

In many areas where these sophisticated weather and snow measuring stations are functioning, snow scientists and workers no longer have to ski or snowshoe to the snow study plot to read the instruments. They just have to turn on their computer. Of course even though data loggers and computers eliminate the need to ski to the study plot to change the charts and check the condition of last night's fall of powder snow . . . who ever said that sensors and microloggers didn't need occasional maintenance and attention?

Advances in instrumentation have allowed scientists to study avalanches in motion — impossible in the past since avalanches usually ended the experiments by destroying the instrument. In British Columbia, Peter Schaerer and David McClung, with the National Research Council of Canada, have been studying the dynamics of avalanches trying to learn about avalanche speed, impact pressures on the objects they hit, and depths of the flowing avalanches. Their instruments are mounted on steel frames and secured in the gully of a frequently running avalanche path. On the steel frame are load cells which record the impact pressures of the avalanche flowing down the gully, and geophones, special microphones which record the vibrations of the avalanche. These measurements allow the scientists to determine the speed of the moving avalanche. Moving avalanches on the instrumented slope traveled at speeds ranging from 30 mph to 90 mph, with impact pressures up to about 30 pounds/square inch to 40 pounds/square inch — pressures about ten times greater than those which ordinary buildings — houses and the like — can be expected to withstand. Similar experiments have been conducted in Japan. The results have not been obtained easily, since avalanches occasionally bypass the instruments; or when they do hit, they have been perverse enough to damage the equipment without leaving any data. Freezing rain can also harm the equipment. In spite of the problems, the equipment has held up well enough to produce fascinating results.

Seismometers and geophones, often used for earthquake detection, have found another use in the mountain snowpack. Scientists in the United States and Europe have experimented with methods of detecting the acoustic emissions of a stressed snowpack. Years of data collection with listening devices implanted in the snow on avalanche slopes show that emission activity increases just before the slope avalanches. The increased emissions prior to release indicate that small fractures within the snowpack are beginning to appear. Theoretically, avalanche forecasters with remote listening devices could predict avalanche activity based on pre-release emissions from the snowpack. However, the equipment is expensive, the monitoring is very site-specific, and no operational instruments are currently in use in the United States.

WHAT'S NEXT FOR AVALANCHE RESEARCH?

European scientists built the foundations of snow and avalanche knowledge in the late 1930s and 1940s. The Americans and Canadians joined in in the 1950s. Modern research has made advances and refinements of the basic principles, and we now have a greater understanding of the physical and mechanical processes in the snowpack which lead to avalanche formation, as well as of the complex interactions between weather and avalanches. But there remain many unanswered questions. Many of these ideas on future research came from some of the best scientists in the field, assembled at a workshop in Snowbird, Utah, in April of 1981. Their collective thoughts on the state of snow and avalanche research and where it should be headed are described below.

Much more information is needed before researchers can give practitioners guidelines, or index values, for evaluating and judging snow stability. Research is needed to determine if a relationship exists between the electrical and the mechanical properties of snow. If so, then it is theoretically possible to build instruments that could measure electrical values and then convert these to index values for snowpack strength. This would allow the practitioner to quickly assess snowpack properties over a large area, a regional forecaster's dream.

Work needs to be done to learn about the dissipation characteristics of snow — that is, how much energy is required to change the physical state of snow from, for example, a cohesive snow layer to individual snow particles. This knowledge would be useful in working with blowing snow problems, since wind often erodes the snow surface, picking up the loose particles of snow and depositing them in avalanche release zones.

What happens to snow stability with sudden changes in air temperature? The circumstantial evidence exists, and those who spend a lot of time in the backcountry have observed significant changes in stability of the snow pack with sudden temperature changes, but why this happens needs to be understood so practitioners can anticipate the results of this phenomenon.

An important area for future research should be the measurement of the speed and density of flowing avalanche snow. This information is critical for researchers who seek to model moving avalanches, and practitioners who must use the research for decision-making, such as evaluating maximum avalanche path runout distances for determining where to allow construction or highway development. Schaerer and McClung have gathered data from Rogers Pass, British Columbia, which provide information on flowing snow. From their measurements, they noted that dry snow avalanches look like bursts of particles, while wet snow avalanches appear to have a more continuous type of flow. These descriptive observations are just the beginnings of more quantified research into the characteristics of flowing snow. In Switzerland, Hansueli Gubler is experimenting with radar to measure the velocity of avalanches — just as the police measure the velocity of speeding automobiles. As noted in Chapter 3, this information is necessary to better understand and predict avalanche impact pressures and runout distances.

By describing the advances in instrumentation, providing a few examples of current research, and offering a few ideas on where future research should be headed, we are making the point that research is needed so that practical solutions can be applied to real-life problems. Although much of snow and avalanche research is theoretical, useful applications eventually can exist — and do. The application of research findings comes under the category of technology transfer.

TECHNOLOGY TRANSFER: LAND-USE PLANNING

One very practical application of snow and avalanche research is in its ability to determine how far across the landscape an avalanche will travel. Land-use planners, ski area developers, and individual property owners all need this very essential application of theoretical calculations of avalanche flow mechanics and dynamics. One way of attaining this data is to observe the avalanche over a period of years. Although records go as far back as 500 years in a few areas of the European Alps, and over a thousand years in a few places in Iceland, for most parts of the world, no records exist. Without historical records another technique is to calculate the maximum or extreme runout distance, using a series of equations which take into account the dynamics, the speed, and the density of the flowing avalanche snow. Since 1964 the Swiss Avalanche Institute has prepared avalanche hazard maps which show maximum avalanche runout distance, based on calculations using equations first published by Voellmy in 1955. Avalanche consultants continue to use these equations today, with constant updates and improvements in some of the coefficients. In many areas with strict land-use planning codes, the expert opinions of avalanche consultants are often required by government officials before building permits are issued and construction begins.

In the late 1970s Norwegian researchers developed a method for calculating maximum avalanche runout distance which does not require the often difficult-to-determine coefficients that are essential to the Swiss calculation methods. The Norwegian method (developed by Lied and Bakkehoi, of the Norwegian Geotechnical Institute in Oslo) uses only topographic features of the individual avalanche path to calculate maximum runout distance. The numbers which go into the equation, slope angle and slope of the avalanche path, for example — can be easily obtained from a standard topographic map. The Norwegians tested their method against the known runout distances of over 400 avalanches. These were avalanches that traveled in populated areas, where, for over a century, the local inhabitants had recorded their behavior. Other researchers have tested these equations on avalanche paths in Europe, North America, and New Zealand, and all report a good relationship to observed maximum runout distances. Methods such as this, which do not require complex, theoretical values, can be very useful for all those concerned with avalanche mapping and land-use planning, for recreation, development, and transportation.

TECHNOLOGY TRANSFER: AVALANCHE FORECASTING AND AVALANCHE EDUCATION

Forecasting

Probably the foremost intermediary between the research group and the practitioners is the avalanche forecaster. Coming from a wide variety of disciplines, avalanche forecasters in the United States combine scientific principles, research findings — often their own — their intuitive knowledge and experience, and information gathered from field workers to provide the public with snow-stability forecasts on a real-time basis. Avalanche forecasting traces its beginnings to Europe, specifically to Switzerland, where the Federal Institute for Snow and Avalanche Research has been issuing avalanche warnings for the Swiss Alps since the 1950s. Swiss avalanche forecasters gather, on a daily basis throughout the winter, reports from about 50 stations that provide information on current snowpack conditions, weather, and avalanche occurrence. The forecasters judge the current state of snow stability based on these observations and their own field tests. The avalanche forecast is then made based on how the existing snowpack will react to the anticipated weather conditions. The information includes the evaluation of current snowpack stability, the mountain weather forecast, and the avalanche hazard prediction (issued to the public on a regular basis). When avalanche hazard is forecast to increase to a dangerous level, the forecasters issue avalanche warnings through the media.

With some refinements, improvements and regional differences, this is how avalanche forecasters work today at most of the avalanche forecast centers of the world. In this computer age, don't avalanche forecasters use a model for decision-making? The answer to that question today is No, at most forecast centers. Modeling avalanches is very difficult, as is modeling snow, and for the same reasons. The difficulties lie in the complex nature of seasonal snow and weather patterns, which can change not only from hour to hour but also from one side of the mountain to another. This is due to the interactions of physical parameters like wind, temperature, and solar radiation, and mechanical forces acting within the snow cover. So many constantly changing variables are involved that no practical physical model yet exists which can be used on an operational basis.

Yet avalanche forecast models have evolved considerably; early statistical models forecast if one or more avalanches would fall on a given day, yes or no. These early models, developed in the early 1970s, were the predecessors of more sophisticated computer models. Relying on years of meteorological and avalanche event records from stations in the European Alps, these statistical models analyzed what combination of weather factors correlated best with recorded avalanches. To use such a model, the forecaster would "plug in" the present or forecasted weather factors, and the model would give either a yes or no to avalanche events, or in the more sophisticated models, a predictive probability .

Nearly all of these models took into account only the meteorological parameters and contained no snowpack parameters. This is the heart of the problem. Although it is valid to generalize about weather influences, even though terrain and topography can alter and influence them to some degreee, it is extremely difficult to generalize about the mountain snowpack from one place to another. This is why most statistical models have avoided the problem of including the snowpack. But, Othmar Buser of the Swiss Federal Snow and Avalanche Institute has developed a statistical model that does look at all available information. Called the "nearest neighbor" model, this approach serves primarily as a computerized memory for the forecasters.

Here's how it works. Daily meteorological and snowpack information is stored in the computer's memory — maximum, minimum, and mean air temperature; average and maximum wind speed and direction; new snowfall; snowfall from the past 24-hour period; condition of the snow surface; snow settlement, etc. In a separate memory file, daily avalanche data are stored. To use the model, the forecaster enters the parameters for the current or forecasted weather, and the computer searches for days with similar parameters — the "nearest neighbors" to the current data. The computer lists the 10 nearest days, then goes off to find the avalanche record for those days. Suppose the results show that eight of the 10 "nearest neighbor" days had no avalanche events, indicating insignificant avalanche activity. The forecaster then knows that, on past days, with conditions similar to today's weather, avalanche activity was minimal. The forecaster can then make a forecast, based on actual past records alone.

At this point in computer avalanche forecasting, human forecasters predict as well as, or better than, the models, with accuracy of 80 to 85 percent. Although the current models can be valuable aids for decision-making, the burden of responsibility lies with the forecaster in using *all* available information, including forecast model results, to make the correct evaluation.

Education

Regional avalanche forecast centers operate in four metropolitan areas of the western United States — Denver, Salt Lake City, Seattle, and Anchorage — and report on conditions over thousands of square miles of mountains. The forecasters themselves are a diverse group, coming from the varied academic disciplines of geophysics, atmospheric sciences, meteorology, and geography — or from the practitioner end — experienced ski patrollers bringing years of experience in avalanche control to the forecasting centers.

The goal of all the forecasting centers is to provide the public with enough information so they can make informed and intelligent decisions, whether they are driving their car on a mountain highway, planning a ski tour or snowmobile ride, or undertaking a rescue mission in avalanche-prone terrain. This is achieved in several ways. First, all the centers provide free recorded telephone messages, which are updated twice daily, seven days a week, for the winter season. These messages typically contain information on current snow and weather conditions, a brief weather forecast and an avalanche forecast. Often the messages will refer to specific geographic areas when conditions are not uniform throughout the forecast area. Forecasters issue avalanche warnings when hazard is likely to increase to high, and terminate them when hazard has moderated. With the help of radio, television, and the newspapers, they get these warnings out to the public, who then knows a problem exists and can call the recorded telephone message to learn the details of where and why.

Avalanche forecasters become proficient and occasionally brilliant public speakers, by bringing the message of avalanche awareness to the public. Forecasters speak before diverse groups: grade-school students, university classes, mountain-club members, business groups, and special interest groups such as highway workers or power company representatives whose jobs bring them into the mountains. Forecasters also instruct at avalanche awareness schools and present the results of their work and research at workshops and seminars. And what do they do during the summer? All sorts of things, from mundane but necessary tasks like analyzing data, writing reports, and working on instrumentation, to the more exotic — like traveling to the mountains of the Southern Hemisphere for more winter (and more skiing), or taking kayak trips to wild and untamed areas.

Forecasters in Anchorage, Alaska forecast for the Kenai, Chugach, and Talkeetna ranges of Alaska. Although the numbers of people traveling through and recreating in the mountains is small compared to those of the other forecast centers, the area of mountainous terrain is huge, and keeping track of the various snow climates in each mountain range is quite a task.

In the Washington State-Oregon areas, the Northwest Avalanche Center forecasts for the Cascade and Olympic Mountains. Operating out of Seattle, the forecasters keep grueling hours during their operational season to send out their messages to the public. Twelve- to 14-hour days are pretty common for this crew, who arrive on the job shortly after 4 a.m. when it is their day to forecast. No *Tonight Snow* for these folks. When they aren't forecasting, climbing towers to fix stubborn wind sensors, or sampling the Northwest powder, they find the time to write technical papers, passing on information to their colleagues and compatriots so that everyone won't have to reinvent the wheel.

The Utah Avalanche Forecast Center is located in Salt Lake City and serves the Northern Wasatch Mountains. Although one of the smaller mountain regions, the center has a large number of users, with hundreds of daily calls to the recorded message phones in Salt Lake, Ogden, Logan and Provo.

The first and oldest regional avalanche center is located in Colorado, the state which holds the dubious distinction of tallying the highest number of avalanche fatalities. This forecast center brought the European concept of public avalanche warnings to Colorado, and developed the framework for issuing public avalanche bulletins which would be imitated and expanded on by the other American avalanche centers. When the Forest Service relinquished administration of Colorado's Avalanche Warning Center, the State of Colorado's Department of Natural Resources jumped in to save the group. Renamed the Colorado Avalanche Information Center, it continues its mission of informing the public of current mountain conditions and forecast dangers.

All the centers stress the importance of education — giving the public enough basic knowledge to understand and use the information issued from the avalanche centers. Their forecasters reach thousands of people each winter through talks, lectures, workshops, and recorded messages — and millions over the radio and television air waves. The importance of widespread, basic knowledge was readily learned when the Colorado Avalanche Center interviewed hundreds of backcountry skiers and snowmobilers, during surveys we conducted at popular trailheads in Colorado. The survey showed that those people with a basic knowledge of avalanches were more likely to heed avalanche warnings, when issued.

It's the old story of you don't know what it is until it bites you. But in this situation, a little bit of knowledge is not a dangerous thing; in fact, it just might save a life. Just knowing what an avalanche is and a few basic facts about what to look for and where to go have saved many lives. Stories abound of people who have sat through just an hour's talk on avalanches but, when caught in the panic situation of an avalanche, have remembered enough to save their own lives.

Why are we proselytizing here, so close to the conclusion of this book? Because it is our job to save lives and, although it is pretty hard to count how many we have saved, we can point out that the avalanche fatality rate in the United States has not increased at nearly the same rate as the numbers of winter recreationists have. We attribute the containment of avalanche fatalities to education, pure and simple.

For education's sake then, we hope you will examine the appendices which follow this chapter. We have listed not only the references used but also included suggestions for further reading in *Appendix A (Bibliography and Additional Reading)* ; *Appendix B (Public Information and Education)* is a listing of the regional avalanche center's recorded message telephones, as well as several avalanche education courses and their locations; *Appendix C (Equipment)* offers a list of the manufacturers and suppliers who provide avalanche safety equipment. We encourage you to read some of these books, go to mountaineering shops and examine the safety equipment, listen to a short talk on avalanches, or take a course or workshop.

CONCLUSIONS

We conclude this chapter, and this book, with some thoughts on the state of the science, or the state of the art, or both. The field of avalanche studies is imperfect and difficult to quantify. Experts in our field must have the scientific background to understand the physical and mechanical processes of the evolving winter snowpack, and to assimilate this understanding with a knowledge of mountain weather patterns which influence the snowpack's growth and development. But while quantifying these factors is science, it is truly an art to combine, almost intuitively, all the many variables into a forecast of snow stability.

During the last few hundred years, the field has made great advances, from blaming witches and spirits for causing avalanches, to a clear understanding of the climatic and snowcover conditions that combine to give snow on an incline either stability or instability. Even in this age of computer avalanche-forecast models and satellite transmission of weather and snow data , there is still an element of "art." Whether it is the avalanche forecaster preparing daily messages, the ski patroller deciding whether to open slopes to the public hungry to ski the powder, the highway worker plowing snow on highways occasionally threatened by avalanches, the planner deciding whether to issue building permits for property where avalanches may occasionally travel, the backcountry skier wondering about the slope about to be crossed, all must make decisions — occasionally life or death decisions — and this is where the buck stops! All the "information in" — the research results, education, reading, schools — must be boiled down to the right decision — the "information out."

We have shown you good decisions and bad, with the bad ones causing death or, for the lucky ones, just close calls. We would like to see many more good decisions, but this can happen only if the decision-makers are armed with the best information available, the latest research, the most current analyses of the experts, and the ability to assimilate all of this intelligently. The conclusion we draw from writing this book is that we must not lose ground, after gaining so much. Support — financial support — on the local, state, and federal levels must continue, and hopefully increase, to maintain research into snow and avalanche problems and to educate the public.

Appendix A: Bibliography and Additional Reading

1. Why Tell of Avalanches

McClung, D. 1981. *American Alpine Journal*, p. 138-145.

Fraser, Colin. 1978. *Avalanches and Snow Safety*. John Murray Publishers, Ltd., Great Britain. 269 p.

2. History and Avalanches

Armstrong, B.R. 1976. *Century of Struggle Against Snow: A history of avalanche hazard in San Juan County, Colorado.* University of Colorado Institute of Arctic and Alpine Research, Occasional Paper No. 18, 97 p.

Armstrong, B.R. 1977. *Avalanche Hazard in Ouray County, Colorado: 1877-1976*. University of Colorado Institute of Arctic and Alpine Research, Occasional Paper No. 24, 125 p.

Bader, H. and others. 1939. *Snow and its Metamorphism* (Der Schnee und Seine Metamorphose). Translation 14, January 1954, Snow, Ice and Permafrost Research Establishment, U.S. Army, 313 p.

Björnsson, Helgi. 1980. Avalanche activity in Iceland, climatic conditions, and terrain features. *Journal of Glaciology*, Vol. 26, No. 94, p. 13-24.

Björnsson, Helgi. 1977. Snow avalanche studies in Iceland. In: *Avalanches. Glaciological Data Report* GD-1, World Data Center A for Glaciology, University of Colorado, Boulder, Co., p. 39-42.

Fraser, Colin. 1978. *Avalanches and Snow Safety*. John Murray Publishers, Ltd., Great Britain. 269 p.

Fraser, Colin. 1966. *The Avalanche Enigma*. John Murray Publishers, Ltd., Great Britain, 301 p.

Friedl, John. 1974. *Kippel: A Changing Village in the Alps*. Holt, Rinehart and Winston, Inc., New York, 129 p.

Gallagher, Dale, ed. 1967. *The Snowy Torrents: Avalanche Accidents in the United States 1910-1966*. Alta Avalanche Study Center, U.S.D.A. Forest Service, 144 p.

Gibbons, Rev. J.J. 1898. *In the San Juan, Colorado: Sketches*. St. Patrick's Parish, Telluride, Colorado (reprinted in 1972), 194 p.

Harper, Frank. 1943. *Military Ski Manual: A Handbook for Ski and Mountain Troops*. The Military Service Publishing Company, Harrisburg, Pa, 393 p.

Laely, A. *Lawinenchronik der Landschaft Davos* (Avalanche history of the Davos area), Davos, Switzerland (in German, no publication date).

Leaf, C. F. and M. Martinelli Jr. 1980. Historic Avalanches of the Northern Front Range and of the Central and Northern Mountains of Colorado. Unpublished manuscript, 220 p.

Netting, R. M. 1981. *Balancing on an Alp*. Cambridge University Press, Cambridge, 278 p.

Peattie, Roderick. 1936. *Mountain Geography: A Critique and Field Study*. Greenwood Press, New York, 249 p.

Perla, R. and M. Martinelli, Jr. 1976. *Avalanche Handbook*. Agriculture Handbook 489, U.S.D.A. Forest Service, 238.

Ramsli, G. 1975. Report on Avalanche Zoning in Norway with Reference to other Scandinavian Countries. Special Report for Meeting in Davos, Switzerland, July 1975.

Scheuchzer, Johan. 1706. Description of the Natural History of Switzerland, Part I, Zurich. IN: *Snow and its Metamorphism* (H. Bader and others, with introduction by P. Niggli). Translation 14, January 1954, Snow, Ice and Permafrost Research Establishment, U.S. Army, 313 p.

Ward, R. G. W. 1980. Avalanche hazard in the Cairngorm Mountains, Scotland. *Journal of Glaciology*, Vol. 26, No. 94, p. 31-42.

Zinsli, Paul. 1968. *Walser Volkstum in der Schweiz* (Valais Human History in Switzerland). Verlag Huber & Co., Frauenfeld, Switzerland (in German: Alpine migration and settlement history).

3. THE MOUNTAIN SNOWPACK

Bentley, W. A. and W. J. Humphreys. 1931. *Snow Crystals..* McGraw-Hill Book Co., New York (paperback edition, Dover T287, 1962)

Nakaya, U. 1954. *Snow Crystals: Natural and Artificial.* Harvard University Press, Cambridge, Mass.

5. THE RIGHT CHOICE

Powder Magazine, January 1980.

6. WHEN THINGS GO WRONG

Western Skier magazine, January 1968.

7. GETTING THINGS UNDER CONTROL

Armstrong, B.R. 1977. *Avalanche Hazard in Ouray County, Colorado: 1877-1976*. University of Colorado Institute of Arctic and Alpine Research, Occasional Paper No. 24, 125 p.

Atwater, Montgomery. 1968. *The Avalanche Hunters*. Macrae Smith Company, Philadelphia, Pa., 235 p.

Fraser. Colin. 1978. *Avalanches and Snow Safety*. John Murray Publishers, Ltd., Great Britain. 269 p.

Perla, R. and M. Martinelli, Jr. *1976. Avalanche Handbook.* Agriculture Handbook 489, U.S.D.A. Forest Service, 238.

U.S. Department of Agriculture. 1975. *Avalanche Protection in Switzerland.* (translated by U.S. Army) USDA Forest Service General Technical Report RM-9, 168 p.

8. AVALANCHES AND THE LAW

Armstrong, B.R. 1976. *Century of Struggle Against Snow: A history of avalanche hazard in San Juan County, Colorado.* University of Colorado Institute of Arctic and Alpine Research, Occasional Paper No. 18, 97 p.

Armstrong, B.R. 1977. *Avalanche Hazard in Ouray County, Colorado: 1877-1976.* University of Colorado Institute of Arctic and Alpine Research, Occasional Paper No. 24, 125 p.

Breu, K. 1975. Avalanche Damage, In: *Avalanche Protection in Switzerland.* General Technical Report RM-9, USDA Forest Service, Rocky Mountain Forest and Range Experiment Station, p. 1-5.

deCrécy, L. 1980. Avalanche zoning in France-regulation and technical bases. *Journal of Glaciology*, Vol. 26, No. 94.

Freer, G.L. and P.A. Schaerer. 1980. Snow-avalanche hazard zoning in British Columbia, Canada. *Journal of Glaciology*, Vol. 26, No. 94, p. 345-354.

Frutiger, H. 1975. Historical background of Swiss avalanche control projects. In: *Avalanche Protection in Switzerland.* General Technical Report RM-9, USDA Forest Service, Rocky Mountain Forest and Range Experiment Station, p. 38-44.

Frutiger, H. 1977. Avalanche damage and avalanche protection in Switzerland (translated by Richard Armstrong). In: *Avalanche-s. Glaciological Data GD-1*, World Data Center A for Glaciology, University of Colorado, Boulder, Co., p. 17-32.

Frutiger, H. 1980. History and actual state of legalization of avalanche zoning in Switzerland. *Journal of Glaciology*, Vol. 26, No. 94, p. 313-324.

deCrécy, L. 1980. Avalanche zoning in France-regulation and technical bases. *Journal of Glaciology*, Vol. 26, No. 94.

Ferguson, Sue, publisher and editor. The Avalanche Review, Volumes 1-3, Numbers 1-7, 1982-1985. Salt Lake City, Utah. (for specific reference to avalanche litigation, see Vol. 3, numbers 3 and 4).

Fraser, Colin. 1978. *Avalanches and Snow Safety*. John Murray Publishers, Ltd., Great Britain. 269 p.

Hestnes, E. and K. Lied. 1980. Natural-hazard maps for land-use planning in Norway. *Journal of Glaciology*, Vol. 26, No. 94, p. 331-344.

Ives, J.D. and M. Plam. 1980. Avalanche hazard mapping and zoning problems in the Rocky Mountains, with examples from Colorado, U.S.A. *Journal of Glaciology*, Vol. 26, No. 94, p. 363-376.

LaChapelle, E. R. 1967. Timberline reforestation in the Austrian Alps. *Journal of Forestry,* p. 868-872.

Mears, Arthur I. 1980. Municipal avalanche zoning: contrasting policies of four western United States communities. *Journal of Glaciology*, Vol. 26, No. 94, p. 355-362.

Mellor, Malcolm. 1968. Avalanches. Cold Regions Science and Engineering, Part III: Engineering, Section A3: Snow Technology. Hanover, N.H. 215 p.

9. AVALANCHE STUDIES

Atwater, Montgomery. 1968. *The Avalanche Hunters*. Macrae Smith Company, Philadelphia, Pa., 235 p.

Bader, H. and others. 1939. *Snow and its Metamorphism* (Der Schnee und Seine Metamorphose). Translation 14, January 1954, Snow, Ice and Permafrost Research Establishment, U.S. Army, 313 p.

Brown, R. L., S. C. Colbeck and R. N. Yong, editors. 1982. *Proceedings of a Workshop on the Properties of Snow, 8-10 April 1981, Snowbird, Utah.* U.S. Army CRREL Special Report 82-18, Hanover, N.H. 135 p.

Bryson, Sandy. 1984. *Search Dog Training*. Boxwood Press, Pacific Grove, California. 368 p.

Buser, O. and Frutiger, H. 1980. Observed maximum run-out distance of snow avalanches and the determination of the friction coefficients (u and e). *Journal of Glaciology*, Vol. 26, No. 94, p. 121-130.

Buser, O. 1983. Avalanche forecast with the method of nearest neighbours: an interactive approach. *Cold Regions Science and Technology*, Vol. 8, No. 2, p. 155-163.

Fraser, Colin. 1978. *Avalanches and Snow Safety*. John Murray Publishers, Ltd., Great Britain. 269 p.

Gubler, H. and M. Hiller. 1983. Use of microwave FMCW radar in snow and avalanche research. *Cold Regions Science and Technology*, volume 9, no. 2, p. 109-119.

LaChapelle, Ed. 1984. The Alta Avalanche Study Center. *The Avalanche Review*, Vol. 2, No. 6, p. 7.

Lied, K. and S. Bakkehøi. 1980. Empirical calculations of snow-avalanche run-out distance based on topographic parameters. *Journal of Glaciology*, Vol. 26, No. 94, p. 165-178.

Schaerer, Peter. 1984. Measurements of the amount of snow brought down by avalanches. *Proceedings of International Snow Science Workshop, October 24-27, Aspen, Colorado*, p. 78-79.

Scheuchzer, Johann. 1706. Description of the Natural History of Switzerland, Part I, Zurich. IN: *Snow and its Metamorphism* (H. Bader and others, with introduction by P. Niggli). Translation 14, January 1954, Snow, Ice and Permafrost Research Establishment, U.S. Army, 313 p.

Seligman, G. 1936. *Snow Structure and Ski Fields*. (reprinted in 1962 and 1980, 555 p. (references to early snow scientists are found here.)

ADDITIONAL READING

Atwater, Montgomery. 1968. *The Avalanche Hunters.* Macrae Smith Company, Philadelphia, Pa., 235 p.

Bryson, Sandy. 1984. *Search Dog Training.* Boxwood Press, Pacific Grove, California. 368 p.

Colbeck, S.C., Ed. 1980. *Dynamics of Snow and Ice Masses.* Academic Press, 468 p.

Daffern, Tony. 1983. *Avalanche Safety for Skiers & Climbers.* .Rocky Mountain Books, Calgary, Canada, 172 p.

Ferguson, S., publisher. *The Avalanche Review.* P.O. Box 51904, Salt Lake City, Utah 84151 (volumes 1-4, 1982-83 through 1985-86).

Fraser, Colin. 1978. *Avalanches and Snow Safety.* John Murray Publishers, Ltd., Great Britain. 269 p.

Fraser, Colin. 1966. *The Avalanche Enigma.* John Murray Publishers, Ltd., Great Britain, 301 p.

Fredston, Jill and Doug Fesler. 1985. *Snow Sense: a guide to evaluating avalanche hazard.* AEIDC, University of Alaska and Alaska Department of Natural Resources, Anchorage, 48 p.

Gallagher, Dale, ed. 1967. *The Snowy Torrents: Avalanche Accidents in the United States 1910-1966.* Alta Avalanche Study Center, U.S.D.A. Forest Service, 144 p.

LaChapelle, E.R. 1985. *The ABC's of Avalanche Safety.* Second Edition. The Mountaineers Books, Seattle, Washington, 112 p.

Perla, R. and M. Martinelli, Jr. 1976. *Avalanche Handbook.* Agriculture Handbook 489, U.S.D.A. Forest Service, 238 p.

Seligman, G. 1936. *Snow Structure and Ski Fields*. (reprinted in 1962 and 1980. 1980 edition available from International Glaciological Society, Lensfield Rd., Cambridge CB2 1ER, U.K.).

Williams, Knox. 1975. *The Snowy Torrents: Avalanche Accidents in the United States 1967-71*. USDA Forest Service General Technical Report RM-8, Fort Collins, Colorado, 190 p.

Williams, Knox and Betsy Armstrong. 1984. *The Snowy Torrents: Avalanche Accidents in the United States 1972-79*. Teton Bookshop Publishing Co., Jackson, Wyoming, 221 p.

Appendix B: Public Information and Education

Public Information

24-hour regional avalanche information is available generally from December through April, by calling these recorded messages. Additional information can often be found through local forest service ranger districts, parks or ski areas.

ALASKA
South-Central Alaska Mountain
(907) 271-4500
(Anchorage)

CALIFORNIA
Lake Tahoe/Donner Summit area
(916) 587-2158
(Truckee)
Central-Eastern Sierra near Mammoth Lakes
(714) 934-6611
(Mammoth Lakes)

COLORADO
Colorado Rockies
(303) 236-9435
(Denver/Boulder)
Colorado Rockies
(303) 482-0457
(Fort Collins)
Colorado Rockies
(303) 520-0020
(Colorado Springs)

Colorado Rockies
(303) 468-5434
(Dillon)
Colorado Rockies
(303) 827-5687
(Minturn)
Colorado Rockies
(303) 920-1664
(Aspen)

IDAHO
Smokey, Sawtooth, and Pioneer Mountains
(206) 622-8027
(Ketchum)

MONTANA
Northwest Montana Rockies
(406) 257-8606
(Whitefish)

OREGON
Southern Washington Cascades and Mt. Hood area
(503) 221-2400
(Portland)
Mt. Bachelor/Three Sisters area
(503) 382-6922
(Bend)

UTAH
Sundance/Mt. Timpanogos area
(801) 374-9770
(Provo)
Tri-Canyon area
(801) 364-1581
(Salt Lake City)
Mt. Ogden south to the Tri-Canyons
(801) 621-2362
(Ogden)
North Wasatch
(801) 752-4146

WASHINGTON
Washington Cascades and Olympics
(206) 526-6677
(Seattle)
Snoqualmie Pass area
(206) 442-7669

WYOMING
Teton, Wyoming and Wind River Mountains
(307) 733-2664
(Teton Village)

ALBERTA, CANADA
Columbia Ice Fields to Sunshine area
(403) 762-3600
(Banff)

AVALANCHE EDUCATION

Several organizations teach basic and advanced avalanche awareness and training courses. Beyond those listed here, many local colleges and universities, ski patrols and recreation departments offer courses.

Alaska Avalanche School
State Department of Natural Resources Division of Parks and Outdoor Recreation
Pouch7-001
Anchorage, Alaska 99510
(907) 762-4530

Alpine Skills Institute
National Ski Patrol c/o Rodney Babcock
P.O. Box 2027
Arnold, CA 95223

American Avalanche Institute, c/o Rod Newcomb
Box 308
Wilson, WY 83014
(307) 733-3315

Backcountry Avalanche Institute
Box 1050
Canmore, Alberta, Canada TOL OMO
(403) 678-4102

Blue Lake Centre
Box 850
Hinton, Alberta Canada TOE 1BO
(403) 865-4741

British Columbia Industry Services
School of Engineering Technology, Attn: Avalanche
3700 Willington Avenue
Burnaby, B.C. Canada V5G 3H2
(604) 434-5734

Brighton Ski Touring Center
P.O. Box 17848
Salt Lake City, UT 84117
(801) 531-9171

The Mountain School, Inc.
P.O. Box 728
Renton, WA 98057
(206) 266-2613

National Ski Patrol c/o Rob Faisant
750 Welch Road, Suite 321
Palo Alto, CA 94304

National Avalanche School, c/o Warren Walters
2638 Dapplegray Lane
Walnut Creek, CA 94596-6699
(415) 937-9338 or 933-3560

Sierra Wilderness Seminars
P.O. Box 707
Arcata, CA 95521
(707) 822-8066

Silverton Avalanche School,
c/o San Juan Mountain Search and Rescue
Silverton, CO 81433

Summit County Search and Rescue
P.O. Box 1794
Breckenridge, CO 80424

Snow-Motion Avalanche Seminars
P.O. Box 2027
Arnold, CA 95223

Colleges and universities that offer avalanche and snow related courses:

Montana State University, Department of
Engineering and Engineering Mechanics
Bozeman, MT 59715

Sierra College, Forestry Department, 5000 Rocklin Road, Rocklin, CA 95677

University of Utah, Department of Geography, Salt Lake City, UT 84102

Utah State University, Forestry Department, UMC 52, Logan, UT 84322

Utah Technical College at Provo, P.O. Box 1609, Provo, UT 84603, Attn: Wayne Kearny

University of British Columbia, Department of Geophysics, Vancouver, B.C. V6T 2A4, Canada

Wenatche Valley College, c/o Lee Rowe, 5th Street, Wenatche, WA 98801

Appendix C: Avalanche Safety Equipment Manufacturers and Suppliers

Alpine Research, Inc.
1930 Central Avenue, Suite F
Boulder CO 80301
(303) 444-0660

[backcountry ski equipment, survival gear, Echo and Ortovox rescue beacons]

Cascade Toboggan
25802 West Valley Highway
Kent WA 98032
(206)852-0182

[shovels, probes, Pieps rescue beacons, other rescue equipment]

Chouinard Equipment, Ltd.
P.O. Box 90
Ventura CA 93002

[backcountry ski equipment, clothing, survival gear, Echo and Ortovox rescue beacons]

Climb High
P.O. Box 9210
South Burlington VT 05401
(802) 864-4122

[backcountry ski and expedition equipment, Ortovox rescue beacons, shovels, probes and clothing]

Eastern Mountain Sports
1 Vose Farm Road
Peterborough NH 03458
(603)924-9571
(or local retail store)

[backcountry ski equipment, clothing, survival gear, rescue beacons]

Hydro-Tech
4658 N.E. 178th St.
Seattle WA 98155
(206)362-1074

[snowpit instruments]

Lawtronics
326 Walton
Buffalo NY 14226
(716)839-0630

[Skadi rescue beacons]

Life Link
P.O. Box 2913
Jackson Hole WY 93001
(800)443-8620

[snowpit instruments, shovels, probes, other rescue equipment]

Mountain Safety Research
1212 1st Avenue South
Seattle WA 98134
(206)624-8573

[survival gear, probes, other rescue equipment]

Mt. Tam Sports
Box 111
Kentfield CA 94914
(415)461-81111

[snowpit instruments, rescue equipment, first aid equipment]

The North Face
999 Harrison St.
Berkeley CA 94710
(800)323-8333
(or local retail store)

[backcountry ski equipment, clothing, survival gear, rescue beacons]

Recreational Equipment, Inc.
P.O. Box C-88125
Seattle WA 98188-0125
(206)323-8333
(or local retail store)

[backcountry ski equipment, clothing, survival gear, rescue beacons]

Sear Search and Rescue Equipment Ltd.
2818 Bayview Street
Surrey, B.C., Canada V4A 2Z4
(604)531-7300

[probes, other rescue equipment]

Strong Stitch Fabric Products
1415 East 3045 South
Salt Lake City UT 84106
(801)494-9436

[snowpit instruments]

INDEX